Turbo Pascal® for the Mac®

A Quick Path to Programming Power

Paul Goodman
Alan Zeldin

A Brady Book
New York, New York 10023

BRADY

Simon & Schuster, Inc.
Gulf + Western Building
One Gulf + Western Plaza
New York, New York 10023

DISTRIBUTED BY PRENTICE HALL TRADE

Manufactured in the United States of America

10 9 8 7 6 5 4 3 2 1

Library of Congress Cataloging-in-Publication Data

Goodman, Paul, 1958–
Turbo Pascal for the MAC: a quick path to programming power
Paul Goodman, Alan Zeldin.
p. cm.
"A Brady book."
Bibliography: p.
Includes index.
ISBN 0-13-933011-9
1. Macintosh (Computer)—Programming. 2. PASCAL (Computer program language) 3. Turbo Pascal (Computer program) I. Zeldin, Alan, 1957– .
II. Title.
QA76.8.M3G664 1987
005.265—dc19

CONTENTS

Other Brady Books by Paul Goodman and Alan Zeldin
The MacPascal Book, 1985

Other Brady Books by Paul Goodman
The Commodore 64 Guide to Data Files and Advanced Basic, 1984

TRADEMARK LIST

Limits of Liability and Disclaimer of Warranty

PREFACE

On a cold day in the winter of 1642, in the northwest corner of France, a young man put the finishing touches on a strange device built from gears, pegs, and dials.

On a snowy day in 1971, in Zurich, Switzerland, a university professor put the finishing touches on a paper for publication.

On a sunny day in 1976, in a garage in northern California, two young men wearing jeans put the finishing touches on a computer no one could have predicted would cause a revolution.

History has ways of connecting events that take place hundreds of years and thousands of miles apart. None of these men could have realized the importance of their work in the future, nor completely understood their connection to the past.

On a hot day in 1986, in Lexington, Utah, a team of computer scientists at Borland International linked the works of Blaise Pascal, the seventeenth-century mathematician, natural philosopher, and inventor of the first adding machine, to Nikolas Wirth, designer of the Pascal computer language, and to Steven Jobs and Steven Wozniak, founders of Apple Computer, and completed an extraordinary computer language, Turbo Pascal for the Macintosh.

That is the legacy of this book. *Turbo Pascal for the Mac* is intended for both the novice who wants to learn how to program and the experienced Pascal programmer who wants to use Turbo Pascal. A highlight of the book is its discussion of how to use QuickDraw graphics to produce animation and interesting graphics effects. Graphics are integrated into each chapter to demonstrate the topic and to provide some entertainment. A separate graphics chapter includes a video game program and ideas for others.

As a full implementation of Pascal, Turbo Pascal allows a programmer to express problems in a natural form that is similar to how people think. As Macintosh software, Turbo Pascal takes full advantage of the unique features of the Macintosh, making it easy to learn, to use, and to debug the occasional programming mistakes that inevitably occur. This book contains all that you will need to become a proficient Pascal programmer.

INTRODUCTION

Start your engines. The Macintosh, with its plethora of sophsiticated concepts and its rich repertoire of routines built into ROM, presents a truly exhilarating programming environment to use and explore. Unfortunately, the would-be explorer has had trouble finding a suitable programming language to work with. Certainly most programmers have outgrown BASIC, and the C language implementations for the Macintosh have been complex, tedious to use, and expensive. Many feel that the ultimate Macintosh programming language now exists for the Macintosh: Turbo Pascal from Borland International. *Turbo Pascal for the Mac* was written to help those who wish to learn how to harness the full power of the Macintosh with Turbo Pascal. The reader of this book may have no programming experience and limited exposure to the Macintosh, or the reader may already have some mastery of the Pascal language and want to learn how to use the Mac's more advanced features. The approach of this book is broad enough for both.

The book's goals can be summarized as follows:

- To teach Pascal programming from the simplest concepts to the most complex;
- To introduce the reader to the Macintosh User Interface Toolbox and QuickDraw and explain the procedures and functions they contain;
- To teach data file programming;
- To teach sophisticated Pascal programming topics such as pointers, handles, and recursion;

- To show the reader how to develop "real" Macintosh applications with Turbo Pascal that implements pull-down menus, event handling, file handling, and sophisticated graphics.

Turbo Pascal represents a significant advance in programming language systems. As a programming language, Turbo Pascal is a full implementation of the ANSI Pascal standard. Add to this full IEEE numeric standards for accuracy, and you have a Pascal system suitable for either scientific or business applications.

As a programming environment, Turbo Pascal combines a powerful and fast compiler with easy generation of double-clickable applications and desk accessories.

As a way to explore the Macintosh, Turbo Pascal provides a safe, easy environment to work with. Full access is provided to the Macintosh's User Interface Toolbox and QuickDraw graphics package, allowing programs that conform to the standards of the Macintosh User Interface. Turbo Pascal provides a programming safety net by softly landing a programmer back into the editor when serious programming errors occur.

Turbo Pascal for the Mac is written to fill the needs of new and experienced programmers by introducing the reader to all these areas of Turbo Pascal. No knowledge of Pascal or previous exposure to the Macintosh is assumed . Chapter by chapter, the reader will advance in Pascal programming skills and knowledge and will learn all concepts hand in hand with how to take advantage of the unique features of the Macintosh. It is expected that after reading this book, the new programmer will be able to design and develop true Macintosh applications.

Chapter 1 introduces the reader to Turbo Pascal and the Macintosh as a programming environment including QuickDraw and the User Interface Toolbox. The reader learns to enter, compile, and run a simple Turbo Pascal program that utilizes QuickDraw graphics.

Chapter 2 presents the fundamentals of Turbo Pascal, covering data types, input and output, variables, assignment statements, and expressions. In this chapter the fundamentals of programming errors are discussed, and Turbo Pascal's "dirty dozen," the twelve most common syntax errors, are included.

Chapter 3, entitled "Pascal Structures," presents the basic building blocks of a Pascal program. Covered is decision making with the If-then-else statement and looping with the For loop and the While loop.

This chapter takes the first serious look at the QuickDraw graphics package, covering the use of the mouse and the rectangle data type. Example programs show animation and the use of the mouse in interactive graphics programs.

Chapter 4 will introduce the reader to functions, both those built into Turbo Pascal and those defined by the programmer. Simple Toolbox routines are introduced along with programming examples. The chapter also expands the concept of data types, covering the extended real and integer types that are part of the Standard Apple Numerical Environment and the enumerated data types.

Chapter 5 is devoted to procedures, the mechanism for dividing large programs into smaller, more manageable sections. The use of procedures will allow for the development of more sophisticated programs throughout the remainder of the book.

In Chapter 6 attention is focused on two of Pascal's more sophisticated data structures, arrays and strings. They provide the programmer with the tools necessary to handle and process large amounts of text and numerical data. Other related topics in this chapter include sorting and checking input validity.

Chapter 7 continues the book's examination of more sophisticated programming and data structures with coverage of the Repeat loop, records, and sets. These structures are explained in relation to how they can be used in developing programs. This Chapter also takes a unique look at recursion, a programming technique where procedures and functions invoke themselves. Recursion is one of the most powerful programming techniques available in Pascal, but unfortunately it is also one of the most confusing to learn. Unique examples are presented that use QuickDraw routines to graphically indicate the operation of recursive procedures. These examples help make this difficult concept easy to understand and enjoyable to learn.

Chapter 8 presents a formal look at QuickDraw graphics. Many of the graphics concepts explained earlier in the book are reviewed and reinforced with a deeper level of understanding. Two graphics applications, a free-hand sketching program and a video game, are developed as examples of QuickDraw programming.

Chapter 9 covers files and file programming techniques. Files are the key to writing useful programs, yet information on their use and operation is scarce. This chapter teaches the techniques needed to store and retrieve data from both sequential and random files on the Macintosh. Besides data files, the important text files are covered with special emphasis placed on the use of devices such as the printer and modem. A major file application is developed and presented in its entirety.

Chapter 10 completes the book's discussion of Pascal language structures by presenting three topics used extensively in Toolbox programming and throughout the remainder of the book. Variant records are an extension on the concepts of records. Pointers and handles, along with dynamic memory allocation, are the way flexibility can be added to programs. They allow memory space to be created and destroyed during program execution as needed, a feature necessary to do complex things such as windows. Macintosh memory management techniques and the Mac's Memory Manager is explained in relation to these concepts.

Chapter 11 moves from Pascal programming into Macintosh programming and covers events and event programming, the key to developing true Macintosh applications. Events allow a program to respond directly to user action such as keyboard and mouse input. The Toolbox routines that manage the event queue and report on events to programs are presented along with helpful programming examples. The chapter continues by covering the Toolbox's Menu Manager, and programming examples which utilize pull-down menus are presented, developed, and explained. Supporting desk accessories from a program is also explained in detail.

Finally, Chapter 12 presents a complete Macintosh application combining the Toolbox, QuickDraw, events, and file handling. The program called TurboDraw is an object-oriented programming graphics program suitable for use in flow charting and graphing. The reader is taken through the entire process of planning and programming a Macintosh application. Emphasis is placed upon selecting the proper data structure for an application and the use of the Toolbox and QuickDraw to follow the Mac's User Interface guidelines.

Pedagogically speaking, *Turbo Pascal for the Mac* is the type of book that teaches with the aid of small programming examples that demonstrate the concepts without confusion. These are later combined into larger examples. Normally, routines are introduced, explained, and then used in a program. Much care has been taken to make sure that the little questions do not go unanswered. An example of this might be when the fact that a value is passed as a variable parameter could be overlooked. The authors firmly believe that it is better to take the time to point out these possible oversights than to let the reader develop a program with hard-to-detect bugs.

SPECIAL FEATURES OF THE BOOK

Complete Pascal Coverage. The book includes the topics neglected by many Pascal texts; sets, variant records, pointers, and SANE (the Apple Standard Numeric Environment) are all covered.

Emphasis on Program Development. Starting with the first chapter, program development is stressed by encouraging top-down programming design and by pseudocoding many of programs.

Total Coverage of Files. The use of files occupies a complete chapter rather than the five or six pages usually devoted to this important topic. The reader is presented with the information and programming techniques necessary to develop programming systems to solve substantial data storage applications.

In-Depth Look at Graphics. A majority of the QuickDraw routines are presented. A difficult topic to grasp, QuickDraw concepts are introduced in the first chapter and built upon from chapter to chapter. A separate chapter is devoted to a formal description of QuickDraw and includes two interactive graphics programs, SketchPad, a free-hand drawing program and PaddleBall, a challenging video game.

Event Handling. Events are the key concept in all true Macintosh applications. The book presents events and event handling and presents the programming structures needed to develop Macintosh applications.

The Toolbox. Along with events, this book presents the Macintosh User Interface Toolbox and those routines that deal with the mouse, events, pull-down menus, printing graphics, and the clock.

Double-Clickable Applications. Very few Macintosh programming languages can produce double-clickable applications. Turbo does it easily, and it is fully covered by this book.

Complete Programming Systems Presented. The book progresses from simple programs to complete, true Macintosh applications utilizing event handling, pull-down menus, and files. The book's final chapter develops from scratch a sophisticated, object-oriented drawing program

Appendices. Turbo Pascal for the Mac contains appendices that complement the book with easy-to-reference information on menu commands, documenting a program, differences with Macintosh Pascal, syntax diagrams, QuickDraw procedures, SANE procedures, error messages, bibliography, and the Macintosh character set.

It is expected that after reading *Turbo Pascal for the Mac*, the reader will be able to race through the challenges of programming the Macintosh and take the checkered flag. Always buckle your seat belt!

1
Turbo Pascal for the Macintosh

WHY TURBO PASCAL?

Turbo Pascal for the Macintosh is one of the most unique programming environments developed to date. It combines the programming elegance of Pascal, the power of the Macintosh, and the speed of a finely tuned race car along with the Macintosh's familiar User Interface and text editing. This combination provides a Pascal system that is easy to use but also has remarkable power and flexibility.

Turbo Pascal presents the programmer with a unified environment to work with. Its own Macintosh-style editor allows up to eight programs to be developed, compiled (translated to machine language,) and executed side by side. If an error occurs, Turbo is right there, returning you to the editor and directing you to the source of the error. Turbo even handles with elegance those nasty System Errors by allowing you to restart the program without having to turn off the computer and without any loss of data. This ability to edit, compile, execute, and debug in one context saves considerable time over other languages where a programmer must work in several different contexts in a short period of time. With other development systems, the program is written with a text editor or word processor and saved as an ASCII file. This file is passed to a Pascal compiler, which checks it for syntax and if no mistakes exist translates it into machine language. After compilation the machine language program is not yet ready for execution and is saved in a second file passed to a program known as a link/loader, which takes the machine language program and prepares it for execution by linking it together with subroutines and run-time libraries. The output of the loader is placed either directly in memory or into a file for later execution. Turbo avoids all this without sacrificing the power of a compiler. In fact, Turbo Pascal for the Macintosh may be the fastest compiler ever developed, parsing over 12,000 lines a minute.

For the novice programmer, Turbo provides a supportive environment excellent for learning. Turbo allows programs to be written forgetting about the Macintosh environment by providing its own window for all output. The major advantage is that much of the overhead involved in writing programs for the Macintosh is eliminated. This is significant because even the seemingly simple task of creating a new window and displaying it is complex enough to befuddle a sophisticated programmer, requiring extensive knowledge of the Macintosh's Window Manager, QuickDraw, and Event Manager.

For the experienced programmer, Turbo allows the development of double-clickable applications and provides complete access to all of the Macintosh's User Interface Toolbox. The compiler even supports development of specialized Macintosh programs such as desk accessories and device drivers.

MACINTOSH OVERVIEW

The designers of the Macintosh wished to provide programmers with more than just a box containing basic computer components, as is done by most other computer manufacturers. They wanted to include in a computer all that would be needed for programmers to write programs based on a group of elemental building blocks. Their goal was to establish a consistent look and feel for all programs that would run on this computer. For instance, the way a user saves a file would be exactly the same in all application programs. This decreases the time needed to learn a program and makes it easier to remember how to use a program. This was accomplished on the Macintosh by including in read-only memory (ROM) a large set of program routines that can be freely used by the programmer. These routines, most of which were originally written for the Macintosh's revolutionary predecessor the

Lisa, can be broken down into two parts, the operating system and the User Interface Toolbox.

The operating system lies on the lowest level of the ROM software. It performs basic tasks such as the handling of files and memory. Unlike other computers, the user of the Macintosh has very little interaction with the operating system, dealing with it through a program called the Finder, which provides an easy-to-use graphical interface to perform actions such as copying a file or changing a filename. A program written with Turbo Pascal will also have very little contact with the operating system relying on Pascal to indirectly use it to do things such as open and close files.

The next level up is the User Interface Toolbox, the set of routines that provides a way of constructing programs that conform to the standards established by Apple Computer. These standards are undoubtedly familiar to you already and include the use of pull-down menus, windows, text editing, controls, and dialog boxes. The Toolbox is divided into a set of managers, each one performing one of the standard functions. There is a Window Manager, a Menu Manager, and so on. The complete documentation for the Toolbox is found in a publication written by Apple Computer known as *Inside Macintosh*. This book has existed in a number of incarnations since the introduction of the computer, including a three-binder edition, a phonebooklike edition, and a version from a major book publisher. While invaluable to the Macintosh programmer, *Inside Macintosh* is not the last word in clarity or simplicity. It has been accurately described as 25 chapters, each one assuming that you have already read the other 24. For more information on obtaining a copy of *Inside Macintosh*, contact Apple Computer or your local bookstore.

An important part of the Toolbox is the QuickDraw graphics package. QuickDraw is responsible for the drawing of all graphics on the screen, including text. Built into QuickDraw is the ability to draw a variety of graphical shapes and objects, to manipulate these objects, and to draw text in a variety of shapes, sizes, and typefaces. QuickDraw itself is called upon by many of the Toolbox routines to do graphical operations. Writing a program using QuickDraw is covered intensively throughout this book.

Turbo Pascal provides direct access to all of QuickDraw and the Toolbox. By direct access, it is meant these routines can be used in a program as though they were a part of standard Pascal. By the time the reader completes this book he will be fully familiar with the use of both QuickDraw and the Toolbox.

WHY THIS BOOK?

This book is intended for all programmers from the complete novice to those who are experienced programmers and want to know more. The overall theme of this book is to integrate the concepts of Turbo Pascal programming with the aspects of the Macintosh environment. For example, most Pascal concepts are backed up by examples that rely upon special features of the Macintosh not found on the IBM PC such as QuickDraw graphics or other Toolbox features.

Turbo Pascal for the Macintosh teaches Pascal programming in the Macintosh context from start to finish, meaning that by the last chapter you will be developing programs that meet the standards of the Macintosh User Interface. No knowledge of computer programming, Pascal or otherwise, is required or assumed. The book provides in-depth coverage of all Pascal concepts but merges this with the special and intriguing features of the Mac. In fact, within the next few pages you will be writing and running your first Pascal program using QuickDraw graphics.

STARTING UP

The best way to learn Turbo Pascal programming is to jump right in by entering and running a program. Let's start by a quick summary of how to start up the Turbo Pascal environment. The concepts involved are simple, and you will quickly learn how to handle Turbo Pascal like an expert. This chapter will serve as a handy reference later on.

Turn on your computer, then insert your Turbo Pascal program disk into the disk drive slot and start up the Turbo icon. The window that appears is where you will enter the Turbo Pascal program. It will be titled Untitled. Up to eight of these programming windows may be open at once, each containing a different program. The Turbo editor has features to help you easily manage the eight windows simultaneously.

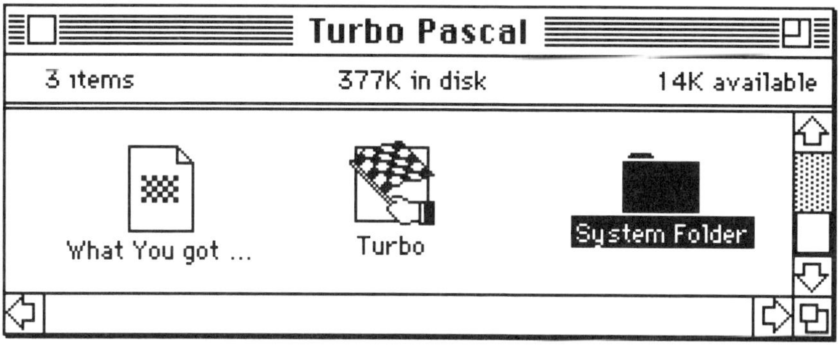

Figure 1-1. The Turbo Icon

If you are at all familiar with text editing on the Mac, you will have no problem entering and editing a Turbo program because it follows the standard text editing conventions. However, if you are not that familiar with the Mac, have no fear and read on. Locate the pointer on the screen. When you move it into the window, it changes shape. Place the pointer in the upper left-hand corner of the window and click the mouse button. A blinking vertical line called the cursor will appear at that spot. The cursor indicates the current insertion point for new text being typed. Anything typed will be inserted starting at that spot in the window. Any text to the right of that spot will be moved over. Now that the cursor is waiting for text to be entered, let's enter a program. Type the following exactly:

```
program FirstTime;
uses
 MemTypes, QuickDraw;
var
 Oval :rect;
 I :Integer;
begin
 for I:1 to 10 do
   begin
     SetRect(Oval, 10,10, 5*I, 5*I);
     FrameOval(Oval)
   end
end.
```

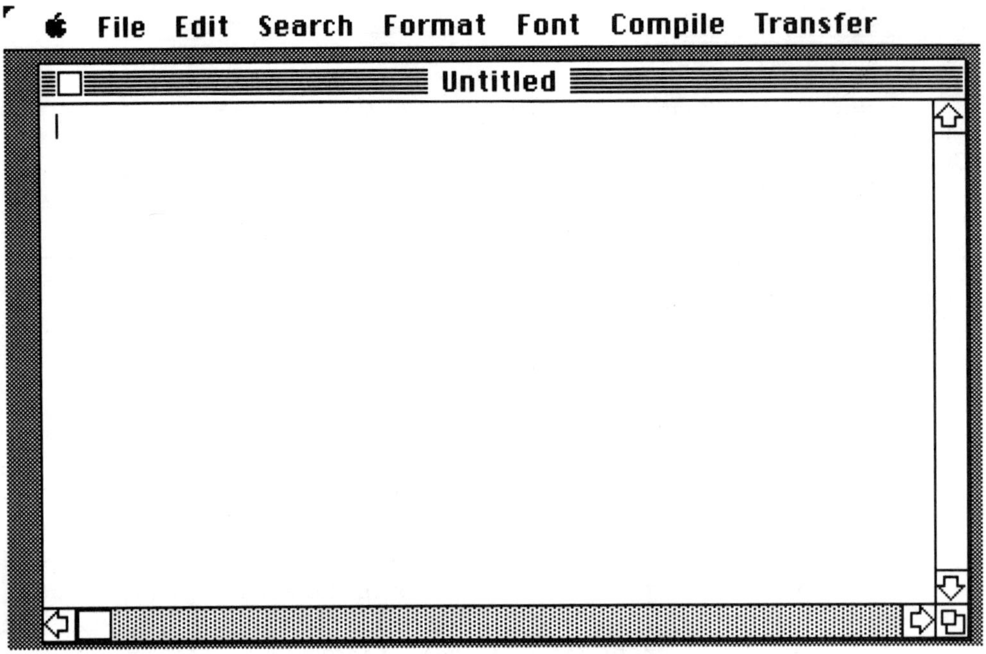

Figure 1-2. An Editing Window.

If you make a mistake as you type, the Backspace key will erase one character to the left. When you are done the window shown in Figure 1-3 should appear.

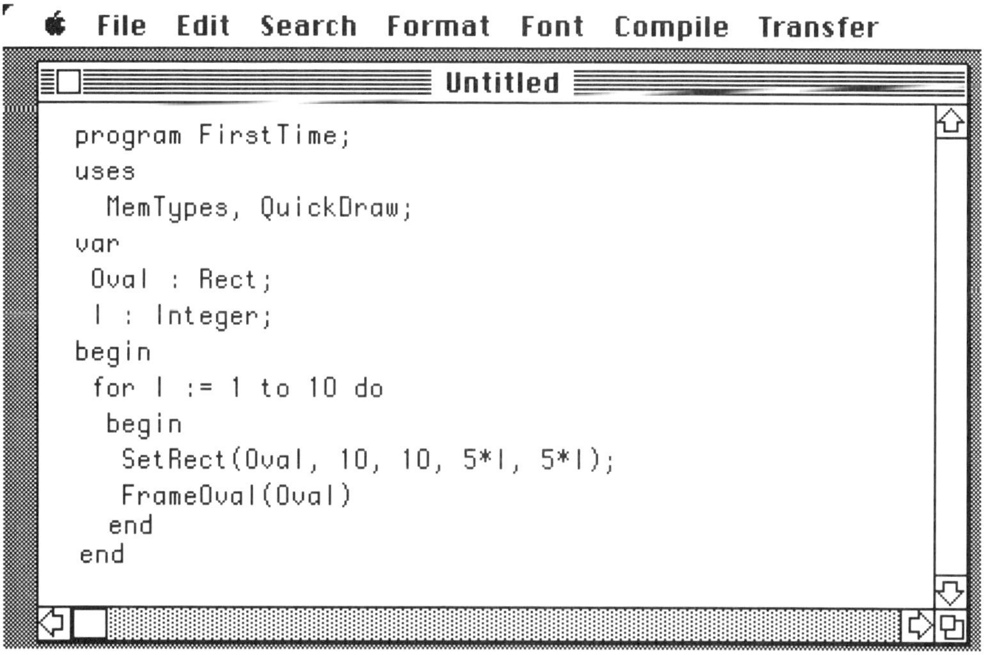

Figure 1-3. Program in the Window.

RUNNING A PROGRAM

Once you are satisfied that you typed the program correctly, we are ready to run it. There are several ways to run a program from Turbo. The first and fastest is to compile the program to memory. Compiling causes the Turbo to translate your program from Pascal into machine language. The To Memory option will cause the machine language program to be stored in a section of memory from where it can be executed. While the program is compiling, the checked flag will wave on the screen. If you mistyped any of this program, an alert box such as this will appear:

Figure 1-4. A Bug Box

In computer lingo, one would say that the program has a "bug." The bug box indicates that a syntax error exists in the program. Hitting the Enter key or the mouse button will clear it, but the real task is to locate the source of the error and correct. Errors detected by the compiler are known as "syntax errors" since they are triggered by improper program syntax. Syntax is the set of rules that define the proper construction of a language (more on this later). In a short program such as this, a syntax error is easy to find. Turbo helps out by attempting to point out the line that caused the trouble. We will not try here to explain how to correct all syntax errors. Much of the rest of the book is devoted to writing Pascal programs correctly. If you have an error, correct that line to make it conform to the program above and recompile. In the next chapter you will find a section label "The Dirty Dozen," which discusses the twelve most common syntax errors and has suggestions for solving them.

Once any error is corrected, recompile the program. After a successful compile you will notice that once the flag stops waving nothing else happens. This is because we have told Turbo to compile the program but haven't yet given the command to run it. The compiled code will sit in memory but will be erased when the program is edited.

We are now ready to run the program. Choose "Run" from the Compile menu. The program window will quickly disappear, and a new window will be opened where the output of the program will be displayed as is shown below.

This window is automatically provided by Turbo for both text and graphics output of a program. Once the program has completed, Turbo will quickly replace the program window. There is a technique for "freezing" the program's display on the screen, and we will soon see what that is. What is important is that you entered the program correctly and that the program worked as expected. If the program did not work as expected, check the program carefully and make sure that it is exactly the same as the example.

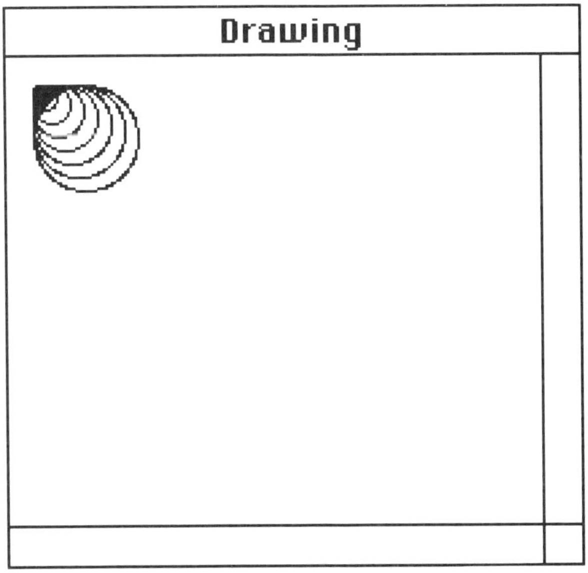

Figure 1-5. Tangential Circles

The compiling and running of the program could have been performed in just one step by just choosing the Run option. If no compiled code is in memory, Turbo will compile the program in the active window to memory and then run it. All this is done at blinding speed. Borland International, the manufacturer of Turbo Pascal, claims that Turbo for the Mac can compile 12,000 lines per minute, and there seems to be no reason to dispute this claim. If you have ever worked with other programming language systems, you will quickly learn to appreciate this type of speed. If this is your first programming language experience, consider yourself lucky. You have avoided having to go out for coffee as the program compiles.

As mentioned, there is another way of compiling a program. The To Disk option in the Compile menu will save the compiled program to a file on the disk. The compiled program will appear with a generic icon with the name given the program in the first line of the program such as this:

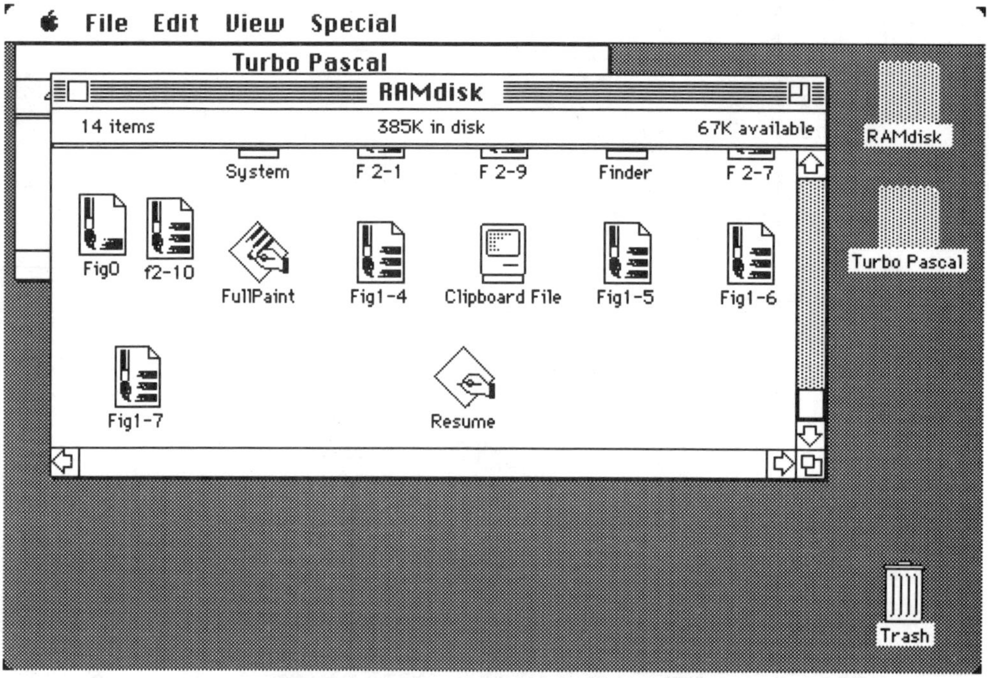

Figure. 1-6. Program Compiled to Disk

This program is ready to be executed by double clicking on the icon. A window will come up, display the circles, and then disappear as the Finder comes back. No interaction with Turbo will occur; the program is now a true double-clickable application. This represents the simplest way to create a double-clickable application in the entire Macintosh universe. With other programming languages a programmer must be extremely knowledgeable about Toolbox to create such a standalone application, but Turbo sets it up automatically.

EDITING A PROGRAM

If a mistake is made while entering a program, or a change in the program needs to be made, the following editing techniques are available.

To Insert Text

1. Move the pointer to the desired spot in the program and click the mouse button to place the insertion point.

2. Enter the text.

To Delete Text

There are two different techniques for deleting text. For a small amount of text:

1. Move the pointer to the right of the characters you want to delete and click the mouse button to place the insertion point.

2. Use the Backspace key to delete the characters.

For a large amount of text:

1. Select the text to be deleted by placing the pointer at the start of the text to be deleted and holding down the mouse button.

Figure 1-7. Selecting Text

2. Now drag the pointer across the text. Notice that, while dragging, the area selected is displayed inverted (white characters on a black background). At the end of the portion to be deleted, release the button. The text to be deleted should now be in reverse video.

3. Delete the selected area by pressing the Backspace key.

Figure 1-8. Highlighting Text

To Replace Text

1. Select the text to be replaced by using the dragging technique described above.

2. Start typing the new text. The old text is replaced automatically.

To Move Text

1. Select the text to be moved.

2. Choose "Cut" from the Edit menu.

3. Place the insertion point where you want the text to go and click.

4. Choose "Paste" from the Edit menu.

To Copy Text

1. Select the text to be copied.

2. Choose "Copy" from the Edit menu.

3. Place the insertion point where you want the text to go and click.

4. Choose "Paste" from the Edit menu.

Shortcut

Double clicking the mouse button on a word automatically selects the word.

These editing procedures are exactly the same as those used in MacWrite and in many other places in the Macintosh such as the Notepad.

PRINTING A PROGRAM

A copy of your Turbo Pascal program (the text itself, not the output) can be printed on the printer connected to your Macintosh. Select "Print" from the File menu. A dialog box will then appear on the screen.

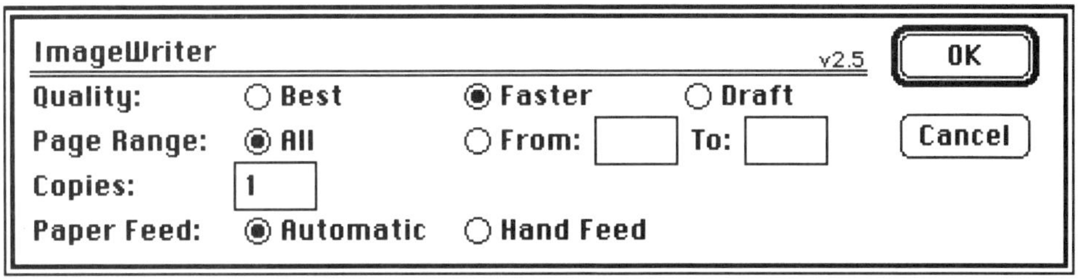

Figure 1-9. The ImageWriter Dialog Box

What you see may vary slightly depending upon the version of the print driver you are using and whether you have an ImageWriter or are lucky enough to have a LaserWriter. The boxes for the number of copies and the range of pages to print can be filled in by placing the cursor in the box and clicking. The Tab key will move the cursor from box to box without the use of the mouse.

PRINTING THE ACTIVE WINDOW

The active window is the frontmost window on the screen. The contents of the active window can be printed by simultaneously holding down the Shift, Command, and four keys simultaneously. You can make any window the active window by clicking the pointer anywhere inside of it.

THE MACINTOSH SCREEN

Turbo Pascal is capable of displaying high-quality graphics and animation. Before we can write graphics programs we must first take a look at the Macintosh's graphics coordinate system. The Macintosh's screen can be thought of as a grid of 512 vertical lines by 342 horizontal lines not much different from graph paper. The vertical lines (X coordinates) are numbered from 0 to 511, and the horizontal lines (Y coordinates) are numbered 0 to 341. The location where a horizontal line and a vertical line intersect is called a point and noted as (X, Y). The upper left corner of the screen, the origin, is where vertical line 0 and horizontal line 0 intersect, point (0,0). The lower right-hand corner of the screen is where vertical line 511 intersects horizontal line 341, point (511, 341). Below and to the right of each point on the screen is a dot that can be displayed on the screen as either white or black. These dots are called **picture elements**, or **pixels** for short. For each of the 175,104 (342 by 512) points on the screen there is a corresponding pixel.

The coordinate system actually extends beyond what is visible on the screen. For instance, the coordinate (-10, -10) is above and to the left of the origin. These points exist to help in calculating complex geographic constructs that may extend beyond the visible portion of the screen.

The Macintosh's ROM contains a very complete and powerful graphics package called QuickDraw. Turbo Pascal allows access to QuickDraw by simply using QuickDraw commands in a program as if they were Pascal statements. The program that you typed and ran used two different QuickDraw commands to define the size of an oval and then to draw it in the window:

```
SetRect(Oval,10,10, 5*I, 5*I);
FrameOval(Oval)
```

The first of the commands, SetRect, defines a rectangle, one of QuickDraw's graphic types. The size of this rectangle will vary as the program executions. The second command, FrameOval, actually draws an oval on the screen whose size is the same as the rectangle defined.

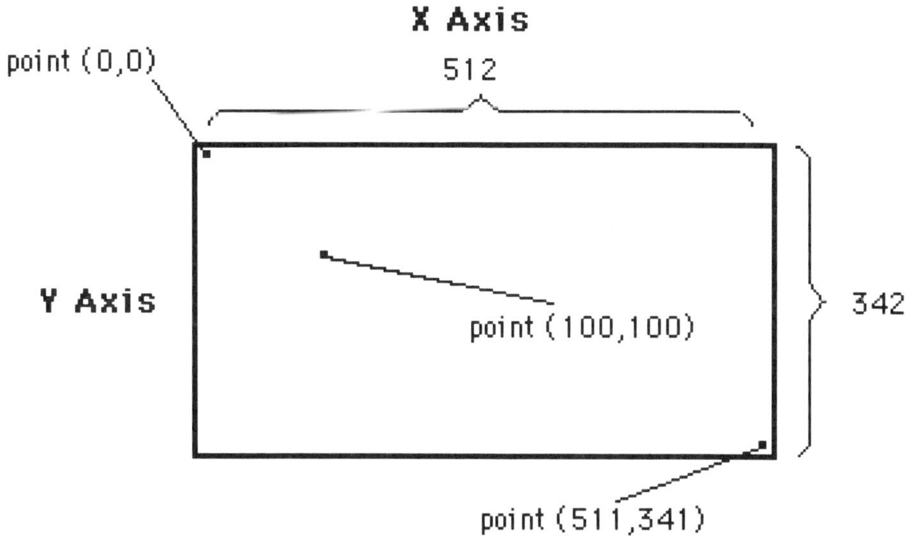

Figure 1-10. The Mac Coordinate System

CHAPTER SUMMARY

In this chapter we have seen how to enter, compile, and run a program with Turbo Pascal. We even quickly looked at a small program using QuickDraw graphics. All the commands and programming techniques used will be explained in much greater detail in future chapters.

2
Turbo Pascal Fundamentals

INTRODUCTION

In Chapter 1 we saw how to work with the Turbo Pascal environment and how to enter and run a short Turbo program. In this chapter, we will start to explore the basic elements of the Pascal programming language. You will be introduced to the concepts of different types of data, storing data in the computer, and the input and output of data.

A FIRST PROGRAM

The best way to go about learning Pascal is to dive right in, so here is the simplest program possible in Pascal.

```
program Good_For_Nothing;
 {This is our first program }
 begin
 end.
```

If you enter and run it, you will see that it does absolutely nothing. However, it is useful to explore the required elements of a Pascal program. All programs must begin with a program declaration consisting of the word "program" followed by one or more spaces and then a program name. This program's name is Good_For_Nothing, and it is followed by a semicolon (;). Together they form what is known as the **program declaration**. The semicolon is used in Pascal to separate consecutive statements or declarations and must be present. A name in Pascal is called an **identifier**. In Turbo Pascal, identifiers can be made up of combinations of letters, numbers, and underscores. While an identifier can be of any length, it must start with a letter, and only the first 63 characters are significant (any two identifiers with the same first 63 characters are considered the same). We doubt this will create much of a problem for you. In practice, an identifier will contain from one to about fifteen characters (who wants to type very long names?). It is good practice to use identifiers that have a meaning that corresponds to the functions they perform or the objects they represent.

The word "program" cannot be used as an identifier because it has a special meaning in the language. Words like "program" are called **reserved words** and are used by the compiler to be able to understand the structure of the program. The 48 reserved words in the Turbo Pascal language are listed in Appendix A.

After the program declaration a program may contain other optional declaration sections. These are absent in Good_for_Nothing because it is so simple they are not needed. Other possible declarations will be discussed later. Following the declaration section in our program are the reserved words "begin" and "end." These mark the start and the finish of the program's instructions, those statements that perform some action. This program contains no instructions whatsoever. The reserved word "end" is followed by a period indicating the end of the program.

SYNTAX

All languages need a set of rules that define the language. We can communicate with other people who speak the same language we do because they use the same rules for constructing sentences. Syntax is the set of rules for constructing valid statements in a language. In natural languages such as English, we call these rules grammar. Programming languages also have rules of syntax, but they are much more restrictive and simpler than those of natural languages. Pascal's syntax is so simple and well defined it can be expressed in a series of diagrams. For instance, here is the syntax diagram for a digit:

DIGIT

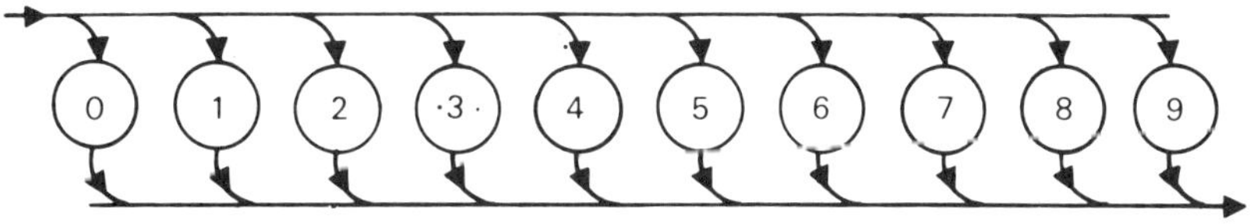

Figure 2-1. Syntax Diagram : Digit

To construct a syntactically correct digit, follow the diagram from the starting point on the left to the end point on the right. Many paths are possible. Any path that starts on the left and ends on the right describes a digit that is syntactically correct. Notice that in this diagram any single digit from 0 to 9 is a valid digit. A slightly more complex syntax diagram is that of an unsigned integer (a whole number).

UNSIGNED INTEGER

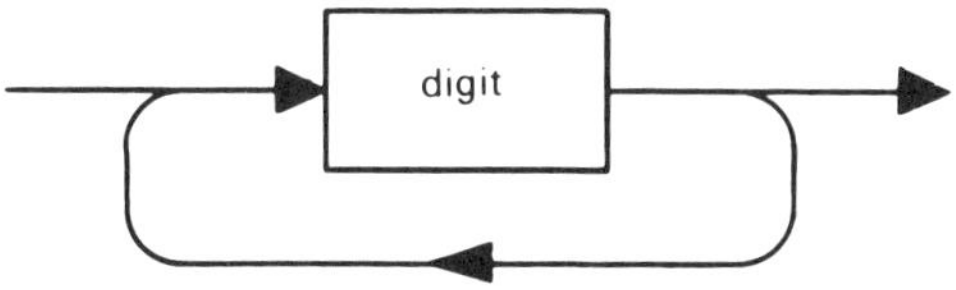

Figure 2-2. Syntax Diagram : Unsigned Integer

Once again, any path that goes from the start to the end defines a syntactictally correct unsigned integer. To confirm that a number such as 327 is a valid unsigned integer, we would follow the diagram traversing the middle section three times and then exit. You may think of the box labeled "digit" as an abbreviation for Figure 2-2 above.

The syntax diagram for a signed integer is built with the rules for an unsigned integer:

SIGNED INTEGER

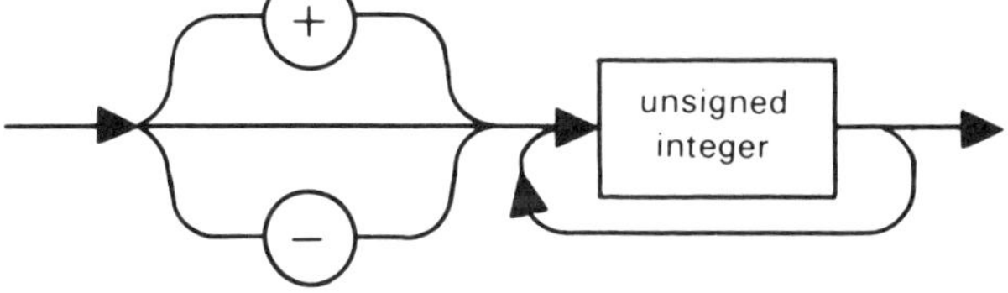

Figure 2-3. Syntax Diagram : Signed Integer

In a syntax diagram, the elliptical symbols are atomic,—that is, they cannot be subdivided into smaller diagrams. Rectangular symbols are those that can be subdivided. For example, in the signed integer diagram, the unsigned integer symbol was defined previously.

MORE ON IDENTIFIERS

Not all words can be used as identifiers. A numeric digit or an underscore cannot be the first character of an identifier. Spaces, punctuation characters, and other special characters cannot be used in identifiers either. A special character is any character that is not a letter, space, or underscore. The following are all valid identifiers:

```
Big Bucks          Total          Rate3          One4all
```

These, however, are not valid Pascal identifiers:

```
22go               Big:Bang                      Counter$
```

Lowercase and uppercase characters are equivalent in an identifier; therefore, the following two identifiers are treated as one and the same by Turbo Pascal:

```
GrossPay           grosspay
```

The underscore character is sometimes used as a separator between words to make identifiers easier to read. The following identifiers are considered to be different by Turbo Pascal:

```
Gross_Pay                    GrossPay
```

Here is the syntax diagram of an identifier:

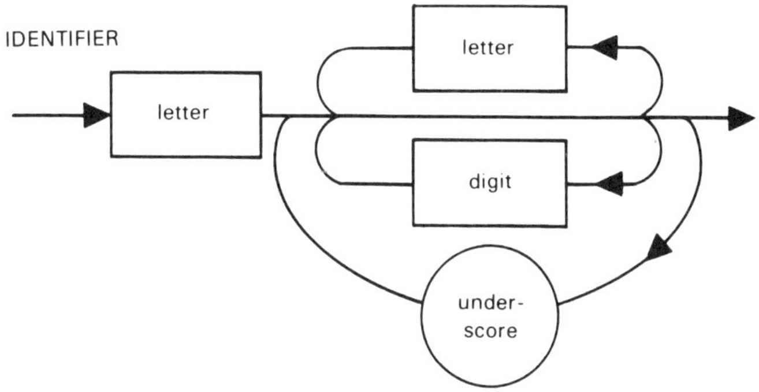

Figure 2-4. Syntax Diagram : Identifier

From now on we will not bore you by including syntax diagrams for each Pascal feature. A complete listing of the syntax diagrams for Turbo Pascal can be found in Appendix G.

COMMENTS

In a Pascal program, information that is enclosed between curly braces { and } are comments. Comments are used to document the workings of a program and are meant for people, rather than computers, to read. The Turbo Pascal compiler completely ignores all comments. It cannot be emphasized too strongly that comments are required for writing clear, maintainable programs that can be understood when examined later. For historical reasons, a parentheses asterisk pair, '(*' and '*)' can be substituted for the curly brace pair, '{' and '}'. This is because many input devices used with early computers in the 1970s could not read the brackets. The start and end of a comment must be matching delimiters: '{' and '}' or '(*' and '*)', but not '{' and '*)' or '(*' and '}'.

DOCUMENTING A PROGRAM

When you write a program, it is important that you include an explanation of how the program works. This may not seem important or necessary when the program is written, but you will be grateful sometime in the future when

Figure 2-5. The Programmer's Commandment

you look back at your work. The Eleventh Commandment should read, "Thou shalt document thy programs."

There are two aspects to properly documenting a program. The first is to make your program self-explanatory by using meaningful identifier names. Below are instructions that perform the same task.

```
X := Y + Z;
SalePrice := Price + Tax;
```

The only thing that can be ascertained from the first statement is that two variables are being added together and the result assigned to a third. However, from the second statement the reader can tell you why that statement is being executed.

The second aspect of documentation is the use of **comments**. These should be used when the identifier names alone cannot indicate the purpose of a statement or a group of statements. Comments should describe what the program is doing, not how it is doing it. Here is an example of a well commented program section; its function is self-evident:

```
ConversionRate := 21374; {# of lire in a dollar}
{Calculate import cost}
Dollars := Lire * ConversionRate;
Duty := Dollars * TaxRate;
Cost := Dollars + Duty;
```

Comments should not just redescribe what can be ascertained from the instructions themselves. This is the way not to write comments:

```
{ multiply lire by conversion rate to get dollars }
Dollars := Lire * ConversionRate;
{ multiply dollars by tax rate to get duty }
```

```
Duty := Dollars * TaxRate;
{ add dollars to duty to get cost }
Cost := Dollars + Duty;
```

Appendix E contains an entire program meticulously documented to serve as a guide.

WRITE AND WRITELN

Now let us look at a program that actually does something. For a computer to be useful it must be able to output information for people to see. The Macintosh can generate two different types of output: graphics and text. These can be freely intermixed in a Turbo program. Since text output is simpler, we will tackle it first. The two most common statements in Pascal that output text are the **Write** and **Writeln** (pronounced "write line") statements.

To demonstrate the Write statement, enter and run the following program:

```
program MyName;
begin
  Write('I am a Macintosh computer');
  Readln
end.
```

If you made no errors, the Mac's screen will clear and a new window will appear. This is the console window used by Turbo Pascal as the place that output is displayed. At this point you may not appreciate the beautiful simplicity of the console window, but suffice it to say that most programming languages on the Macintosh force the programmer to learn how to use the most complex features of the Toolbox to run even the simplest program. The following will be displayed:

```
'I am a Macintosh Computer'
```

This program now contains two instructions, more accurately referred to as **statements**, sandwiched in between the "begin" and "end." The Writeln statement was responsible for producing the output. The last statement in the program (Readln) forces the computer to wait for you to hit the Return key before returning to the Turbo environment. If the Readln had not been in the program the message would have flashed on the screen and the program would have returned to the Turbo Pascal environment almost instantly.

TRIAL AND ERROR—SEMICOLONS

Try removing the semicolon after the Writeln statement. Running the program should now produce this error:

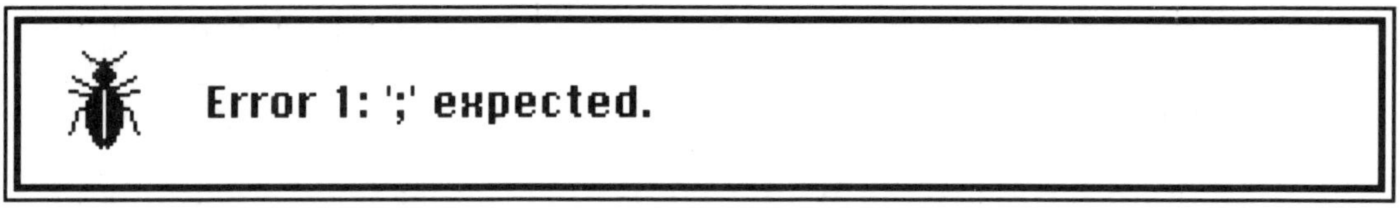

Figure 2-6. Missing Semicolon Error

The "; expected" message will probably be the one you most encounter in Pascal programming. When it occurs, look in the vicinity of the insertion point for a statement that requires a semicolon but is missing one.

Let's try a second program:

```
program MyNameAgain;
begin  Write('I ');
 Write('am ');
 Write('a ');
 Write('Macintosh ');
 Write('Computer ');
 Readln
end.
```

Program MyNameAgain does the same exact thing as MyName. Why? The Write statement acts just like Writeln except that no carriage return is performed after the information is displayed. Thus, all the information is displayed on the same line in the console window.

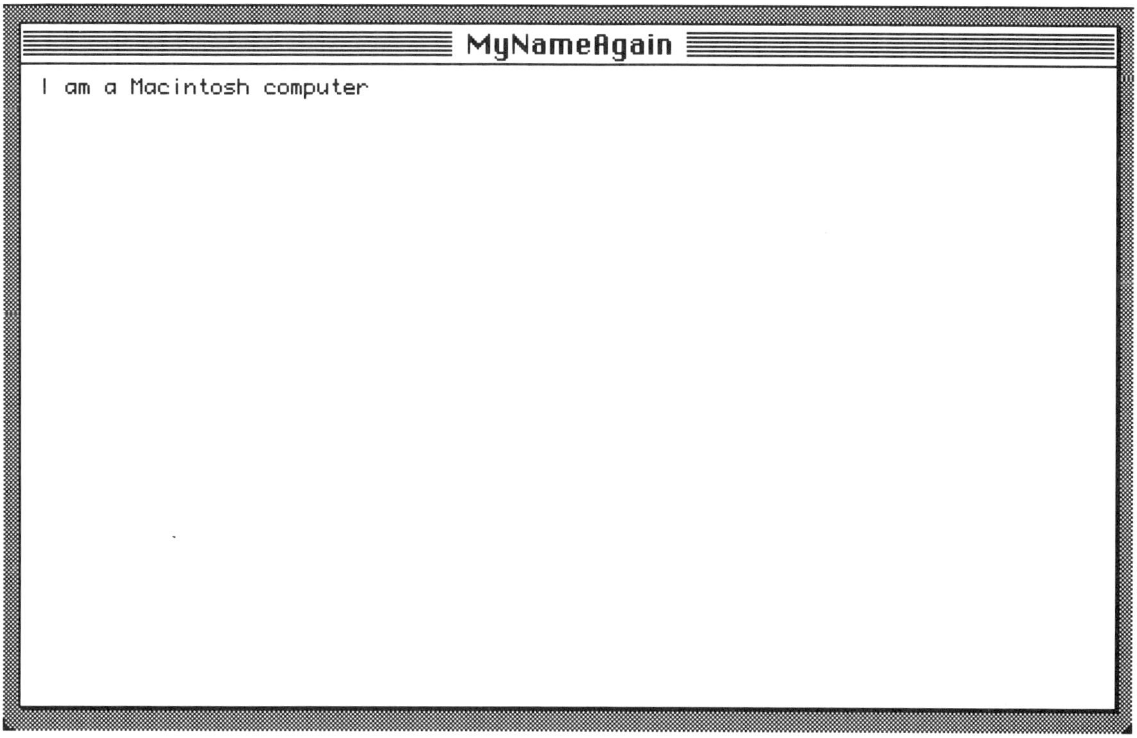

Figure 2-7. Displayed by MyNameAgain

Use the Change feature of the Turbo editor to change all the Write statements in the program to Writeln. Now try running it.

```
program MyNameAgain;
begin  Writeln('I ');
 Writeln('am ');
 Writeln('a ');
 Writeln('Macintosh ');
 Writeln('Computer ');
 Readln
end.
```

It now displays:

```
I
am
a
Macintosh
Computer
```

The program now places each word on a separate line. The difference between Write and Writeln should now be clear. After a Writeln statement is executed, the text insertion point returns to the beginning of the next line, and whatever is displayed next will be on a new line. However, whatever is displayed after a Write statement appears on the same line.

More than one item can be used in a Write or Writeln statement as long as each item is separated by a comma, such as

```
Writeln('I ', 'am ', 'a ', 'Macintosh ','Computer ');
```

All items contained within each Writeln statement will be displayed on the same line. Write and Writeln can be mixed in the same program. Now that we have a way to display information, let us examine the kinds of information Pascal can handle.

DATA TYPES

In our everyday lives we deal with many types of information: sounds, pictures, words, numbers, and so forth. Information used by a computer is called **data**. Computers process many different kinds of information, or data, including numbers, characters, strings of characters, pictures, sounds, and so on. Several different types of data can be represented in Pascal.

Integers

The most basic data type is **integer**, which includes positive and negative whole numbers (numbers that don't have fractional parts). Examples of integers are

```
1     23     -252     0     1398     -12
```

Notice that integers contain no decimal points. Commas are not used or allowed in integers. The largest integer that can be used by the Pascal language is called **Maxint**. This number is dependent on the machine being used. On the Macintosh system MaxInt is 32767. The smallest number that can be represented is −MaxInt−1 or −32768.

Reals

At one time computers could only process integer data, but today we can also represent numbers that have both a whole part and a fractional part. Turbo Pascal lets us represent these numbers with the **real** data type. Real numbers have a much larger range of values than integers and are thus useful for representing very large or very small quantities.

Examples of real numbers are:

```
3.14        -87.0        242.34        1.324e+6        -7.43e-2
```

The first three numbers listed are in the notation with which you are most familiar, that is, numbers with digits to the left and right of the decimal point. The last two numbers are in a form known as "scientific notation." The "e" stands for exponent and is always preceded by a sign. A number in scientific notation is interpreted by multiplying the number on the left of the "e" by ten raised to the number following the "e." Thus, 1.324e+6 is equivalent to 1.324×10^{6} or 1324000.0 and −7.43e−2 is equivalent to -7.43×10^{-2} or 0.0743. Other examples are

```
-12.34e+2   equivalent to   -1234.0
34.567e+1   equivalent to   345.67
-932.13e-4  equivalent to   -0.093213
```

In Pascal, real numbers can be always be expressed in either standard or in scientific notation. When expressing a real number there must always be at least one digit before the decimal point. For example, 0.5 is a valid representation of one-half, whereas .5 is not.

Characters and Strings

Computers need to process information other than numbers in order to communicate effectively with people. Pascal has two data types that handle text information, the **character** and the **string** data types.

Characters are upper- and lower-case letters, numbers, and punctuation symbols. Character data is enclosed in single quotes. Examples of characters are the following:

```
'a' 'D' '!' ';' '3' '%' ' '
```

Since quotes are used to delineate a character, to represent a quote we must use two consecutive quotes between quotes for a total of four, such as

```
''''
```

Strings are sequences of characters and are useful because they let us combine individual characters into words or sentences. This allows manipulation of more meaningful units than individual characters. As with characters, strings are written between single quotation marks:

```
'This is a sample string'
'testing 123 testing!!!'
```

VARIABLES

In order for a program to use data, it must be stored in the computer's memory. The computer's memory can be thought of as being divided into many different compartments, each holding a single piece of information of a specific data type. These compartments are called **variables**.

Pascal uses identifiers to name each variable. The value of a variable can change during the execution of a program, (hence the name) and is used as sort of a working storage of information during the execution of a program. To be used, a variable must be declared in a variable declaration section, as demonstrated in the next program.

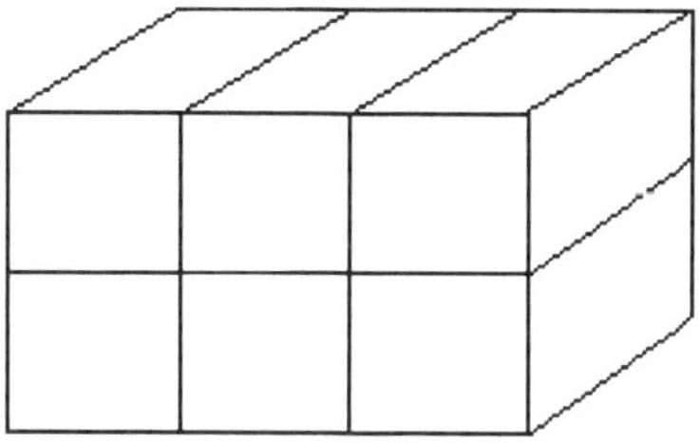

Figure 2-8. Compartments in Memory

```
program ShowVars;
var
  Number : Integer;
  Ch : Char;
begin
  Readln(Number, Ch);
  Write(Number,' ',Ch);
  Readln
end.
```

In this program two variables were declared: Number, which will hold an integer, and Ch, which will hold a character. Variables are declared after the program declaration but before the "begin" of the program. The variable declaration section is indicated by the reserved word "var" and consists of the variable's identifier and its type, separated by a colon (:).

```
var
identifier1 : DataType1;
identifier2 : DataType2;
```

Many separate declarations can exist with a semicolon separating each individual variable declaration. If there are several variables of the same data type, they may be declared together by separating them with a comma. For example:

```
var
x1, x2 : Real;
count, sum : Integer;
```

When you run the program, it will wait until you enter at the keyboard an integer, a space, and a character followed by a return. The integer value entered will be placed in the variable Number, and the character will be placed in the variable Ch. Whatever is entered is echoed to the screen by the Write statement. Whenever a variable is listed in a Writeln statement, the contents of that variable are displayed. The details of Readln will be explained later in this chapter.

TRIAL AND ERROR—IMPROPER DATA

Run the program again and enter data of a type other than that expected. What happened? When you hit the Return key, the System Error dialog box appeared. What you have encountered is your first run-time error.

RUN-TIME ERRORS

Unlike syntax errors that can be detected by the compiler during compilation, a run time error occurs during the execution of the program. There are several possible situations that can cause a run-time error. The one we just encountered is the entering of illegal input. Unlike other programs, Turbo protects from System Errors by allowing a graceful exit through the Resume option in the dialog box. This will deliver you back into the editor with the source of the error highlighted. (If you compiled to disk, you will go directly back to the Finder.) One of the chief goals of a programmer is to prevent program "crashes" caused from illegal input. Several techniques have been developed to protect against this; they are covered in later chapters.

Other sources of run-time errors include

- Dividing by zero
- Using variables that are out of their range (more on this later)
- Improper use of Toolbox functions.

Figure 2-9. I/O Error

ASSIGNMENT STATEMENTS

In the program that you were just playing with, variables were given values via the keyboard during program execution. Data can be placed in a variable in the program itself with an assignment statement such as

```
Number := 23;
Ch := 'A';
```

The function of an assignment statement is to place the value on the right-hand side of the assignment operator (:=) into the variable on the left-hand side. The variable retains the assigned value until it is altered by some other statement in the program. Notice that in the assignment operator there is no space between the colon and the equal sign. An assignment statement is not an algebraic equation, and it is not solved as one. This is the reason the assignment operator looks different from an equal sign. The assignment operator is interpreted to mean "gets the value." Hence, Number :=23 can be read as the variable Number gets the value 23. It may be helpful to think of the integer value 23 as being placed into the memory compartment that is labeled Number. Likewise Ch := 'A' can be thought of as the character "A" being put in the compartment labeled Ch.

The value assigned to a variable must be of the same data type as that variable (an integer value must be assigned to an integer variable, a real value to a real variable, and so on). Given the following variable declarations:

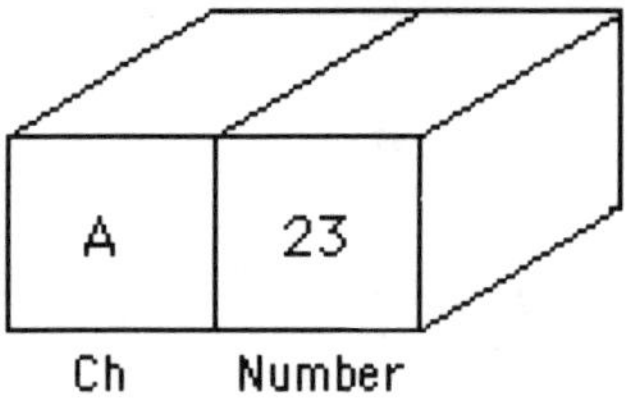

Figure 2-10. The Assignment Operator

```
var
 I : Integer;
 R1, R2 : Real;
 Ch : Char;
```

the following assignment statements are all legal:

```
I := 17;
R1 := 2.03;
R2 := 15.0;
Ch := 'B';
```

while, the following assignment statements are all illegal:

```
I := -17.17; -17.17 is not an integer
R1 := 15;    15 is not a real value
Ch := 22;    Ch is a character variable
Ch := '22';  '22' is a character string, not a
                   character
```

Improper assignments will be revealed as syntax errors by the compiler. This is one of the unique features of Pascal. Many other languages permit this type of statement to be performed without any kind of checking.

EXPRESSIONS

The value of an arithmetic expression can also be assigned to a variable. For example:

```
NewNumber := 5 + 3;
```

In this assignment statement, the variable "NewNumber" is given the value of the expression on the right-hand side of the assignment operator {:=}. This statement can be read as "the variable NewNumber gets the value obtained by adding together 5 and 3." That value is, of course, 8.

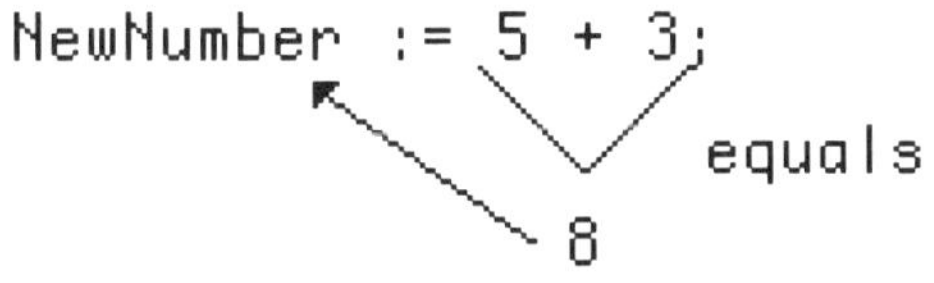

Figure 2-11. NewNumber := 5 + 3;

An expression can contain variables as well as constants.

```
NewNumber := OldNumber + 17;
```

This statement adds 17 to the value of the variable OldNumber and assigns that value to the variable NewNumber. There is no change in the value of OldNumber since it appears on the right side of the assignment operator; only a variable on the left side of the assignment operator will be changed in an assignment statement. The value of one variable can be assigned to a second variable in the same way.

```
NewNumber := OldNumber;
```

Here the value of OldNumber is assigned to NewNumber. They will now both have the same value. It is quite common to have assignment statements with the same variable on both sides of the operator. This may seem strange at first, but on closer examination its use will become apparent.

```
Number := Number + 3;
```

This statement simply adds 3 to the value of Number. It is interpreted just like any other assignment statement. The expression on the right side is evaluated and assigned to the variable on the left side. That is, add 3 to the value of Number and place the resulting value back into Number. Another way of describing this statement is that the "new" value of Number is the "old" value of Number plus three. For example, if Number contained seven before the statement was executed, it would contain ten after it was executed.

OPERATIONS

Addition is not the only operation that can be performed in an expression. Several other arithmetic operators are available in Pascal:

```
+   real or integer addition
-   real or integer subtraction
*   real or integer multiplication
/   real division
div integer division
mod modulo division (remainder of integer division)
```

The *, +, and − operators work as expected on both integer and real numbers, but different divisions exist for real and integer values. The div operator is used to divide one integer by another. When two integers are divided using div, the remainder is discarded. Some examples are shown in Table 2-1.

Table 2-1. Integers Divided Using DIV

Expression	Value
8 div 2	4
8 div 3	2
8 div 9	0

The mod operator is used to find the remainder of an integer division. For instance, 10 mod 3 is 1, because 10 divided by 3 leaves a remainder of 1. (Table 2-2)

Table 2-2. The Mod Operator

Expression	Value
8 mod 8	0
8 mod 2	0
8 mod 9	8
8 mod 3	2

Both 8 div 0 and 8 mod 0 are illegal since you cannot divide by 0. Either would generate an error.

Real division (the / operator) divides two real values giving a real result: 5.0/2.0 yields 2.5 and 10.0/1.0 yields 10.0

MIXING DATA TYPES

With any of the operations, real values can be mixed with integer values. When this is done the integer value is automatically converted to a real prior to the operation. For instance, in the addition of 4 + 3.7 an integer and real are both used. The integer 4 will first be converted to the real 4.0 and then added to 3.7. The result is 7.7 . The result of an expression can only be assigned to variables of the same data type. Breaking this rule will cause an error during compilation. Given these variable declarations:

```
var
I, J : Integer;
X : Real;
```

the following statements are all legal:

```
I := J + 3;   Integer result assigned to an integer
X := I + 2.0; Integer result assigned to an integer
X := 5 / 2;   Integer result assigned to an integer
X := J;       Integer result assigned to an integer
```

while the following statements are all illegal:

```
J := X;          Can't assign a real value to an
                 integer variable
J := 3.0 div 2;  Div needs two integer operands
J := J / I;      Real division produces a real result
```

Table 2-3 summarizes the data type of the result of different operations.

Table 2-3. Data Types

	Type of Operand			
	Real	Real	Integer	Integer
Operator	Real	Integer	Real	Integer
+	Real	Real	Real	Integer
−	Real	Real	Real	Integer
*	Real	Real	Real	Integer
/	Real	Real	Real	Real
DIV	error	error	error	Integer
MOD	error	error	error	Integer

OPERATOR PRECEDENCE

How is the value of an expression calculated when more than one operator is used? For instance, in the following expression the order of operations is significant.

```
7 + 2 * 4
```

If the addition is done first, the result is 36. If the multiplication is done first, the result is 15. However, Pascal has rules of operator precedence that are used to decide what is done first. Operators with a high precedence get evaluated before operators with a low precedence. Multiplication, real division, div, and mod have a higher precedence than addition and subtraction.

Operator Precedence Table

```
High Precedence *, /, mod, div
Low Precedence +, -
```

When operators of the same precedence are found in an expression, they are evaluated from left to right.

The natural precedence of the operators can be overcome by the use of parentheses. For instance:

```
(7 + 2) * 4
```

Some more examples:

Table 2-4. The Use of Parenthese

Expression	Value
3 + 2 * 3	9
(3 + 2) * 5	25
14 mod 3 + 1	3
1 + 2 * 3 + 4	11
(1 + 2) * 3 + 4	13
1 + 2 * (3 + 4)	15

CONSTANTS

Constants, as the name implies, are values that never change. Pascal can also have named constants that are represented by identifiers. Examine the following program:

```
program Constant;
const
 TwentyThree = 23;
 Ayyy = 'A';
var
 Number : Integer;
 Ch : Char;
begin
 Number := TwentyThree;
 Ch := Ayyy;
 Write(Number,' ',Ch);
 Readln
end.
```

This program would display

```
23 Ayyy
```

Constants are declared after the program declaration but before the variable declaration section. The reserved word "const" is used to indicate the constant declaration section, which consists of the constant's identifier and the value of the constant separated by an equals sign (=). The assignment operator is not used. A semicolon separates each of the constant declaration statements.

Once a constant is defined it cannot be changed later in the program; in fact, trying to assign a new value to a constant will produce an error when you compile your program. Try it and see. Constants are used rather than the values themselves to make a program more readable. Additionally, the use of constants can prevent errors since any erroneous attempt to alter its value will result in a program error when you attempt to compile the program. It is far better to detect an error in this fashion than to hunt for the source of an improper calculation or rely on the result of that calculation.

MORE ON WRITE AND WRITELN

Write and Writeln allow an optional parameter called the **field width**, which is used to provide control over how data is displayed. The field width parameter is specified by following any item in a Write or Writeln statement with a colon (:) and a positive integer. The integer determines how many spaces are allocated for displaying the item. The easiest case to look at is that of displaying strings. The field width parameter indicates how many spaces are used to display the string. If the string does not take up all the spaces allocated, it is right-justified within the field as demonstrated in Figures 2-12 and 2-13.

```
Write('Cantaloupe' : 15)
```

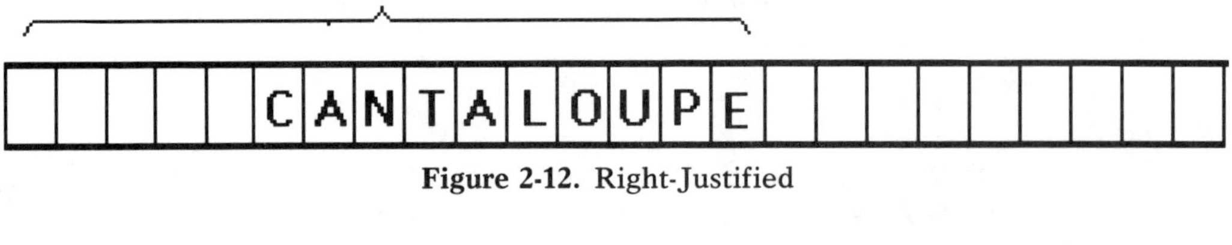

Figure 2-12. Right-Justified

```
Write('Cantaloupe:20)
```

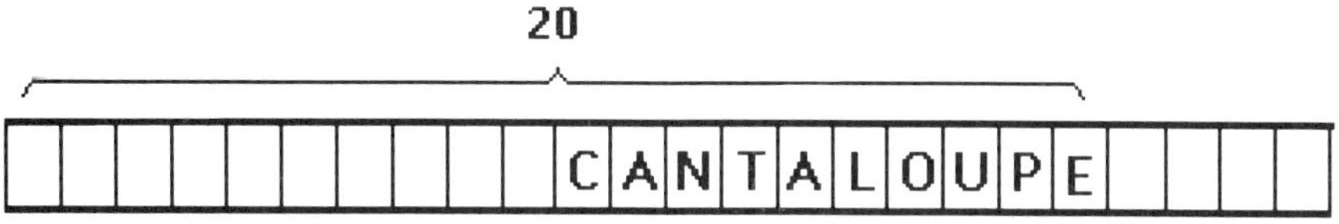

Figure 2-13. More Spaces

If the number of characters in the string exceeds the field width parameter, the excess characters on the right side are truncated. Figure 2-14 demonstrates this:

```
Write('Cantaloupe':5)
```

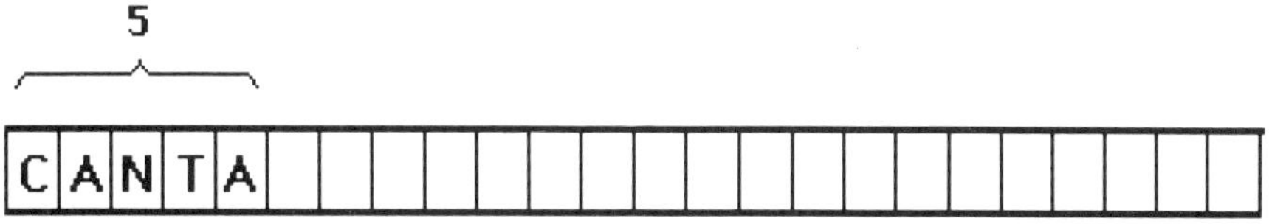

Figure 2-14. Truncation

In order to display real numbers in standard notation, two field width parameters are used. The first represents the total field width, not including the decimal point, and the second is for the number of digits to be included after the decimal point. It is important to remember that reals are right-justified in the number of spaces indicated by the first parameters. Consider the following assignment statement:

```
R := 2.55;
```

the following Writeln statement:

```
Writeln(R:4:2)
```

displays the following:

```
2.55
```

If the total field width given is too small for a real number or an integer, the entire value will be printed anyway. The following sequence of statements:

```
I := 10;
R := 10.04;
Writeln(I :1);
Writeln(R : 3 : 2);
```

will display:

```
10
10.04
```

In displaying a real, the value will be rounded off to the number of decimal places specified by the second field width parameter, rounding off the number if necessary.

The effect of omitting a field width parameter differs with each data type. A string will be printed in precisely the number of characters required. Integers will occupy a minimum of eight spaces, but more are used if needed. An integer will never be truncated. Reals will be displayed in scientific notation.

READ AND READLN

So far in all the programs we have seen, variables were given values via assignment statements. However, in Pascal there is a way to provide a variable with a value during execution with the **Read** and **Readln** statements.

As we have already seen, the Readln statement stops and waits for information to be entered from the keyboard. When a Readln statement is executed, the information that is entered on the keyboard is placed into the variable specified in the statement and echoed to the console window. The user signals that he has finished the entry by pressing the Return key. Below is an example of using Readln in a simple program:

```
program CircleArea;
const
```

```
 Pi = 3.14159;
var
 Area, Radius : Real;
begin
 Write('What is the radius of the circle ?:');
 Readln(Radius);
 Area := Pi * Radius * Radius;
 Write('The area of a circle with radius ',Radius,' is
',Area);
 Readln
end.
```

The Read statement works in the same fashion as the Readln except that the input does not have to be terminated by hitting the Return key. Instead, the data entry is terminated when a space or comma is entered.

Read and Readln can work with all of the data types already discussed. More than one variable can be used by separating them with commas. For example:

```
program MoreThanOne;
var
 Moe, Shep, Curly : Integer;
begin
 Readln(Moe,Shep,Curly);
 Writeln(Moe,Shep,Curly);
 Readln
end.
```

The user must type some nonnumeric character between the three integers to indicate where one integer ends and the next begins. Because we are using a Readln statement, a carriage return must follow the last value entered.

REVIEW OF PROGRAM STRUCTURE

The four sections of a program we have examined so far are

1. the program declaration;

2. the constant declarations;

3. the variable declarations;

4. the program body (everything between "begin" and "end").

Remember that the variable and constant declaration sections are optional and not required by a syntactically correct program, although every program that is nontrivial will have both these sections.

THE DIRTY DOZEN—THE MOST LIKELY SYNTAX ERRORS

While 99 possible syntax errors can be triggered in your programs, there are 12 that are most likely to occur, especially for new programmers. Here is a list of the "dirty dozen" and possible solutions.

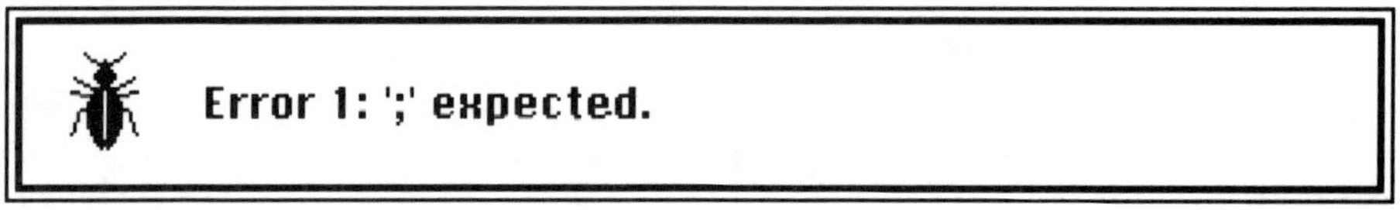

Figure 2-15. Missing Semicolon Error

The missing semicolon is probably the most common error encountered in Pascal programming. Its source is obvious: there is no semicolon where there should be one. When this is the cause, Turbo will return you to the editor with the start of the line after the missing semicolon highlighted.

There is a common but more subtle way to trigger this error. When the begins and ends of a program are not balanced—that is, do not match up—this error can be triggered. Consider the following program.

```
program SubtleError;
var
 I, Sum : Integer;
begin
 for I := 1 to 10 do
```

```
begin
Sum := Sum * 2;
Sum := Sum + I
end.
```

Close examination of the program will show that there is a missing end statement, the one needed to close the compound statement in the For loop. The missing semicolon error will be triggered, and Turbo will highlight the last end.

Figure 2-16. Unknown Identifier Error

The unknown identifier error is caused by not declaring a variable that is used in the program. For instance:

```
program UnknownI;
var
 I : Integer;
begin
 for I := 1 to 10 do
 Sum := Sum + 1
end.
```

In this simple program, the identifier Sum is not declared and thus will cause this error. The solution: simply add it to the variable declaration.

Figure 2-17. Colon Expected Error

The colon expected error is most often caused by failing to use a data type in a variable declaration. For instance:

```
var
 K ;
```

Here K is declared as a variable, but no data type is given. Since the compiler is expecting a colon after the identifier, this error is triggered. Note that using the equal sign for the assignment operator will not cause this error but instead will trigger Error 07, := expected.

Figure 2-18. Period Expected Error

The period expected error most often occurs when there are too many ends in a program. For instance:

```
program TooEndorNotTooEnd;
var
 I : Integer;
begin
 for I := 1 to 10 do
 Sum := Sum + 1
 end
end.
```

In this program, there are two ends but only one begin. The programmer apparently forgot that a compound statement was not used with this For loop. Since the compiler expects a period after the first end encountered, this is the error triggered.

Figure 2-19. Expected Error

Right parenthesis expected is caused when the parentheses in a statement are not balanced. This can occur either in an expression such as

```
Total := ((Height * Weight) + (Age * Waist);
```

or, in a Writeln statement such as

```
Writeln (Name, Address, ZipCode;
```

This error happens more frequently than left parenthesis expected since we type from left to right.

Figure 2-20. Error in Expression Error

The error in expression error is caused by improperly using operators in an expression:

```
Dog := Cat div mod Bird;
```

Figure 2-21. Unexpected End of Text Error

The source of this error is almost always just a missing period at the end of a program. Since this very subtle to catch, it can lead to great frustration.

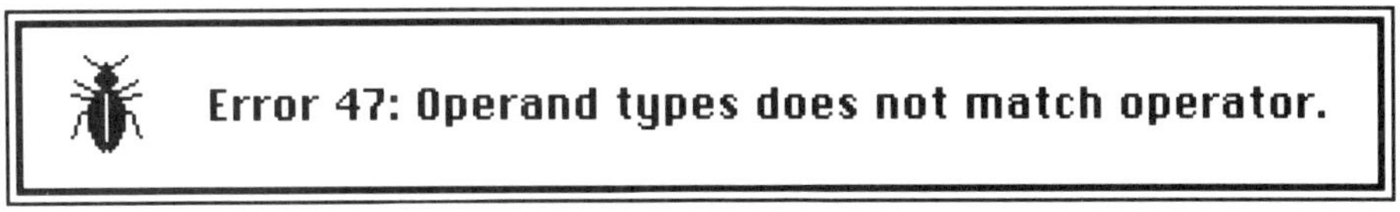

Figure 2-22. Operand Types Do Not Match Operator

This is a simple error caused by using the wrong operator with a value. For instance, all of these will trigger this error:

```
R := R Not 4;
Int := 4.0 div 12;
Ch := 'C' + 'A';
```

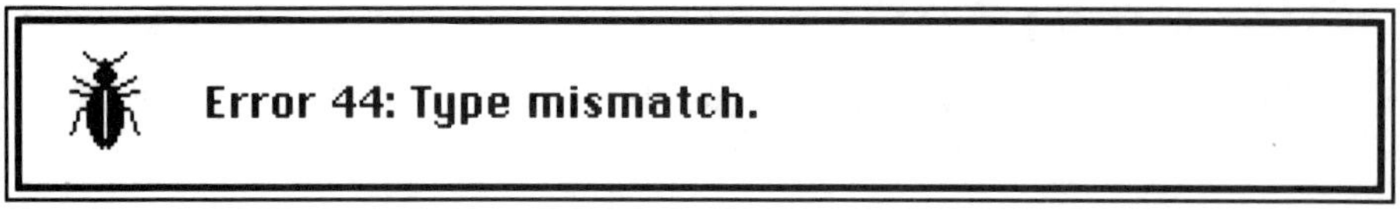

Figure 2-23. Type Mismatch Error

This error happens when a value of one data type is assigned to a variable of another. For instance, given the following variable declaration:

```
var
 Int : Integer;
 R : Real;
```

the following expression would trigger this error:

```
Int := R + 1.2;
```

since it is attempting to assign a real value to an integer variable. If this operation need take place, either the real value must be converted to an integer with the Round or Trunc functions, or a real variable must be used instead.

Figure 2-24. Unit Missing Error

This error occurs when a Toolbox or QuickDraw routine is used, but the proper Uses statement has not been included in the program. For most of the Toolbox routines this Uses is required:

```
Uses MemTypes, QuickDraw, ToolIntF, OsIntF;
```

Figure 2-25. Duplicate Indentifier Error

There are two common sources of this error. First is declaring the same identifier for two variables as in the following:

```
var
J, K, L : Integer;
L, M, N : Real;
```

The other, more subtle, source is forgetting to start the program with a begin. For instance:

```
program ANewBeginning;
var
Larry, Moe : Integer;
Moe := 15;
```

Since the compiler found no begin, it assumes that the assignment statement is just another variable declaration and will trigger duplicate identifier.

Figure 2-26. Comma Expected Error

This error can occur in a multitude of situations. The most common is failing to separate items in a Write statement with a comma.

```
Write(First Second);
```

A more subtle occurence is when a built-in function is used with the wrong number of arguments. For instance, the GoToXY routine requires two arguments, X and Y. If one is missing, this error is triggered:

```
GoToXY(Y);
```

Turbo will apply this same standard to all the Toolbox routines and thus provides a very high level of type checking for the use of the Toolbox.

This error is caused by using a control variable that is not an enumerated type. For instance:

```
var
R : real:
begin
For R := 1.0 to 5.0 do
```

Here a real variable is being used as the control variable for the For loop.

3
Pascal Structures

INTRODUCTION

We have already seen the basic building blocks of a Pascal program; how a program is formed; how values are assigned to variables; and how simple input and output is done. More will be needed to write programs that are capable of doing more complex tasks. This chapter will introduce you to some Pascal's structures, the building blocks of programs. We will see how decisions can be made in programs, how statements can be repeated and we will be introduced to rectangles, the first of QuickDraw's many drawing shapes.

DECISION MAKING—IF-THEN

The If-then structure allows for execution of different statements depending upon the result of a conditional test. A conditional test is an expression that can have a value of either True or False. The form of the If statement is

```
IF conditional test is True
   THEN statement1;
statement2;
```

If the result of the test is True, then Statement1 is executed; otherwise it will be skipped. Statement2 is executed no matter what the value of the test. The following program uses an If-then statement to make a decision based upon a value that is entered. Enter it and then run it several times with different values.

```
program FirstIF;
var
  Num : Integer;
begin
  Write('Enter a number any number : ');
  Readln(Num);
  Write(Num,' is a ');
  if Num > 100 then
      Write('BIG ');
  Writeln('number');
  Write('Press <Return> to continue ');
  Readln
end.
```

Here the If statement reads:

```
if Num > 100 then
     Write('BIG ');
```

The value of Num is entered by the user. If the input is less than 100 (for instance 79), the Write statement that is part of the If will be skipped, and the output would read: 79 is a number. However, if the value is greater than 100, the Write statement contained in the If statement would be executed, and the output would read: 179 is a big number.

Conditional Tests

Several different types of comparisons called **conditional tests** can be made in an If statement. Following are the possible conditions that can be tested:

```
=     Equal to
<>    Not equal to
<     Less than
>     Greater than
>=    Greater than or equal to
<=    Less than or equal to
```

In Table 3-1 are some examples of conditional expressions and their values. Assume I has a value of 3 and J has a value of 4.

Table 3-1. Conditional Expressions

Expression	Value
3 > 2	True
I * 2 = 4	False
I <> J	True
I - J <= J	True

The following program reads three positive integer values from the keyboard and finds the largest of the three:

```
program Iffy;
var
  Num1, Num2, Num3 , Biggest: Integer;
begin
  Write('Enter 3 integer numbers separated by spaces ');
  Readln(Num1, Num2, Num3);
  Biggest := 0;
  if Num1 > Biggest then
      Biggest := Num1;
  if Num2 > Biggest then
      Biggest := Num2;
  if Num3 > Biggest then
      Biggest := Num3;
  Writeln('The largest of the numbers is ',Biggest);
  Write('Press <Return> to continue ');
  Readln
end.
```

In this program each value is compared against the current largest value to see if it is larger. The variable representing the largest value, Biggest, is initialized to zero, which we will assume is smaller than any value entered. This assures that the first meaningful value of Biggest will be the value of Num1. Try to enter several sets of values and see if you can get the program to "crash." What input produces undesirable results, and how can the program prevent itself from crashing?

Compound Statements

If we were only allowed a single statement to be executed as part of an If-then, its usefulness would be severely limited. There exists a way to execute many statements rather than just one. Wherever a single statement can be used, it can be replaced by a compound statement. A compound statement is a sequence of statements separated by semicolons and bracketed by a begin and end. Thus, a program can have many begin and ends sets. The statements contained in a compound statement are always executed together. Here is a short example of a compound statement:

```
program CompoundExample;
var
  Num : Integer;
  Abs : Integer;
begin
  Write('Please enter number : ');
  Readln(Num);
  if Num < 0 then
      begin  {Start of Compound statement}
          Abs := Num * -1;
          Write(' The absolute value of ',Num);
          Writeln(' is ',Abs)                {No semicolon}
      end; {End of Coumpound statement}     {Uses a semicolon}
  if Num >= 0 then
      Writeln(' The absolute value of ',Num,' is ',Num);
  Write('Press <Return> to continue ');
  Readln
end.
```

This program finds the absolute value of a number (that number without any sign). If the value entered is a negative value, the compound statement in the If-then is executed multiplying the number by −1 and then displaying it. If the number is positive, the number is just displayed as is. This program also demonstrates one of the rules of good programming. Whenever a value is to be entered, the program should prompt the user with a message telling what is expected.

A short note on semicolons. A statement before an end never gets a semicolon. An end that comes before a statement gets a semicolon.

If-then-else

The If-then statement allows a second clause called else to allow two mutually exclusive statements (or compound statements) as part of the If, one executed if the condition is True, the other executed if the condition is False.

The form of the If-then-else is:

```
if condition then
   Statement1
else
   Statement2;
Statement3;
```

For example:

```
if Hours <= 40.0 then
   Pay := Hours * Rate
else
   Pay := 40 * Rate + (Hours - 40) * Rate * 2.0;
```

In this example from a hypothetical payroll program, the If statement is used to determine pay based on the number of hours worked. If the value of Hours is 40 or less, the statement after the then, Pay := Hours * Rate; is executed calculating the paycheck. If the value of Hrs is greater than 40, then the else clause, Pay := 40 * Rate + (Hours − 40) * Rate * 2.0; is executed and adds in overtime pay.

Nested If Statements

The statement that follows after a then or else can also be an If statement. The nesting of If statements can be used to make multiple decisions based on the same data. Type the following short program:

```
program CaliforniaDreaming;
var
  Temp : Integer;
begin
  Write('WHAT'S TODAY'S TEMPERATURE?  ');
```

```
  Readln(Temp);
  if Temp > 70 then
      if Temp > 80 then
          Writeln('GO TO THE BEACH')
      else
          Writeln('GO TO THE POOL')
  else
      Writeln('GO TO THE MOVIES');
  Write('Press <Return> to continue ');
  Readln
end.
```

Table 3-2 shows a list of some possible inputs and their associated output:

Table 3-2. Possible Inputs and Outputs

Input	Output
75	GO TO THE POOL
60	GO TO THE MOVIES
89	GO TO THE BEACH

In the program two "elses" are used. An "else" always belongs to the If-then that is physically closest to it. In order to see what belongs to what, it is important that a program be properly indented. The reader of a program should immediately be able to tell which "else" belongs to which If statement based upon the way it is indented. Fortunately, Turbo Pascal's editor has an auto indent feature that makes it easy to properly format a program. Here is a look at another way of structuring the If statements to get the same result.

```
if Temp > 80 then
 Write('GO TO THE BEACH')
else if Temp > 70 then
 Write('GO TO THE POOL')
else
 Write('GO TO THE MOVIES');
```

Notice the indenting in this example. Each Write statement is indented the same number of spaces to emphasize that each is dependent on the value of temperature.

What do the following statements print?

```
Stars := 4;
if Stars >= 3 then
  if Stars = 5 then
      Write('much better than');
else
  Write('worse than');
Writeln('average');
```

If you said "average," then you are wrong. If you said "worse than average," you are correct. Remember the rule that an "else" belongs to the closest If statement? That rule applies here also; the "else" clause belongs to the if Stars = 5 clause. This segment is tricky because the indenting fools us into interpreting the code in the wrong way. You can bracket an If statement in a begin-end pair and override the "else" to the nearest If statement rule. The program should be rewritten as follows to have the "else" belong to the if Stars >= 3 clause:

```
Stars := 4;
 if Stars >= 3 then
    begin
        if Stars = 5 then
           Write('much better than')
    end
 else
     Write('worse than');
Writeln('average');
```

THE BOOLEAN DATA TYPE

Closely related to conditional tests is the **Boolean** data type. In fact, the result of a conditional test is a Boolean value. A variable of type Boolean can have one of only two possible values represented by the words "true" and "false." They are called Booleans in honor of George Boole, the father of algebraic logic.

A variable is declared as a Boolean with

```
var
 X, Y : Boolean;
```

Here the variables X and Y are both of type Boolean. A value is assigned to a Boolean variable with an assignment statement.

```
X := True;
Y := False;
```

Boolean Operators

Since Booleans are not numeric values, they cannot use the same operators as numeric types and therefore must have operators of their own. These operators are the standard logical operators And, Or, and Not.

Truth Tables

The operator And takes two values and gives a result of True only if both values are True. The operator Or gives a result of True if either value is True. The operator Not simply flips a single value. The table of possible results of a Boolean operator is called a **truth table**. Table 3-3 to 3-5 are the truth tables for And, Or, and Not:

Table 3-3. And

Value1	Value2	Result
True	True	True
True	False	False
False	True	False
False	False	False

Table 3-4. Or

Value1	Value2	Result
True	True	True
True	False	True
False	True	True
False	False	False

Table 3-5. Not

Value1	Result
True	False
False	True

The Boolean operators should not seem all that strange to you since they are used in everyday English. For instance, you might say, "I'm going swimming and I'm going water skiing." If you did neither or only one, the statement is False. On the other hand, if you said, "I'm going bowling or I'm going to play Frisbee," then the statement would be True if you did either.

Boolean Expressions

Just like numeric expressions where many values are reduced to a single value, there are also Boolean expressions. A Boolean expression can consist of

1) a single Boolean value; or

2) a single Boolean variable; or

3) a combination of values and variables connected by operators.

When more than one operator are used together, the order in which the operations are evaluated is significant. All Nots are applied first, followed by And operator and then Or. This order can be altered with the use of parentheses. It is recommended that you always use parentheses in large Boolean expressions to make them more readable and understandable. For example, the following two expressions using Boolean variables X, Y, and Z are equivalent:

```
X OR NOT X AND Y
X OR ( (NOT X ) AND Y )
```

In Table 3-6 are some sample Boolean expressions and their results.

Table 3-6. Boolean Expressions

Expression	Result
True	True
True or False	True
True or False and False	True
(True or False) and False	False
not True or False	False
Assuming	
X := True;	
Y := False;	
True or Y and not X	True

Only a Boolean value can be assigned to a Boolean variable. Pascal goes to quite a bit of trouble to check that all values assigned are compatible with the type of variable used. This is done to prevent erroneous values from being assigned to variables. Because of the large amount of the type checking done, Pascal is referred to as a "strongly typed language."

LOOPS—MORE LIKE AN AIRPLANE THAN A BRICK

Up to this point all the programs we have written have one thing in common. They executed in a sequential order, starting with the first statement and proceeding to the last (although sometimes an If statement provided a fork in the road). You can think of this type of program as being similar to a brick dropped out of a seventeenth-floor window. It starts at the top and quickly descends straight down. There was no way to repeat the execution of some part of the program, just as there is no way for the brick to do a loop-the-loop on an air current. Fortunately, Pascal has three different loop structures to make a program more like a paper airplane than a brick. The loop structure are For, While, and Repeat. Each of the three different loops has its own uses and attributes. The first loop to be discussed is the **For loop**.

To demonstrate the function of the For loop, run this short program, which uses QuickDraw's rectangle commands.

```
program OverlappingRectangles;
uses
  MemTypes, QuickDraw;
var
  Square      : Rect;
  Shift, I     : Integer;
begin
  Shift := 0;
  for I := 1 to 20 do
     begin
        SetRect(Square,10+Shift,10+Shift,
          40+Shift,40+Shift);
        FrameRect(Square);  {Draw Rectangle}
        Shift := Shift + 5
    end;
 Readln;
end.
```

Displayed by the program is the following:

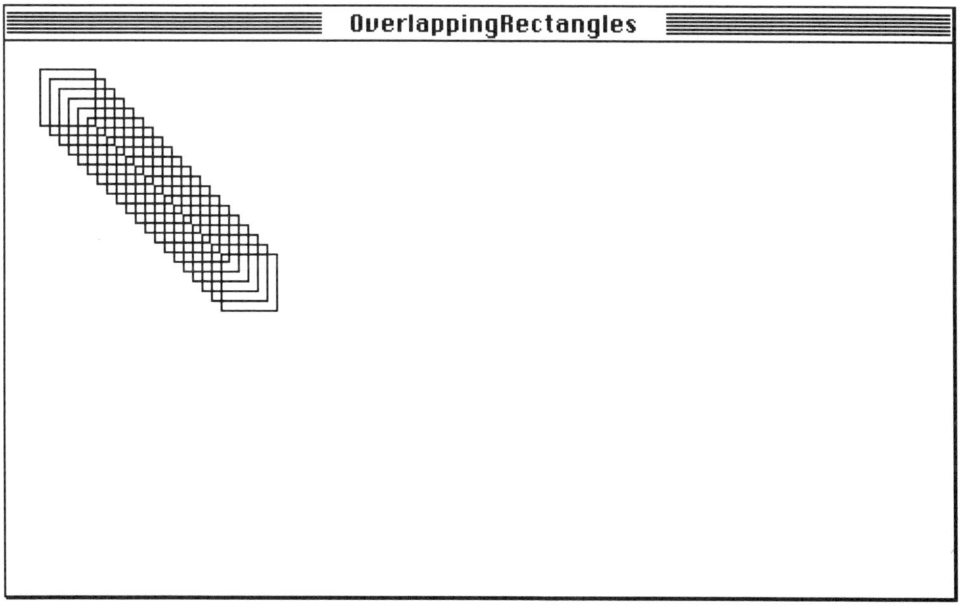

Figure 3-1. Overlapping Rectangles

A For loop is used to repeat the execution of a statement a fixed number of times. In the program the For loops repeat the statements, which draw a rectangle 20 times. The structure of the For loop is

```
for variable := expression to expression do
    statement;
```

The loop uses a variable known as the **control variable**, which is set to an initial value and then successively incremented each iteration of the loop until it hits the final value. Both the initial and final values of the control variable are given as either constants or expressions. Three reserved words are used in the For loop. "For" indicates the type of loop and comes before the initial value of the control variable. This is followed by "to," which comes before the final value for the For loop, and "do," which comes before the statement (or compound statement) that is to be repeated by the loop. This statement is sometimes known as the body of the loop.

Here is an example:

```
for K := 1 to 5 do
  Writeln('The value of K is ',K);
```

In this For loop the initial value is 1 and the final value is 5. The statement after the "do" is executed once for every integer value of control variable from 1 to 5, displayed as

The value of K is 1

The value of K is 2

The value of K is 3

The value of K is 4

The value of K is 5

The value of the control variable K is changed after each execution of the Writeln statement contained in the loop. When the final value of 5 was reached, the Writeln was executed for the last time.

In the next example, the values of the control variable in the For loop are added together.

```
Sum := 0;
for I:= 1 to 3 do
  Sum:=Sum + I;
```

In this loop, the statement after the "do" is executed once for every integer value of the control variable (I) from 1 to 3.

Let's trace the execution of the loop presented in the example.

```
I       Sum
                (entering the For loop)
-        0       (before execution)
1        1
2        3
3        6
```

As you can see, the loop was executed three times, once for each value of I from 1 to 3. This loop does the same thing as the following statements:

```
Sum := Sum + 1;
Sum := Sum + 2;
Sum := Sum + 3;
```

The single statement in the For loop accomplished all three of these additions. The value added to Sum is the same as the control variable, which is modified in the loop.

Nested For Loops

When one For loop is placed inside another, the result is known as **nested loops**. When there are nested For loops, the inner loop is completely executed for each value of the outer loop. To demonstrate this concept, let's examine a program that produces a simple multiplication table, the type you memorized back in grade school, generated by one For loop nested inside another.

```
program MultTable;
var
  Row, Col, Value : Integer;
begin
  Writeln(' ':5, 'Multiplication Table');
  Writeln;
  Write(' ':5); <Generate Heading>
  for Row := 1 to 10 do
  Write(Row:3);
  Writeln;
  for Row := 1 to 80 do
  Write('-');
  Writeln;
  {**Start to build table **}
  for Row := 1 to 10 do
      begin
          Write(Row:4,':');
          for Col := 1 to 10 do
              begin
                  Value := Row * Col;
                  Write(Value :3)
              end;
          Writeln
      end;
  Writeln;
  Write('Press <Return> to continue ');
  Readln
end.
```

The table is generated by the nested For loops:

```
{**Start to build table **}
 for Row := 1 to 10 do
     begin
         Write(Row:4,':');
         for Col := 1 to 10 do
             begin
                 Value := Row * Col;
                 Write(Value :3)
             end;
         Writeln
     end;
```

```
MultTable

    Multiplication Table

         1   2   3   4   5   6   7   8   9  10
----------------------------------------------------------------------------

    1:   1   2   3   4   5   6   7   8   9  10
    2:   2   4   6   8  10  12  14  16  18  20
    3:   3   6   9  12  15  18  21  24  27  30
    4:   4   8  12  16  20  24  28  32  36  40
    5:   5  10  15  20  25  30  35  40  45  50
    6:   6  12  18  24  30  36  42  48  54  60
    7:   7  14  21  28  35  42  49  56  63  70
    8:   8  16  24  32  40  48  56  64  72  80
    9:   9  18  27  36  45  54  63  72  81  90
   10:  10  20  30  40  50  60  70  80  90 100

Press <Return> to continue
```

Figure 3-2. The Multiplication Table

For each value of Row, the inner loop with Col as its control variable is completely executed for all 10 values of Col. It is then reexecuted for the next value of Row. In summary, there are 100 iterations of the inner loop but only 10 of the outer loop.

Downto

A slight variation in the For loop allows the loop to count down, too. For instance:

```
for I := 5 downto 1 do
  Write(I);
```

This loop prints 5 4 3 2 1. The keyword "downto" has replaced the keyword "to," indicating the direction of the counting. The initial value must now be greater than the final value, or the statement will not be executed.

One limitation of the For loop is that the control variable can only be increased or decreased by one. This can be overcome by using a second variable that is independent of the control variable. Let's write a loop to add the even numbers between 1 and 10.

```
EvenNumber :=  0;
EvenSum := 0;
for Count := 1 to 5 do
 begin
   EvenNumber := EvenNumber + 2;
   EvenSum := EvenSum + EvenNumber
 end;
Writeln(EvenSum);
```

Notice that Count goes from 1 to 5, but at the same time the values of EvenNumber are from 2 to 10 by twos.

PROGRAMMING EXAMPLE—CALCULATING BANK INTEREST

A For loop can be used in a program to calculate daily interest on any amount for any period of time. In the following program, the user is asked to enter the principal amount and the number of years for which to compute the interest. The interest is compounded daily, and the information is printed for every 30 days. The formula for compound interest is as follows:

```
Interest := Principal * (1 + Rate / 365)
```

Here is the pseudocode (see below) for the program:

```
Get principal amount
Get number of year
Get interest rate
for each year do
  for every day in the year do
      calculate the daily interest
      add it to the principal
      if the day is divisible by 30 then
          Write (information)
```

In this book we will express algorithms in a cross between Pascal and English known as **pseudocode**. As your programs become more and more complex, it will become increasingly difficult to conceive of the entire program at one time. This is where pseudocode comes in. Pseudocode is a language that is closer to the way people think than Pascal. Pseudocode can be used to bridge the gap between the abstract thoughts in your mind and a more concrete realization of these ideas as a Pascal program. You may not need to write pseudocode for every program you create, but if a program gets large and complicated or you don't know where to start, pseudocode can be a indispensable aid in organizing your ideas.

Now here is the program:

```
program Interest;
const
  DaysInYear = 365;
var
  Day, Years, Yr : Integer;
  Rate, Interest, Principal : Real;
begin
  Writeln('Interest Compounded Daily');
  Writeln;
  Writeln;
  Write('Enter the principal       : ');
  Readln(Principal);
  Write('Enter the number of years : ');
  Readln(Years);
  Write('Enter the interest        : ');
  Readln(Rate);
  Rate:=Rate / 100 ; <Convert rate to a fraction>
  for Yr := 1 to Years do
      for Day := 1 to 365 do
          begin
              {Calculate daily interest}
              Interest := Principal * ( Rate / 365 );
              {Add interest to principal}
              Principal := Principal + Interest;
              if Day mod 30 = 0 then
                  begin
                      Write('For day ', Day:3);
                      Writeln(' The Principal is ',
                        Principal:8:2)
                  end
          end; {FOR loop}
  Write('Press <Return> to continue ');
  Readln
 end. {Program}
```

The While Loop

The second of Pascal's looping structures is the **While loop**. Unlike the For loop, where the number of iterations is known before the loop is executed, the While loop is a free loop dependent on what happens inside the body of the loop.

The structure of the While loop is as follows:

```
while Boolean expression is True do
    Statement1;
Statement2;
```

First, the value of the Boolean expression is evaluated (similar to the if statement); if its value is True, the loop body is executed and the Boolean expression is once again checked. This process continues until the value of the Boolean expression becomes False.

Enter the following program, which uses the While loop as well as one of the special features of the Macintosh:

```
program NewLoop;
uses
  Memtypes, QuickDraw, OSIntF, ToolIntF;
var
  Count  : Integer;
begin
  Count := 0;
  while not Button do
     begin
       Count := Count + 1;
       Writeln ('Iteration Number', Count)
   end
end.
```

If you run the program, you will see a quickly scrolling message in the console window indicating the iteration of the loop. The loop is stopped just by hitting the mouse button. How? Notice that the conditional test in the While loop is not Button. Button is a special Boolean variable maintained by Turbo Pascal (actually it is a Boolean function, which we will discuss later, but for now let us think of it as a Boolean variable). It has a value of False if the mouse button hasn't been pressed since it was last checked and True if it has. Since we want the loop to terminate when the button is pressed, we reverse the value of Button so that it is False after the button has been pressed, terminating the loop. The unusual statement just after the program declaration.

```
uses
  Memtypes, QuickDraw, OSIntf, ToolIntf;
```

is not a Pascal structure but is rather a message to the Turbo compiler that certain features of the language not currently included into a program will be used. The use of Button necessitated this.

Normally, we must alter the value of the condition being checked in the body of the While loop; otherwise an infinite loop will be created. For example, the following loop will never end since the value of the variable Int will never change and thus never be greater than 5:

```
Int := 1;
while Int <= 5 do
  Writeln(Int);
```

This loop will continue forever, or until the frustrated programmer turns off the computer. This is a good time to make an important point: Always save your program before running it. This would prevent loss of the program if you had to reboot the computer to stop a runaway loop. If you plan to do a lot of programming, it will make sense to install the plastic programmer's switch on the left side of your Mac. This will allow you to interrupt the execution of a program by producing a System Error and should allow you to resume using the Turbo editor without powering down the computer and losing any unsaved data.

Our next example of a While loop is used to simulate the div and mod operators.

```
program Divide;
var
  Top, SaveTop, Bottom, Answer, Remainder : Integer;
begin
  Write('Enter the dividend : ');
```

```
    Readln(Top);
    Write('Enter the divisor   : ');
    Readln(Bottom);
    Answer := 0;
    SaveTop := Top;
    while Top >= Bottom do
        begin
            Top := Top - Bottom;
            Answer := Answer +1
        end; {while}
    Remainder := Top;
    Writeln(SaveTop, '/',Bottom, ' = ', Answer:1, ' R ',
      Remainder:1);
    Write('Press <Return> to continue ');
    Readln
  end. {Program}
```

Let us trace the program for the values Top := 18 and Bottom := 5 in Table 3-7.

Table 3-7. Values for Top and Bottom

Top	Bottom	Answer	Remainder	SaveTop
18	5	0	—	18
13	5	1	—	18
8	5	2	—	18
3	5	3	—	18
loop terminates				
3	5	3	3	18

Notice that SaveTop was needed to hold the value of Top since the original value is changed in the loop.

QUICK TO THE DRAW

Perhaps the most important component of the Macintosh is the QuickDraw graphics library stored in the Mac's ROM. QuickDraw forms the foundation on which many of the features are built. Like the other features of the User Interface, QuickDraw was designed to easily interact with programs written in Pascal. This is especially true with programs written with Turbo Pascal. At this point in our familiarity with the Pascal language, we can think of QuickDraw as consisting of a number of "commands" used to generate and display graphics. The first set of commands we will look at are the rectangle commands. The QuickDraw commands operate in part with a special set of graphical data types. To access these commands and data structures, a program needs to communicate with several of Turbo Pascal's units. A unit is essentially a section of the Pascal system not normally connected to a program. To access the units needed to work with QuickDraw, the Uses statement is included right after the Program declaration.

```
uses
  Memtypes, QuickDraw, OSIntf, ToolIntf;
```

The Mouse

We have already seen how the Button function can be used to report on the state of the mouse button. Button and other mouse routines are not actually part of QuickDraw but belong to the Toolbox's Event Manager, of which we will see more later on. The second of the mouse routines is GetMouse, which reports on the position of the cursor on the screen. By successive calls to GetMouse, we can track the cursor as it is moved across the screen by the mouse. GetMouse reports the cursor position in two components, the current horizontal and vertical coordinates relative to the upper left-hand corner of the cursor window. To do this we need to use one of QuickDraw's special data types called point. A variable of type point has two components, horizontal and vertical position. A variable is declared a Point in the variable declaration section.

```
var
 Position : Point;
```

This variable of type Point named position actually has two parts known as Position.H and Position.V.

Position.H—holds the horizontal distance from the upper left-hand corner
Position.V—holds the vertical distance from the upper left-hand corner

The next program displays the position of the cursor in the console window.

```
program MouseDemo;
uses
  Memtypes, QuickDraw, OSIntf, ToolIntf;
var
  Position : point;
begin
 while not Button do
  begin
   GetMouse(Position);
   Writeln('Horizontal = ' : 15, Position.H : 3);
   Writeln('Vertical = ' : 15, Position.V : 3);
  end;
 Writeln('That's all, folks')
end.
```

Run the program and move the cursor around the screen with the mouse. The coordinates of the cursor will be displayed in the window. Notice the speed with which the information is written to the screen. The program is terminated by hitting the mouse button.

Rectangles

The first drawing shape of QuickDraw we have seen are rectangles. Here is the deeper explanation promised. A rectangle is a mathematical structure defined by two points, the point in the upper left-hand corner of the rectangle and the point in the lower right-hand corner.

To display a rectangle in the console window, you must first declare a variable of one of QuickDraw's data types called Rect. The Rect data type is not a standard part of Pascal data type and is used only by QuickDraw.

This variable declaration:

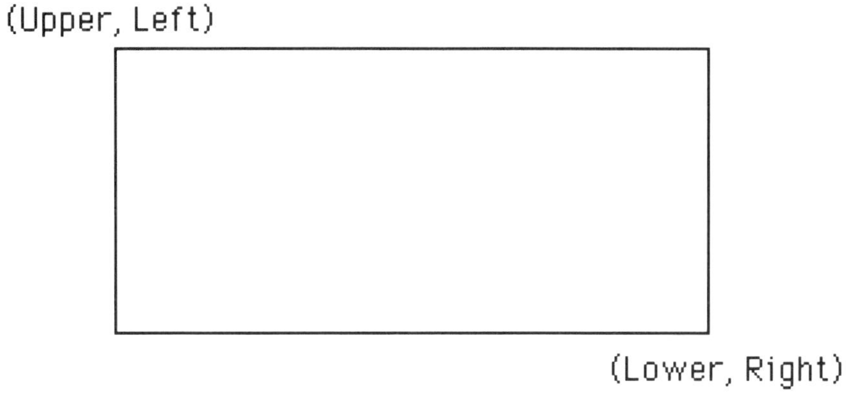

Figure 3-3. Coordinates of a Rectangle

```
var
   Square, Oblong : Rect;
```

declares the variables Square and Oblong to be of the Quickdraw data type Rect.

Once we have defined a rectangle, we are ready to assign coordinates to it. This is accomplished with the use of the SetRect command. SetRect works with five arguments, the name of the rectangle and the upper left-hand and lower right-hand points listed as follows: upper horizontal coordinate, upper vertical coordinate, lower horizontal coordinate, lower vertical coordinate. Here are two SetRect examples:

```
SetRect(Square, 10, 10, 40, 40);
SetRect(Oblong, 50, 50, 80, 90);
```

The first command defines Square as having an upper left-hand corner of 10,10 and a lower right-hand corner of 40, 40. The second command defines Oblong as having an upper left-hand corner of 50, 50 and a lower right-hand corner of 80, 90. Assigning coordinates to a rectangle does not display that rectangle in the window. To do that we need the FrameRect command.

```
program DrawRectangles;
uses
  MemTypes, QuickDraw;
```

```
var
  Square, Oblong : Rect;
begin
  SetRect(Square, 10, 10, 40, 40);
  SetRect(Oblong, 50, 50, 80, 90);
  FrameRect(Oblong);
  FrameRect(Square);
  Readln
end.
```

Displayed in the window by this program is

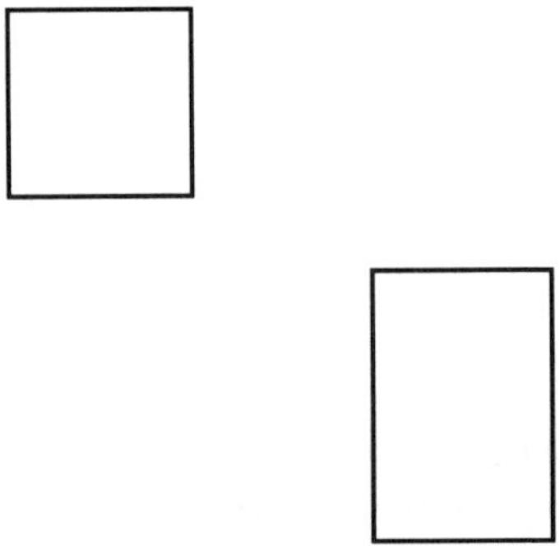

Figure 3-4. Sample Rectangles

Now that we know how to draw a single rectangle, we can create interesting effects by using a For loop to display a series of overlapping rectangles. We simply need to define a rectangle and then redefine it shifted slightly.

An animation effect can be achieved by erasing a rectangle after it has been drawn and then redisplaying it shifted slightly. The EraseRect command is used to erase the rectangle indicated.

```
program MovingRectangles;
uses
  MemTypes, QuickDraw;
var
  Square      : Rect;
  Shift, I    : Integer;
begin
```

```
  Shift := 0;
  for I := 1 to 20 do
      begin
        Shift := Shift + 5;
        SetRect(Square, 10 + Shift, 10 + Shift,
          40 + Shift, 40 + Shift);
        FrameRect(Square);        {Draw rectangle}
        EraseRect(Square)         {Erase rectangle}
    end;
  Write('Press <Return> to continue ');
  Readln
end.
```

This program moves the rectangle across the window at a fast speed. You can slow down the animation by wasting time between the writing and erasing of the rectangle. This can be done by inserting a For loop that does nothing, such as

```
for K := 1 to 20 do;
```

Notice that no statement is actually executed by the For loop.

Experiment with these programs and try to create interesting displays. You might want to use the PaintRect command instead of FrameRect. PaintRect will display a rectangle that is filled in with black.

You should note that the coordinate system in the console window has 0,0 as the upper left-hand point. This will not change even if you enlarge or move the window.

Try More

Develop a program using a While loop that draws increasingly smaller rectangles inside of rectangles until they are too small to draw.

Reach Further

Develop a program that moves a rectangle from the left side to the right side of the screen, but rotate the rectangle as it moves.

Combining the Mouse and a Rectangle

QuickDraw contains a routine called PtInRect, which will tell us if a particular point is in a particular rectangle. PtInRect is a Boolean like Button and returns True if the point is inside the rectangle and False otherwise. PtInRect needs two pieces of information to work, the point and the rectangle. This is deceptively powerful; by connecting this with the GetMouse procedure, we can easily tell the position of the mouse relative to other objects on the screen. A short example program:

```
program Boong;
 uses
  Memtypes, QuickDraw, OSIntf, ToolIntf;
 var
  R : Rect;
  Position : point;
  Done : Boolean;
begin
  SetRect(R, 30,30,40,40);
  FrameRect(R);
  Done := True;
   While not Done do
    begin
     GetMouse(Position);
     if ptInRect(Position, R) then
      begin
       Writeln('Booong');
       Done := False;
       SysBeep(100)
      end; {if}
     end;  {While}
   end.  {program}
```

ple. For instance, SysBeep(100) will sound the speaker for 2.2 seconds. A programming style note: This program had lots of ends, each one labeled with a comment for clarity.

We can make this program slightly more interesting by moving the rectangle across the screen, making it sort of a target to hit with the mouse. This can be done by framing the rectangle, erasing it, changing the coordinates of the rectangle, and then reframing it. An animation effect is created by the continual drawing, erasing, and offsetting of the rectangle.

```
program BooongBooong;
 uses
  Memtypes, QuickDraw, OSIntf, ToolIntf;
 var
  R : Rect;
  Position : point;
  Done : Boolean;
  h,v : Integer;
begin
  h := 30; v := 40;
  Done := True;
  While not Done do
   begin
    SetRect(R, h,h,v,v);
    FrameRect(R);
    GetMouse(Position);
    if ptInRect(Position, R) then
     begin
      Writeln('Booong');
      Done := False;
      SysBeep(100)
     end ;{if}
     h := h + 1;  {move the rectangle}
     v := v + 1;
     {Check to see if the rect has crossed the screen}
     if h > 511 then Done := False;
   end;  {while}
 end.
```

If you run the program, you may think that the box moves too quickly across the screen. This is because of the sheer speed of programs compiled by Turbo. In fact, a precaution was taken to end the program if the horizontal coordinate of the rectangle exceeds 511. A way of slowing down the movement of the box would be to include somewhere in the While loop a statement that does nothing but kill processor time. A single statement just won't do, what is needed is a For loop that just iterates without performing anything. Here is a slower version of the program:

```
program SlowBoong;
 uses
  Memtypes, QuickDraw, OSIntf, ToolIntf;
 var
  R : Rect;
  Position : point;
  Done : Boolean;
  h,v : Integer;
  Wait : Integer;
begin
  h := 30; v := 40;
  Done := True;
   While not Done do
    begin
     SetRect(R, h,h,v,v);
     FrameRect(R);
     GetMouse(Position);
     if ptInRect(Position, R) then
      begin
       Writeln('Booong');
       Done := False;
       SysBeep(100)
      end ;{if}
     h := h + 1;  {Move the rectangle}
     v := v + 1;
     {Check to see if the rect has crossed the screen}
     if h > 511 then Done := False;
     for wait := 1 to 500 do; {Kill some time}
     EraseRect(R);
   end;  {while}
 end.
```

CHAPTER SUMMARY

We have covered much ground in this chapter. First, decision making with the If statement and conditional tests were introduced. Two loops, the For and While, were covered, and many examples of both were presented. We also took our first look at QuickDraw implementing programs using rectangles and the mouse routines Button and GetMouse. Finally, we used much of what was presented in the chapter all together in a program that moved a rectangle across the screen and made the user catch it with the mouse. In the next chapter, we will take a deeper look at data types, see more of the routines available in Pascal and the Toolbox, and design and write our own routines.

4
Functions and More on Data Types

INTRODUCTION

In Chapter 2, the data types Integer, Char, and String were introduced. These are not, however, the only data types available in Turbo Pascal. In this chapter, we will take an in-depth look at all data and the functions, both built-in and user-defined, that can be used with them.

THE CHAR TYPE

We have seen that the data type string can be used to hold a sequence of characters. The type Char also holds character data but is limited to holding just one single character. It may seem strange that both String and the more limited type Char are available. However, historically, standard Pascal only included Char; String is an extension added to the language by many versions of Pascal including Turbo.

The declaration:

```
var
 Ch : Char;
```

declares a variable named Ch, capable of holding a single character. The following statement

```
Ch := 'A';
Writeln(Ch);
```

assigns a character 'A' to Ch and then displays it.

Character data is stored in the Macintosh in a form known as ASCII (which stands for American Standard Code for Information Interchange). This code uses the integers 0 through 255 to represent the different possible characters. If we could look into memory where a character is stored, we would see an integer that in context will be treated as a character.

Ordinal Types

Char and most other data types are known as **ordinal** types. Ordinals are data types where each possible value (except the last and the first) have a unique predecessor and successor. The ordinal types include Integer, Boolean, Char, and the enumerated types (which are discussed in later chapters). Reals are not ordinal types since a unique successor and predecessor of a real cannot be determined; another decimal place always exists. Strings are also not included.

Variables of any ordinal type can be used as the control variable in a For loop. This loop

```
for Ch := 'A' to 'Z' do
  Writeln(Ch);
```

will iterate 26 times and display all the uppercase letters from A to Z.

THE ORD AND CHR FUNCTIONS

We have already seen the built-in function Button; Turbo Pascal has many other built-in functions that can be used in programs. A built-in function is similar to an operator, except that it is invoked differently. Like an operator, a function is given a value to work with, called the **argument**, which is either a constant, variable, or expression. The function then "returns" a value based on the argument. We have already seen several built-in functions such as Button, which returns a

Boolean. When used in an expression, functions have the highest order of precedence. That is, functions are evaluated before any other operations take place. A built-in function can be used in almost any instance that a variable can, such as an expression or a Write statement. A function cannot be placed on the left side of an assignment statement; doing so will generate an error when you try to compile your program.

The built-in function ORD takes a character as an argument and returns the ASCII code for that character as an integer.

ORD('A') returns 65

ORD('a') returns 97

ORD('B') returns 66

ORD('Z') returns 90

ORD('4') returns 52

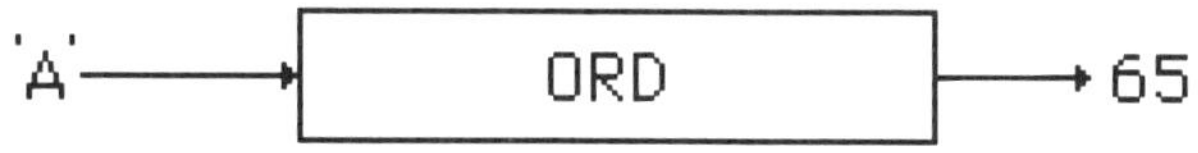

Figure 4-1. The ORD Function

The ASCII code for the characters are in numeric order. This allows us to compare two characters to find which is alphabetically greater.

```
if 'A' > 'B' then
   Writeln('A IS GREATER')
else
  Writeln('B IS GREATER');
```

This If statement will display B IS GREATER since the ASCII code for 'B' is larger numerically than the ASCII code for 'A'. Notice that the letters used in the above example are all uppercase. The lowercase letters have different ASCII codes than the uppercase letters. All the ASCII codes for characters are listed in Appendix J.

The opposite of the ORD function is the CHR function. CHR takes an integer number between 0 and 255, interprets it as an ASCII code, and returns the corresponding character. For example:

```
Write(CHR(65));
```

displays an A.

CHR and ORD are inverse functions; thus

```
Write(CHR(ORD('A'));
```

also prints an A. First, the ORD('A') is done returning 65, then CHR(65) is done returning an A.

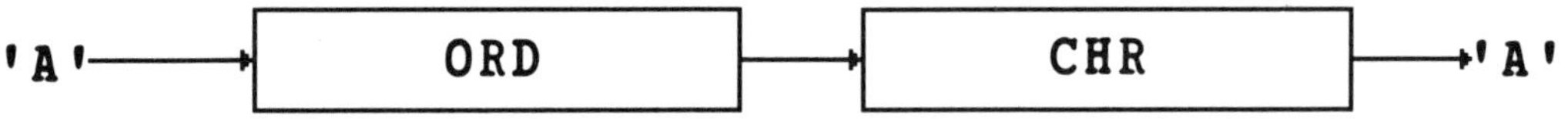

Figure 4-2. The CHR and ORD Functions

The ASCII codes of the characters that represent digits are also in numeric order starting with 0, which is represented by ASCII 48.

```
'0' - 48
'1' - 49
'2' - 50
      .
      .
'9' - 57
```

The difference between a single-digit integer and its ASCII code may not seem clear to you at this point, and rightfully so. The distinction is the set of operations that can be done on either. You can't perform any of the arithmetic operations on characters. Thus, two characters can't be added to find their sum. We can convert the character representation of a number into that number by subtracting ORD('0') from it.

```
I := ORD('8') - ORD('0') assigns the integer 8 (56-48) to I
```

We can use the ORD function to display the ASCII values of a set of characters by using a For loop.

```
for Ch := 'A' to 'Z' do
  Writeln(Ch, ORD(Ch));
```

Inversely, the characters corresponding to ASCII codes can be displayed with the help of the CHR function and a For loop.

```
for I := 0 to 255 do
  Writeln(I, Chr(I));
```

THE SUCC AND PRED FUNCTIONS

The SUCC and PRED functions will return the successor and predecessor values of any ordinal value.

```
PRED('C')         returns 'B'
SUCC (50)         returns  51
SUCC (FALSE)      returns True
SUCC (PRED('B')) returns 'B'
```

The PRED of the first value and the SUCC of the last value of an ordinal type is undefined, and trying to find it will cause an error when the program is run.

OTHER BUILT-IN FUNCTIONS

Besides ORD, CHR, PRED, and SUCC, there are many other built-in functions that can be used. These functions can be broken up into several categories.

The Conversion Functions

The Trunc and Round functions are used to convert a real value into an integer. The Round function rounds off a real to the closest integer.

```
I := Round (4.3)    Assigns the value 4 to the Integer I
Round (3.002)       returns 3
```

```
Round (3.75)         returns 4
Round (20.5)         returns 21
Round (-20.4)        returns -20
Round (-20.6)        returns -21
```

The Trunc function, which stands for truncation, converts a real value to an integer by cutting off the fractional part of the number instead of rounding it.

```
Trunc(4.3)       returns 4
Trunc(20.7)      returns 20
Trunc(-20.7)     returns -20
```

All of these functions are useful in a wide variety of programming situations, including graphics.

MORE ON REALS AND INTEGERS

Pascal is highly regarded as a programming language to express ideas and to teach programming. The major complaint has been that most versions of Pascal did not provide the great accuracy needed in statistical and scientific work or the freedom from rounding errors needed in banking and business work. Thus, old-fashioned and antiquated languages such as FORTRAN and COBOL are still in widespread use. Turbo Pascal has solved these problems by providing easy-to-use extensions to the real and integer data types that provide precision unheard of before in any microcomputer or even minicomputer environment.

The Longint Data Type

A variable of type integer can only represent a value from −MaxInt to MaxInt, which is from −32767 to 32767 ($-2^{15}-1$ to $2^{15}-1$). Many applications require that numbers greater than 32767 be represented. In this instance, the type **LongInt** (for "long integer") is available. A LongInt can hold any value from −2,147,482,647 to 2,146,482,647 ($- 2^{31}-1$ to $2^{31}-1$). A variable is declared a LongInt with

```
var
 L : LongInt;
```

LongInt and integer are fully compatible as long as you don't try to assign to an integer a LongInt too large or small. Doing so will cause a run-time error. Turbo Pascal converts all integer values to a LongInt for all arithmetic operations. If the value is assigned to an integer, it is then converted back. This need not concern a programmer unless the result of an expression returns a value too large or small to be assigned to an integer variable. LongInt is an ordinal type, and all functions that can be used with an integer can be used with a LongInt also. If you are familiar with UCSD Pascal, then note that this type has no relation to that long integer type.

The Extended Real Types

Just like integers, the range of values that can be assigned to a real is limited. Reals are represented in a mantissa (fractional part) and exponent format. The range of positive values that can be stored in a real variable is from $1.5*10^{-45}$ to $3.4*10^{38}$. This is a wide range but only provides accuracy to seven or eight decimal digits. For greater accuracy, two more real types, **Double** and **Extended**, can be used. Double and Extended types work just like real except that the range of values that can be represented is greater.

The range of the real types are shown in Table 4-1.

Table 4-1. Real Types

Type	Range	Accuracy in Decimal Digits
Real	$1.5*10^{-45}$ to $3.4*10^{38}$	7–8
Double	$5.0*10^{-324}$ to $1.7*10^{308}$	15–16
Extended	$1.9*10^{-4951}$ to $1.1*10^{4932}$	19–20

Any negative real number whose absolute value falls within these ranges can also be represented.

The use of these real types is analogous to what happens with integer and LongInt types. All of the three real types are fully compatible, but you can't assign a value to a variable if that value falls outside the range of the variable's type. That would cause a run-time error. Before any real operations are performed, all values are converted to Extended. The result of a real operation is converted to whatever real type is needed. The following example may clarify this situation:

```
var
R : Real;
D : Double;
E : Extended;
    .
    .
R := D + E + R;
```

In this example, the values of R and D will be converted to Extended values before addition with an Extended result produced. The result will then be converted to a real and assigned to the real variable R. This causes no problem unless the result of evaluating the expression falls outside the range that can be represented by a real. In general, you should use the type real unless you need the superaccuracy of the Double or Extended types, since the memory storage requirements of these types are substantial. This system provides the best of both worlds. The high accuracy needed for scientific and statistical work is available without imposing any burden on the programmer. These data types belong to a part of the Toolbox known as SANE (Standard Apple Numerical Interface).

Contrary to what might be expected, calculations actually occur faster when all the variables are of the Extended type. This is because all computations are done only on Extended variables. If variables of other types are used, the Turbo compiler must generate the code necessary to do the data type conversion. When this code is executed it slows down the execution of the program.

A fourth real type, called **Comp** (for "computational"), is like a double LongInt that is converted to Extended for computations. It is provided for applications such as accounting, which require calculations to be done without any rounding errors being introduced into the fractional part of the number. With the Comp type, values are stored and calculations are done as decimal numbers without any decimal points. No rounding errors will occur as long as the values are in the range of -2^{63-1} to 2^{63-1}. The largest-possible value is 9,223,372,036,854,775,807. This number is larger than the American National Debt multiplied by one million and then expressed in Italian lire. Since values are stored without a decimal point, dollars and cents can be represented by assuming a decimal point between the second and third digits. To display Comp values with a decimal point placed between the second and third digits, you can divide the value by 100 in the Writeln statement. For instance:

```
var
C : Comp;
   .
   .
C := 12345; {Assumed to be 123.45}
Writeln(C/10 : 8:2);
```

will display

```
123.45
```

The Summation of an Infinite Series

Mathematicians tell us that when you add together the values of an infinite series such as 1+1/2+1/4+1/8+1/16+1/32 . . . the answer is a finite value, which in this case is 2. This was proved through mathematical induction long before the invention of computers. We can use Turbo Pascal to confirm this with the use of a For loop. The loop will successively add together the terms of the series and print both the terms and the current sum. This example is limited by the accuracy of the real data type, which is seven to eight decimal places. Once that accuracy is exceeded values are rounded off.

Here is the pseudocode for the infinite series program, followed by the program itself:

```
Set first term to 1
  for I := 1 to 30 do
   add the term to the sum
   divide the term in half to get the next term
   write the information

program Prove_An_Old_Theory
var
   I           : Integer;
```

```
   Sum, Term    : Real
begin
   Term := 1;
   Sum := 0;
   for I := 1 to 30 do
      begin
         Sum := Sum + Term;
         Term := Term / 2;
         Writeln (I, Sum : 9 : 7, Term : 9 : 7)
      end
end.
```

The output of the program appears on the next page.

```
Prove_An_Old_Theory
 1 1.00000000 0.50000000
 2 1.50000000 0.25000000
 3 1.75000000 0.12500000
 4 1.87500000 0.06250000
 5 1.93750000 0.03125000
 6 1.96875000 0.01562500
 7 1.98437500 0.00781250
 8 1.99218750 0.00390625
 9 1.99609375 0.00195312
10 1.99804688 0.00097656
11 1.99902344 0.00048828
12 1.99951172 0.00024414
13 1.99975586 0.00012207
14 1.99987793 0.00006104
15 1.99993896 0.00003052
16 1.99996948 0.00001526
17 1.99998474 0.00000763
18 1.99999237 0.00000381
19 1.99999619 0.00000191
20 1.99999809 0.00000095
```

Figure 4-3. Prove an Old Theory

Experiment by changing the number of iterations and the data types used (try Double and Extended).

THE ARITHMETIC FUNCTIONS

Turbo Pascal's repertoire of built-in functions includes a set of arithmetic operations.

SQR

The SQR function returns the square of a number. The value used can either be a real or an integer. The result is either a LongInt or an Extended real.

```
SQR(5)   Returns 25
SQR(1.3) Returns 1.69
```

SQRT

The SQRT function returns the square root of the value given. The value (argument) can be either a real or an integer, the result is always an Extended real.

```
SQRT(9)  Returns 3.0
SQRT(30) Returns 5.5e+0
```

ABS

The ABS function returns the absolute value of the value given. The absolute value of a number is that number regardless of its sign. The argument may be either a real or an integer, the result is always the same type as the argument.

```
ABS (5)      Returns 5
ABS (-5)     Returns 5
ABS (0)      Returns 0
ABS (-1.32) Returns 1.32
```

ODD

The ODD function tests an integer to see if it is odd or even. Odd returns a Boolean value True if the integer is odd and False if the integer is even.

```
ODD (1)  Returns True
ODD (6)  Returns False
```

Float

The Float function converts an integer value into a real value. This is normally not necessary to do when an integer is mixed with reals in an expression since the compiler will automatically convert the integer into a real for the computation.

```
Float(12)  Returns 12.0
```

ORD4

The ORD4 function performs the same task as the Ord function except that it returns a LongInt as its result. This is most useful when dealing with a pointer type; the ORD4 function will return the value of the address pointed to by the pointer. We will discuss pointers in later chapters.

INT

The Int function returns the integer part of the expression passed to it. No rounding takes place.

```
Int(12.3)      Returns 12
Int(12.8)      Returns 12
```

THE TRIGONOMETRIC FUNCTIONS

The Sin, Cos, and ArcTan functions are used for trigonometric operations. They take either a real or an integer as an argument and assume it to be an angle expressed in radians. The result is always an Extended real.

```
Cos(x)       Returns the cosine of x.
Sin(x)       Returns the sine of x.
ArcTan(x)    Returns the arctangent of x.
```

Any of the other trigonometric functions can be synthesized by using the existing ones.

```
To find a tangent of x,     Sin(x)/Cos(x)
To find the cosecant of x,   1/Sin(x)
```

THE LOGARITHMIC FUNCTIONS

Turbo has the EXP and LN natural logarithmic functions. Both take either an integer or a real as an argument and always return an Extended real.

```
LN(x)    Returns the natural logarithm of x.
EXP(x)   Returns the value of e^x.
```

CONSOLE FUNCTIONS

Turbo Pascal contains a set of procedures and functions used to control the output in the console window. The built-in procedures work just like functions except that they return no value and therefore cannot be used in expressions. They are complete statements by themselves. Examples of procedures with which you are already familiar is Write and GetMouse.

ClearScreen

The ClearScreen procedure clears the contents of the console window and places the cursor in the upper left-hand corner of the window. All that is needed to use it is the procedure name.

ClearEOL

The ClearEOL procedure clears all the characters from the cursor position to the end of that line without moving the cursor.

DeleteLine

The DeleteLine procedure erases the line containing the cursor and moves all below it up one.

InsertLine

The InsertLine procedure inserts a blank line at the cursor position and moves all the lines below it down one line.

GotoXY (X, Y)

The GotoXY procedure moves the position of the cursor in the console window. It takes two values, the horizontal position X and the vertical position Y, in which to place the cursor. If X is out of the range of 1 . . . 80 or if Y is out of the range 1 . . . 25, the cursor will not be moved. The major use of GotoXY is to position the cursor at a specific position in the window prior to writing text.

KeyPressed

The KeyPressed function returns True if a key has been pressed on the keyboard and False otherwise. A typical use of this function is to "freeze" a program until the user hits a key. This can be accomplished with the help of a While loop.

```
Writeln('Hit any key to continue');
while not(KeyPressed) do {do nothing};
```

TOOLBOX FUNCTIONS

The Macintosh's Toolbox contains several functions that are not part of standard Pascal. Two functions, SysBeep and TickCount, are presented here. Other Toolbox features will be introduced in later chapters of the book.

To use either of these functions, you will need to have the following Uses statement right after the program declaration:

```
program Example;
  uses MemTypes, QuickDraw, OSIntF, ToolIntF


(statements in your program.)
```

SysBeep

```
SysBeep (duration);
```

The SysBeep function causes a tone to be generated on the Macintosh's speaker. The duration of the tone is determined by the integer value passed to the function. The length of the tone will be duration *0.022 seconds. For example:

```
SysBeep(100); creates a tone that will last 2.2 seconds.
```

TickCount

The TickCount function returns a LongInt representing the elapsed time since the machine was turned on in increments of 1/60 of a second. This information is probably of little use by itself, but TickCount can be used to time the execution of Turbo Pascal statements or to compare the execution speeds of different Pascals for the Mac. For instance, the following program was executed with both Macintosh Pascal version 2.0 and Turbo Pascal (with, of course, small variations needed to make the program work within the different environments):

```
program TimeIt;
uses
   Memtypes, QuickDraw, OSIntf, ToolIntf;
var
   I, start, stop : integer;
   R, S : real;
begin
   Start := tickcount;
   for I := 1 to 1000 do
     R := R + 10;
   Stop := tickcount;
   writeln(Stop - Start);
   Readln
end.
```

The first call to TickCount marks the elapsed time before the loop starts. The second call marks the elapsed time after the loop terminates. The difference between the two represents the amount of time needed to execute the loop.

When run in Macintosh Pascal this program took 203 ticks, or 3.83 seconds, to perform the 1000 calculations. The Turbo version took only 97 ticks, or 1.61 seconds. If Extended values were used rather than Reals, the execution speeds would have been quicker since, as mentioned above, all real values are first converted to extended prior to arithmetic operations. By starting with Extended values, no conversion needs to take place. When the variables were changed to integers rather than reals, the execution times were 106 ticks for Macintosh Pascal and less than 1 tick for Turbo. Generally, integer operations are faster than real since there is no need to handle the fractional parts of the numbers.

USER-DEFINED DATA TYPES

When programming in Pascal, the programmer is not limited to using Pascal's standard data types. You are free to declare your own ordinal data types in a Pascal program with the Type statement. Any programmer-declared data type of this kind is called a **user-defined type**. The Type statement appears between the Const and the Var statements.

```
program Typexample;
const
   C=1;
type
   Days = (Sun, Mon, Tue, Wed, Thur, Fri, Sat);
```

This declares a new data type called Days. The set of possible values of a variable of type Days is enumerated inside the parentheses in the statement. A type where every possible value that a type can take on is explicitly listed in the declaration is called an **enumerated** type.

Variables can now be created of type Days.

```
var
 PayDay: Days;
```

The variable PayDay is of data type Days. The operations that can be performed on enumerated types are limited, but several are possible. An assignment statement looks the way you might expect it to.

```
PayDay := Thur;
```

Notice that there are no quotation marks around Thur. This is because it is not a string value and should not be confused with one. It is one of the possible values that can be assigned to a variable of the data type Days. This is not any different from using an assignment statement with a Boolean variable.

```
Switch := TRUE;
```

Here, one of the possible Boolean values is assigned to the Boolean variable Switch. As a matter of fact, the type Boolean can be thought of as a predeclared enumerated type with the declaration

```
Type
 Boolean = (FALSE, TRUE);
```

Since enumerated types are ordinal types, the SUCC and PRED functions are available. Assuming PayDay := Thur;

```
SUCC(PayDay)    Returns Fri
PRED(PayDay)    Returns Wed
PRED (Sun)      Is undefined and causes an error
SUCC (Sun)      Returns Mon
```

When given a user-defined type, the ORD function returns an integer representing the value's position in the declared list of values. The ORD of the first value declared is zero. Here is the declaration of type Days and the ORD of the values.

```
Days = (Sun, Mon, Tue, Wed, Thur, Fri, Sat);
ORDs     0    1    2    3    4     5    6
```

The following loop will print the ORDs.

```
for PayDay:= Sun to Sat do
 Writeln(ORD(PayDay));
```

Displayed by the loop is:

```
0
1
2
3
4
5
6
```

Unfortunately, the actual value of a user-defined variable cannot be directly printed by Turbo. A programmer must handle that task herself. Luckily, one of Pascal's structures, the Case statement, can help.

THE CASE STATEMENT

The Case statement is a selection structure that can be used to replace several If statements. The following nested If statements:

```
if I = 1 then
  Writeln('ONE')
else if I = 2 then
  Writeln('TWO')
else if I = 3 then
  Writeln('THREE')
else
  Writeln('NONE  OF THESE')
```

can be replaced with

```
case I of
    1:  Writeln('ONE');
    2:  Writeln('TWO');
    3:  Writeln('THREE');
    Otherwise
     Writeln('NONE OF THESE')
end; {CASE}
```

In the Case statement, the keyword "case" is followed by an expression whose value may be any ordinal type except LongInt. This is followed by the reserved word "of." Between the "of" and the "end" statements is a list of statements, each labeled with a value of the same type as the expression. The expression is evaluated, and then the statement whose label matches the value of the expression is executed. Since an expression can only have one value, one and only one of the labeled statements is executed. If the value of the expression is not found, the statement following the reserved word "otherwise" is executed. If the Otherwise statement is absent (it is not required) and the value of the expression is not found, a run-time error occurs. The Otherwise clause is a Turbo Pascal language extension not found in standard Pascal.

More than one value may be used as a label, as shown by this example:

```
case I of
  1, 2, 3 : Writeln('1 to 3');
  4, 5, 6 : Writeln('4 to 6')
end;
```

If the value of I is from 1 to 3, then the first statement is executed. If it is from 4 to 6, then the second statement is executed. If it's greater than 6 or less than 1, oops.

A Case statement can be used to display enumerated types by finding the Ord of a variable and using separate Write statements for each different value possible. For example:

```
case ORD(Payday) of
  0 : Write('Sun');
  1 : Write('Mon');
  2 : Write('Tue');
  3 : Write('Wed');
  4 : Write('Thur');
  5 : Write('Fri');
  6 : Write('Sat')
end;
```

Notice that no Otherwise statement was necessary. Why not? Since these are the only possible values of Payday, ORD(Payday) would not produce a value not listed in the Case statement.

COMPARING ENUMERATED VALUES

When two enumerated values are compared, their ORDs are used to determine which one is the greater. For instance, Tue is greater than Sun because the ORD(Tue) is numerically greater than ORD(Sun).

```
ORD(Wed) is greater than ORD(Tue)
ORD(Sat) is greater than ORD(Sun)
```

Enumerated types are a feature not available in many other popular programming languages. Although they might appear trivial, they are a powerful programming tool that will make a program easier to write, read, and debug. They should be used wherever possible in your programming.

SUBRANGES

A **subrange** is a subset of a declared ordinal data type. Here are some examples:

```
type
 Letters = 'A'..'Z';
 Cards = 1..52
```

Two subranges, Letters and Cards, have been declared as subsets Char and Integer. The first and last values of the range is given with the two periods (..) standing for all the values in between.

Variable of these subranges can be declared like

```
var
  Deck : Cards;
  Ch : Letters;
```

The possible values of Deck are only the integers from 1 to 52, inclusively, and of Ch from 'A' to 'Z', uppercase only, inclusively. Any attempt to assign a value other than one in the subrange would result in an error. The philosophy behind this is that it is preferable to have an error occur and a program stop than to let the program continue with invalid data. This is an example of Pascal's strong typing, the careful checking of value and data types for compatibility. It is a good programming practice to use subranges wherever a set of possible values will fall into a predictable range. Examples of this might be exam grades, temperatures, ages, models of the Macintosh from 1984 on, and countless others.

Subranges can also be declared for enumerated types.

```
type
 Days = (Sun, Mon, Tue, Wed, Thu, Fri, Sat);
 Weekdays = Mon..Fri;
```

Here the type Weekdays is a subrange of the user-defined type Days.

USER-DEFINED FUNCTIONS

Pascal allows the programmer to define his own functions in a program. Let's look at a user-defined function that raises an integer number to a power, one function that has been left out of Turbo Pascal. A function starts with a function heading, much like a program starts with a program heading. The function heading lists the name of the function, any arguments to be sent to the function, and the data type of the value returned by the function. The rules for naming functions are the same as for any identifier:

```
function Power(Base, Exponent : 1..MaxInt) : Integer;
```

This is followed by the body of the function. That is where all calculations take place and is analogous to the body of a program. It can even have its own variable declarations, for variables that can be used only in the function.

```
var
  I, Ans : Integer;
begin
  Ans := 1;
  for I := 1 to Exponent do
    Ans := Ans * Base;
  Power := Ans
end;{function}
```

Here is the body of the function. The result of the function is assigned to the function name (Power). The entire function declaration is placed after the variable declaration but before the first "begin" of the program.

The user-defined function is used by in the program the exact same way a built-in function is used. For instance to raise 3 to the power of 4:

```
X := Power(3, 4)
```

In the function, the arguments listed become the value of those declared in the function heading. For instance, in this call of the function Base would be equal to 3 and Exponent equal to 4. The value returned by Power is an integer because of the type declaration we used in the function heading. All the rules for assignment hold for the values returned by functions. Why define a function for use in a program? There are two reasons. First, a function can eliminate the need to include the same or similar programming instructions in more than one place in a program. The function is defined once and then called when needed. The second reason is that functions allow us to break down a program into smaller logical units and help make the program simpler to conceptualize and program.

The similarity between user-defined and built-in functions goes more than skin deep. In fact, all of the built-in functions have been declared as user-defined functions and included in the compiler. For example, the built-in function ODD might be written like this:

```
function ODD(N : Integer) : Boolean
 begin
  if (N div 2) * 2 = N then
   ODD := FALSE
  else
   ODD := TRUE;
 end; {ODD}
```

Remember that in integer division the fraction value is lost. When N DIV 2 is done the remainder is lost if N is ODD. For instance, 5 DIV 2 equals 2. When the result is multiplied by 2 it no longer equals the original odd value. This is not true for an even number.

DRAWING OVALS

Along with drawing rectangles, Turbo Pascal can access the QuickDraw routines necessary to draw ovals. The FrameOval, EraseOval, and PaintOval commands are analogous to FrameRect, EraseRect, and PaintRect, except of course they work with ovals rather than rectangles. What exactly is an oval? An oval is defined by QuickDraw as the largest ellipse that can be inscribed inside a particular rectangle.

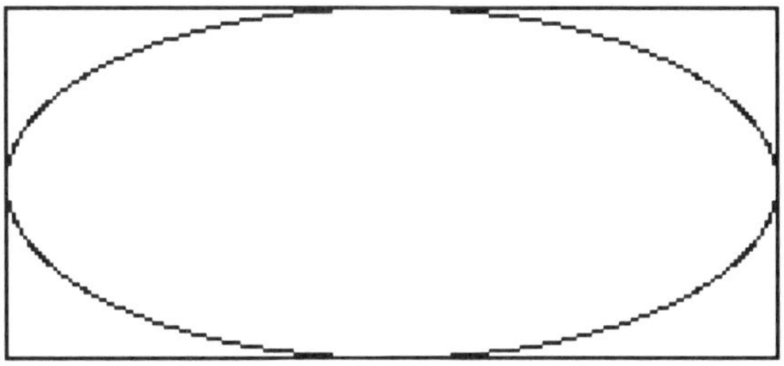

Figure 4-4. Oval Inscribed in a Rectangle

For instance, to draw a circle, define a rectangle that is a square (all sides equal) and then use FrameOval.

```
SetRect(R, 10, 10, 60, 60);
FrameOval(R);
```

Drawn by these two QuickDraw calls is

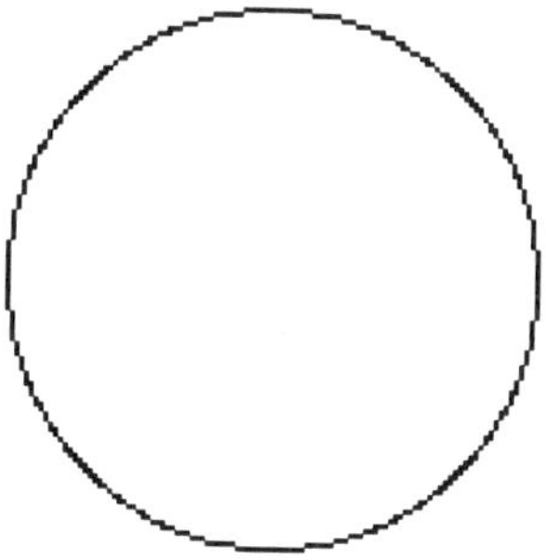

Figure 4-5. Drawing an Oval

The radius of the circle drawn is one-half the length of a side of the square. To display an ellipse, define a nonsquare rectangle instead of a square.

```
SetRect(R, 10, 10, 60, 80);
FrameOval(R);
```

The output would be

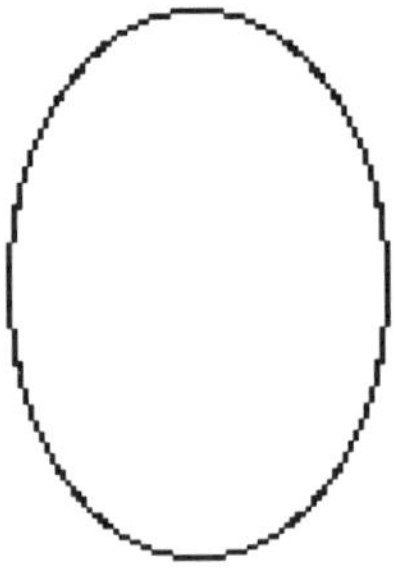

Figure 4-6. An Ellipse

A demonstration that comes to mind when drawing ovals is that of a moon rotating around a fixed planet. The moon will be oriented in an orbit that is a fixed radius from the planet's center. To do this, we must be able to calculate the coordinates for any point along the orbit using the formula for a circle given us by analytic geometry.

```
R² = (X-a)²+(Y-b)²
```

R is the radius, *X* and *Y* are points on the circle, and the constants *a* and *b* are the coordinates of the circle's origin. We can calculate the points on the orbit by using a For loop to iterate through the X coordinates in the orbit and solving the equation for Y.

```
Y = the square root of (R²-(X-a)²)+b
```

Some built in functions will come in handy for calculating Y.

```
Y := Round(SQRT(SQR(Radius)-SQR(X-a))+b);
```

For every X point in the circle there exist two Y points, one on the bottom half of the circle and one at the same position on the top half. The equation above will calculate the Y coordinates on the bottom half of the orbit, but to calculate the points on the top half, we have to subtract from the bottom half point twice the Y coordinate of the origin, or 2 * b.

```
Y := 2 * b - Round(SQRT(SQR(Radius)-SQR(X-a))+b);
```

We can use a second For loop to calculate the points in the top half of the orbit, but we must remember to start calculating the top points at the spot we finished with the bottom points. Therefore, the second For loop will be a Downto loop. The formula for the Y coordinates in the top and bottom halves is very similar, and part of it can be placed into a user-defined function for simplicity.

```
function Coordinate : Integer;
begin
 Coordinate := Round(SQRT(SQR(Radius)-SQR(X-A))+B)
end;
```

This function is simple to write but will make the program easier to implement. The function takes no arguments—all the values it works with will be the variables from the program. That is fine; a function is allowed to use any of the variables defined in the program. The value calculated will be returned using the name of the function.

PROGRAMMING EXAMPLE—KEPLER'S DELIGHT

Here is the program utilizing the oval commands. A new command, InvertOval, is used to erase the moon right after it is drawn, providing an animation effect. InvertOval simply changes the color of the black circle to white, which essentially erases it.

```
program KeplersDelight;
   uses Memtypes, QuickDraw;
const
   A = 55;
   B = 55;
var
```

```
    R : Rect;
    Radius, X, Y : Integer;
begin
    Radius := 45;
    SetRect(R, 45, 45, 65, 65);
    FrameOval(R); {Draw the planet}
    {Calculate the points in the bottom half of the orbit}
    for X := 10 to 100 do
       begin
          Y := Coordinate;
          SetRect(R, X-5, Y-5, X+5, Y+5);
          PaintOval(R);
          InvertOval(R);
       end;
    {Calculate the points in the top half of the orbit}
    for X := 100 downto 10 do
      begin
         Y := 2*B - Coordinate;
         SetRect(R, X-5, Y-5, X+5, Y+5);
         PaintOval(R);
         InvertOval(R);
      end
end.
```

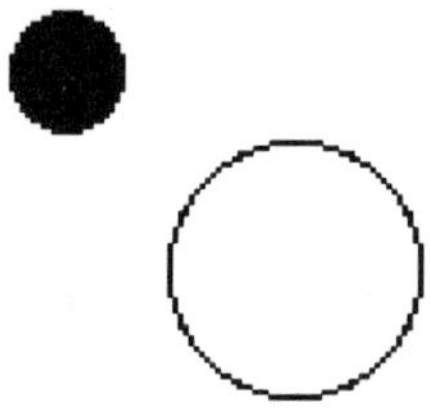

Figure 4-7. Kepler's Delight

Run the program and watch the moon orbit the planet. A real challenge to those comfortable with analytic geometry (and who isn't) would be to have an even smaller moon which orbits the larger moon which as the larger moon orbits the planet. This program can make you stop and think just what the Macintosh would have meant to the early mathematicians if it had been available to them. Wonder about the discoveries that would have been made centuries earlier. Figure out where they would have plugged one in. Would Kepler have turned out to be another Steven Jobs?

CHAPTER SUMMARY

This chapter covered much ground, but the trip was worth it. We are starting to develop programs of increasing sophistication using advanced Pascal structures such as functions and QuickDraw graphics. The next chapter will advance our ability to develop large programs even further with the use of procedures.

5
Procedures

INTRODUCTION

Complex problems are easier to solve if they can be broken down into several components. You have probably noticed this in many facets of life. Once reduced, each component of the problem can then be analyzed separately. Programs, as well as problems, can benefit from being partitioned into smaller and simpler pieces. Pascal provides a way to break a large program into smaller sections called **subprograms**. There are two types of subprograms used in Pascal: **procedures** and **user-defined functions**. We have, of course, already seen the user-defined function in the previous chapter.

Like a function, a procedure has almost the same structure as a program except that it begins with the reserved word "procedure," and the final "end" in a procedure is followed by a semicolon rather than a period. A procedure can contain any statement a program can. When a program contains procedures you usually refer to the non-procedure part as the "main program."

Table 5-1. Comparison of a Program and a Procedure

Structure of a Procedure	Structure of a Program
procedure <procedure name>;	program <program name>;
<type declaration>	<type declaration>
<constant declaration>	<constant declaration>
<variable declaration>	<variable declaration>
<procedure declaration>	<procedure declaration>
begin	begin
<statements>	<statements>
end;	end.

Before a procedure can be used, it must be declared. A procedure is placed after the variable declarations but before the "begin" statement of the main program. A procedure is used by placing its name as a statement into the body of a program, just the way GetMouse was used earlier. Executing a procedure is referred to as "calling a procedure." Here is an example of a simple procedure used in a program:

```
 1.   program Example;
 2.   var
 3.      X, Y, Z : Real;
 4.
 5.    procedure Add;
 6.    begin {Procedure Add}
 7.        Z := X + Y;
 8.    end;  {Procedure Add}
 9.
10.    begin {Main program}
11.        Writeln('Enter two numbers');
12.        Readln(X,Y);
13.        Add;
14.        Writeln('The sum is',Z:6:2);
15.        Readln
16.    end. {Main program}
```

SEQUENCE OF EXECUTION

Procedures change the sequence in which statements are executed in a program. Our example has each line numbered to make it easier to describe. As always, execution of a program starts with the first executable statement in the main program (line 11). It then continues sequentially (one line after another in order) until line 13, where the statement simply reads "Add." This statement calls the procedure named Add and transfers execution to the first executable statement in the procedure (line 7). The procedure is executed sequentially until the last statement in the procedure (also line 7; this is a very small procedure). Control returns to the main program, and execution resumes at the statement following the one that called the procedure (line 14). The main program then continues.

This was a short and simple example of a procedure, yet it illustrates how procedures are written and called.

USING PROCEDURES

Procedures are best used in a program to either divide a complex task into subtasks or to handle a task that must be repeated several times in the program. The procedure allows us to avoid using the same sequence of statements in several places in the program. Let's create a program that draws triangles in the console window. To do so, we must further explore some features of QuickDraw.

Drawing Lines

Lines, like the other graphics we have seen, are drawn with QuickDraw's pen. Obviously there is physically no pen drawing on your screen. The pen is a metaphor for describing drawing operations as though they were done on paper with an ink pen.

To draw lines, we utilize the old saying that the straightest path between two points is a line. First we position the pen with the MoveTo command.

```
MoveTo(X, Y);
```

MoveTo picks up the pen and moves it to the point X, Y without drawing anything. We do this to position the pen to the starting point of the line. The line is actually drawn with the LineTo command.

```
LineTo(X,Y);
```

LineTo draws a line from the old pen position to the new point given in the command.

For example, to draw a line across the window from 10,10 to 10,100 we would

```
MoveTo(10,10);              {Move to starting point}
LineTo(10,100);             {Draw line to ending point}
```

Let's combine drawing lines with procedures in order to create a procedure that draws an equilateral triangle. An isosceles triangle has two equal sides. The procedure will use three pieces of information,

Figure 5-1. Drawing a Line

the coordinates of the upper left-hand point in the triangle and the length of the sides. Geometry and Pythagoras tell us the coordinates of the other points.

In the procedure, we first position the pen at point X, Y and then draw sides 1, 2, and 3.

```
procedure Tri (X, Y, Side : Integer);
begin
   MoveTo(X, Y);
   LineTo(X + Side, Y);
   LineTo(X + Side div 2, Round(Y + Side / Sqrt(2));
   LineTo(X, Y);
   Readln
end;
```

The procedure heading looks as follows:

```
procedure Tri (X, Y, Side : Integer);
```

After the name of the procedure are the parameters to be used by the procedure (also called arguments). Parameters are a means of passing information from a main program (or procedure) to a proce-

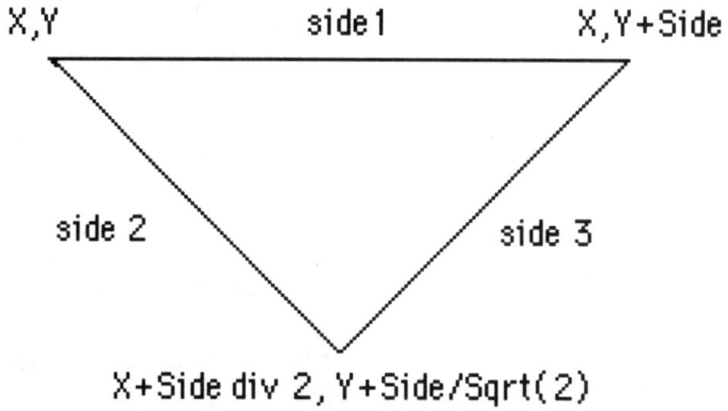

Figure 5-2. An Isosceles Triangle

dure. Placing variable names in the parameter list is similar to declaring them as variables. They are declared by listing the parameter and its type in the procedure heading. However, parameters differ from variables in that they are automatically given values by the statement that calls the procedure from the main program. Let's look at an example.

```
program Triangles;
uses
    MemTypes, QuickDraw;


       procedure Tri (X, Y, Side : Integer);
       begin
          MoveTo(X, Y);
          LineTo(X + Side, Y);
          LineTo(X + Side div 2, Round(Y +
            Side / Sqrt(2)));
          LineTo(X, Y)
         end;


   begin {main program}
      Tri(10,10,10);
      Tri(40, 40, 5);
      Tri(80, 85, 18);
      Readln
   end.
```

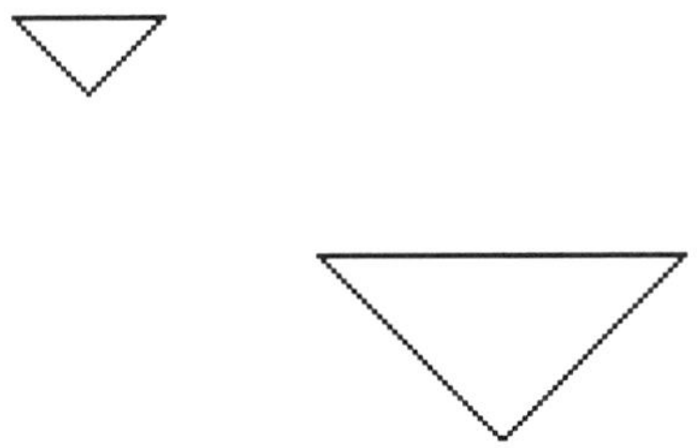

Figure 5-3. Displayed by Triangles

As you can see, our main program draws three triangles by calling the procedure Tri three times. Each statement that calls the procedure has a list of values after it.

```
Tri(10,10,10);
Tri(40, 40, 5);
Tri(80, 85, 18);
```

These values correspond to the parameters in the procedure heading. For each particular call to the procedure, the value of the parameters are as given in Table 5-2.

Table 5-2. Values of Parameters

	X	Y	Side
Call 1	10	10	10
Call 2	40	40	5
Call 3	80	85	18

Scope of Variables

Besides parameters, procedures can have variables declared in them just like a main program. This presents a puzzling question. When a procedure has its own variable declaration, where and when can they be used? Can they be used in the main program? How about the variables declared in the main program—can they be used in the procedure? Pascal has a very strict but easy-to-use set of rules for this situation. It is often referred to as the "scope of a variable."

In our first procedure example, it was obvious that a procedure may use the variables declared in the main program. This is because the main program's variables are declared at the begining of the program. They can be used anywhere throughout a program and are said to be "global" in scope. On the other hand, a procedure's variables can be used only in the procedure in which they are declared. They are said to be "local." The same rules apply to functions. Consider the following diagrams demonstrating the scope of variables in two programs.

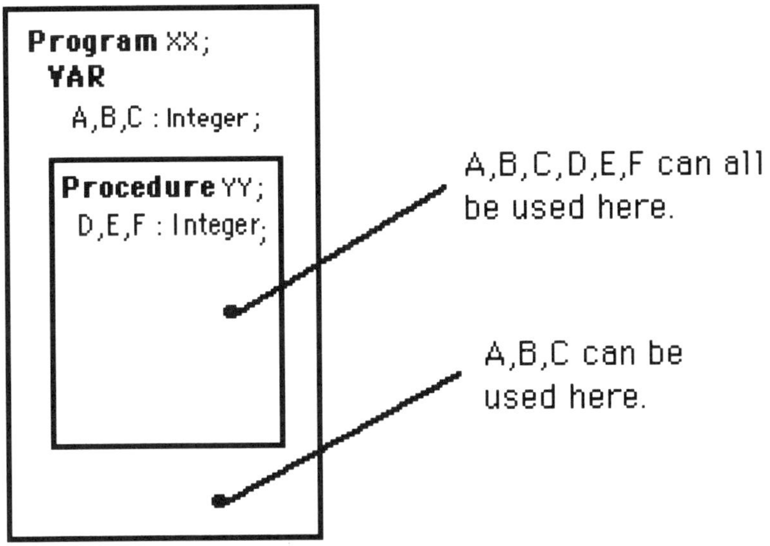

Figure 5-4. Scope of Variables

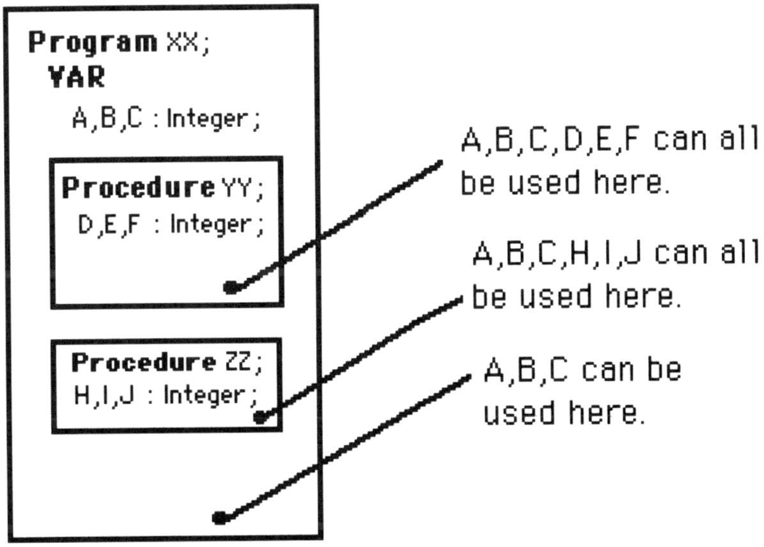

Figure 5-5. A More Complex Situation

To be a little clearer, you can think of variables as having a lifetime, the period between its creation and its destruction. When a procedure that declares variables is called, the variables declared in it are created. While that procedure is executing, the variables are alive, but once the procedure ends, the variables are destroyed and thus can't be used. Even when a procedure is called multiple times, the variables are created and destroyed in each call. This means that a value can't be left in a procedure for subsequent calls to that procedure. Since the main program is always active (until the final "end" is encountered) its variables are always available for use.

Local variables inside a procedure may even have the same name as a global variable. For example:

```
program TwoNames;
var
   X : Integer;

  procedure TheSame;
  var
     X : Integer;
  begin
     X := 1;
     Writeln(X)
  end; {Procedure}

begin
    X := 4;
    Writeln(X);
    TheSame;
    Writeln(X);
    Readln
end.
```

The output is
```
4
1
4
```

In this example, there are two separate variables X. One is the global variable X, declared at the top of the program. Its lifetime is as long as the program runs. The other variable X is the one that is declared in the procedure TheSame. Its lifetime is only while the procedure is being executed. If a local and global variable have the same name, the local variable is the one used in the procedure where it is declared. Hence, in the procedure the local variable named X was used and the value of the global variable named X was not changed. The global variable X is used everywhere in the program except in the procedure where the local variable takes precedence. This exercise was used only to emphasize the difference between global and local variables and constitutes a bad programming practice because of the confusion created.

More on Parameter Passing

We have already seen a simple example of parameter passing. Now for a little more formal discussion. The parameters listed in the procedure declaration are called **formal parameters**, while the values listed in the call to the procedure from the main program are called **actual parameters**. The actual and formal parameters must agree in number and type, and their position in the list is significant. When the procedure is called, the formal and actual parameters are matched up. The first formal parameter is matched with the first actual parameter, the second formal parameter is matched with the second actual parameter, and so on. What happens from then on will depend upon the type of parameter passing being utilized. There are two different mechanisms used with parameter passing. So far we have demonstrated what are known as **value parameters**. When value parameters are used, a copy of the actual parameter is created and is used as the formal parameter. For example, if we use the procedure declared below:

```
procedure Swap(E,F : Integer);
```

and call that procedure from the main program with this statement:

```
Swap(A, B)
```

the corresponding actual parameters are copied into the formal parameters.

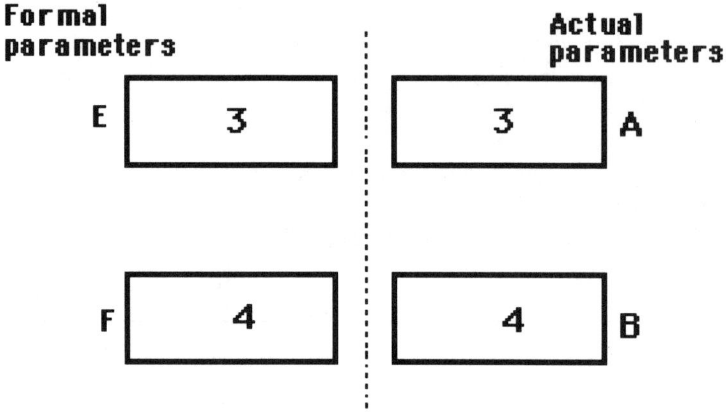

Figure 5-6. Value Parameters

When the values of the formal parameters are changed inside the procedure, the changes do not affect the main program's actual parameters. Therefore, value parameters cannot be used to send information from a subroutine to a main program. When using value parameters, either a constant or expression can be used in the actual parameter list. Some examples of this are

```
Proc1(A, 2)

ColorProc('Blue','Green','Yellow')

DoMath(2*3, X * X, X * 5)
```

In the final example above, the expression is evaluated first, and then the resulting value is passed to the procedure.

Variable Parameters

The second type of parameter passing is known as **variable parameters**. When using variable parameters, no copy of the actual parameter is made, but rather a pointer to the actual parameter is created. This essentially creates two names for the same memory location. A parameter is declared as a variable parameter by including the keyword "var" before its declaration in the procedure heading.

```
procedure Swap(var E,F : Integer);
```

This procedure is called from the main program with the statement

```
Swap(A, B)
```

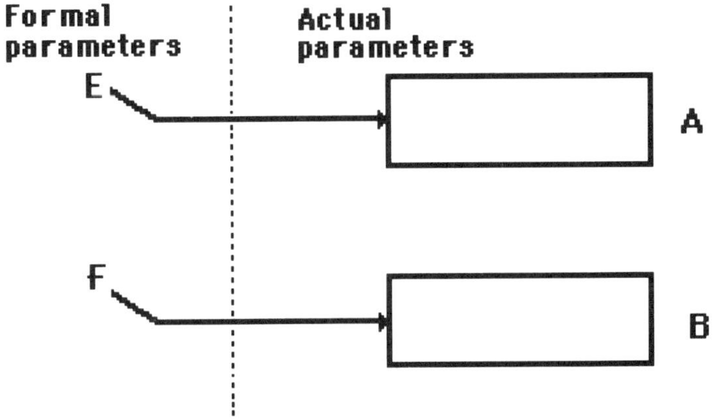

Figure 5-7. Variable Parameters

Here is a program written to utilize parameter passing with several Writeln statements used to help clarify the situation:

```
program Demo;
var
   A, B, C, D : Integer;

   procedure Swap(var E, F : Integer);
   var
      Temp : Integer;
   begin
      Writeln('E= ', E : 1,'  F= ',F : 1);
      Temp := E;
      E := F;
      F := Temp;
      Writeln('E= ', E : 1,'  F= ',F : 1)
   end; {Procedure}

begin {Main}
```

```
    A := 4;
    B := 3;
    C := 5;
    D := 1;
    Writeln('A= ', A : 1, '  B= ',B : 1);
    Swap(A, B);
    Writeln('A= ', A : 1, '  B= ',B : 1);
    Readln
end.
```

The output is

```
A=  4   B=  3
E=  4   F=  3
E=  3   F=  4
A=  3   B=  4
```

We say that E and F point to the variables A and B. When a change is made to E, the change is actually made to the variable that E points to, which is A. When a change is made to F, B is actually affected. When a change in a formal parameter is reflected in an actual parameter, it is referred to as a "side effect." Using variable parameters is also sometimes called passing parameters by reference. From the output you can see how the formal parameters were exchanged and the actual parameters in the main program were affected.

Comparing Value and Variable Parameter Passing

To emphasize the difference between the two methods of parameter passing, Table 5-3 shows two versions of the same program, one using variable parameters, the other value parameters.

Table 5-3. Two Methods of Parameter Passing

Variable Parameters	Value Parameters
program Vars;	program Vals;
var	var
X, Y : Integer;	X, Y : Integer;
procedure PT(var A, B : Integer);	procedure PT(A, B :Integer);
begin	begin

Table 5-3. Two Methods of Parameter Passing (Continued)

A := A + 1;	A := A + 1;
B: = B + 2;	B := B + 2;
Writeln(A : 2, B : 2);	Writeln(A : 2, B : 2);
end;	end;
begin {Main}	begin {Main}
X := 1;	X := 1;
Y := 1;	Y := 1;
Writeln(X : 2, Y : 2);	Writeln(X : 2, Y : 2);
PT(X, Y);	PT(X, Y);
Writeln(X : 2, Y : 2);	Writeln(X : 2, Y : 2);
Readln	Readln
end.	end.

The outputs are

```
1   1                             1  1
2   3   <---from procedure        2  3    <---from procedure
2   3                             1  1    <---no side effect
```

As you can see in the program on the left, variable parameters were used, and the variables in the main program were affected by the operations in the procedure. In the program on the right, value parameters were used, and there was no effect on the variables in the main program. Normally, any time you know that the actual parameter will not be changed by a procedure, you should use value parameters.

Mixing Variable and Value Parameters

In many situations you will mix the use of variable and value parameters. Both types can be included in the procedure's parameter list. Each separate declaration of variable parameters must have its own "var" in front of it.

The following example raises a number to a power (a mathematical operation left out of Pascal). It is a typical example of mixing both value and variable parameter in a procedure. The information sent to the procedure, the number, and the power are both value parameters. The answer is sent back to the main program in a variable parameter (Ans).

```
program PowerTest;
var
   Num,Power : Integer;
   Ans : Real;

   procedure DoPower(var Ans : Real; Base,
     Power : Integer);
   var
      I : Integer;
   begin
      Ans := 1;
      for I := 1 to Power do
      Ans := Ans*Base
   end;
   begin
      Writeln('Enter the number and the power
        to raise it to');
      Readln(Num, Power);
      DoPower(Ans, Num, Power);
      Writeln(Ans);
      Readln
   end.
```

This procedure worked by multiplying the Base by itself Power number of times. Let's trace the procedure for 2 and 3 in Table 5-4 as the values of Base and Power.

Table 5-4. Results of Using 2 and 3 as Base and Power

I	Ans	Base	Power
–	1	2	3
1	2	2	3
2	4	2	3
3	8	2	3 <---Done

When to Use Parameters, Local and Global Variables

The experience of many hours of debugging have taught programmers to use carefully and wisely the various information-passing techniques discussed. There are several guidelines you can follow in choosing how to pass information to procedures that will prevent you from having to spend much time debugging.

Use global variables as little as possible for passing information to procedures. Global variables are visible to every procedure in your program, and a change made to a global variable in one procedure may cause unforeseen changes to other procedures that use that global variable. You should never use global variables to pass information to only one or two procedures. It would be better to pass that information as parameters instead. The only time passing information through globals is desirable is when many procedures in your program access the same information; in this case passing the same parameter to every procedure is a burden, and global variables may be better.

Use variable parameters only when necessary. Only use variable parameters when a procedure must change the value of a variable in the caller. Never use a variable parameter if a value parameter could be used instead. Use value parameters as much as possible. If a value and variable parameter could be used to do the same job, always choose the value parameter. If a local variable will suffice, do not use a global variable.

PROGRAMMING EXAMPLE—MORTGAGE CALCULATOR

Let's turn to a larger, more complex application that requires the use of procedures to help organize the program development process. From time to time people find themselves in a situation where they have to borrow a substantial sum of money. Loans of this type, of which a mortgage is one (the Latin translation of mortgage is "death commitment"; if you have a house, you know what this means), are known as **amortized loans**. In such a loan the monthly payment is constant throughout the life of the loan, but the part of the payment that goes toward interest and the part that goes toward reducing the amount borrowed (principal) varies. In the early years of the loan, the interest component of the payment is high, indicating very little principal is paid off. Little by little, the principal is reduced, decreasing the interest component of the payment and increasing the principal part of the payment. Analyzing this process is complicated, so it would be helpful to have a program to calculate the payments. The program not only calculates the monthly payment and the yearly principal and interest paid, but also reports the true cost of the payments after considering the income tax deduction on the interest paid and subtracting that from the total yearly payment.

The formulas for the calculations are

$$\text{Annual payment} = \frac{\text{Interest rate} * (\text{Interest rate}+1)^{\#\text{of years}} + \text{Principal}}{(\text{Interest rate}+1)^{\#\text{of years}}-1}$$

Monthly Payment = Annual payment / 12

Yearly Interest paid = Interest rate * Principal remaining

Yearly Principal paid = Annual Payment − Yearly interest paid

Principal Remaining = Principal − Principal paid to date

Actual Cost = Interest paid * (1− Tax bracket/100) + Principal paid

The program will prompt the user to enter

- the Principal amount
- the Interest rate (as a fraction)
- the Term of loan in years
- the Tax bracket (as a percentage)

First let's pseudocode the program:

```
Get input
Calculate annual and monthly payment
For I:=1 to Years Do
begin
  calculate yearly principal and interest paid
  calculate yearly cost
  write information
end.
```

Now let's take a stab at writing the main program without the procedures.

```
program Mortgage;
var
    Years : Integer;    { Number of years of mortgage                }
    AnPay,              { Amount of payment each year                }
    MonthPay,           { Amount of payment each month               }
    Principal,          { Amount of principal still owed             }
    AnCost,             { Actual cost after tax is considered        }
    AnPrinPay,          { Amount of principal paid off each year     }
    AnInterestPay,      { Amount of interest paid each year          }
    IntRate,            { Interest rate of loan                      }
    TaxBrac             { Percentage of income paid to Uncle Sam     }
          : Real;

{Procedures will go here}

begin
   GetInfo;
   CalculatePayment(AnPay, MonthPay, Years, IntRate);
   Writeln('The monthly payment is ',MonthPay : 8 : 2);
   PrintTable;
   Readln
end.
```

Now let's put everything together.

Listing 5-1. Mortgage Program with Procedures.

```
program Mortgage;
 var
    Years : Integer;    { Number of years of mortgage                }
    AnPay,              { Amount of payment each year                }
    MonthPay,           { Amount of payment each month               }
    Principal,          { Aamount of principal still owed            }
    AnCost,             { Actual cost after tax is considered        }
    AnPrinPay,          { Amount of principal paid off each year     }
    AnInterestPay,      { Amount of interest paid off each year      }
    IntRate,            { Intereset rate of loan                     }
    TaxBrac             { Percentage of income paid to Uncle Sam     }
          : Real;
  {-----------------------------}
procedure GetInfo;
begin
    Writeln('Enter amount of loan');
    Readln(Principal);
    Writeln('Enter number of years');
    Readln(Years);
    Writeln('Enter interest rate as a fraction');
```

```
    Readln(IntRate);
    Writeln('Enter your tax bracket');
    Readln(TaxBrac)
end;
{-----------------------------}
procedure CalculatePayment (var AnPay, MonthPay : Real;
         Years : Integer;
         IntRate : Real);
var
    TempResult   : Real;
    I            : Integer;
begin
   TempResult := 1;
   for I := 1 to Years do
       TempResult := TempResult * (IntRate + 1);
   AnPay := (IntRate * TempResult * Principal) / (TempResult - 1);
   MonthPay := AnPay / 12
end;




{-----------------------------}
procedure PrintTable;
var
   Temp, I : Integer;
begin
    Writeln('Year', ' ':4, 'Interest', ' ', 'Princ', ' ', 'Cost');
    for I := 1 to Years do
        begin
           Write(I : 3);
           AnInterestPay := Principal * IntRate;
           Write(AnInterestPay : 8 : 2);
           AnPrinPay := AnPay - AnInterestPay;
           Write(AnPrinPay : 8 : 2);
           Principal := Principal - AnPrinPay;
           AnCost :- (TaxBrac / 100 * AnInterestPay) + AnPrinPay;
           Writeln(AnCost : 8 : 2)
        end {For loop}
 end; {Procedure}
{-----------------------------}
begin   { Main program }
   GetInfo;
   CalculatePayment(AnPay, MonthPay, Years, IntRate);
   Writeln('The monthly payment is ', MonthPay : 8 : 2);
   PrintTable;
   Readln
end.     { Main program }
```

If the values entered were an $80,000 loan at 13 percent for a period of ten years and the borrower's tax bracket was 40 percent the program would produce this table:

```
Mortgage
Enter amount of loan:
80000
Enter number of years
10
Enter interest rate as a fraction
.13
Enter your tax bracket
40
The monthly payment is  1228.60
Year Interest  Princ    Cost
  1 10400.00  4343.17  8503.17
  2  9835.39  4907.78  8841.93
  3  9197.38  5545.79  9224.74
  4  8476.42  6266.74  9657.31
  5  7661.75  7081.42 10146.12
  6  6741.17  8002.00 10698.47
  7  5700.90  9042.26 11322.62
  8  4525.41 10217.75 12077.92
  9  3197.10 11546.06 12824.90
 10  1696.12 13047.05 13725.50
The Total Cost is 106972.67
```

Figure 5-8. Mortgage Table

This program could have been written without using procedures, but it would have been harder to organize and write. You will find procedures a great aid to you in your future programs.

6
Arrays and Strings

INTRODUCTION

As our programming skill increases, so does the need to use more sophisticated data types in our programs. In this chapter, we will look at the data type array, which can contain several distinct but related components. This is unlike the other data type we have seen where each variable is a discrete entity. Also discussed in this chapter is the String data type, which is a Turbo Pascal extension to standard Pascal.

ARRAYS

Let's look at an example that will demonstrate the need for arrays by writing a program that will read and average three integers.

```
program Average;
var
  A, B, C : Integer;
  Avg : Real;
begin
  Writeln('Enter three numbers to average');
  Readln(A, B, C);
  Avg := (A + B + C) / 3.0;
  Writeln(Avg : 6 : 2);
  Readln
end.
```

You should recognize this as a straightforward problem whose solution is simple. However, how would you write a program to average 100, 1,000, or 10,000 numbers? It is obvious that it would be extremely impractical to use 100, 1,000, or 10,000 separate variables. That would create quite a long Read statement! What is needed is an array.

An **array** is a group of variables of the same data type, all with a common name. Each individual variable (called an **element**) is referenced by using a subscript along with the array name.

The declaration of an array is as follows:

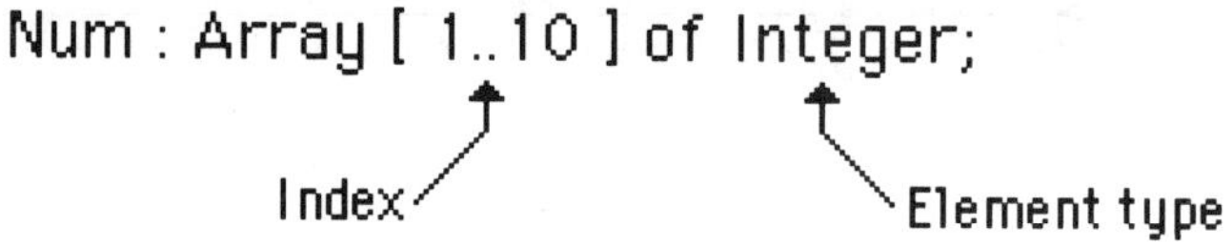

Figure 6-1. Declaring an Array

Here we have declared an array called Num. Num is an array of 10 memory locations, numbered 1 through 10, each holding an integer. The standard form for declaring an array is

```
ArrayName : array [subrange] of DataType;
```

An array is usually pictured as a linear list of variables.

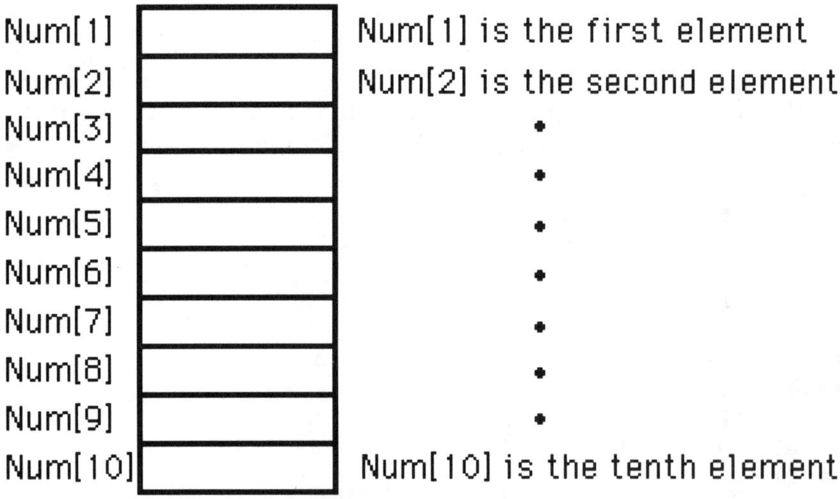

Figure 6-2. An Array

The number of elements in an array and the range of subscripts is determined by the subrange used.

```
A : array [3..7] of Integer;
```

Array A has five elements A[3],...,A[7].

```
B : array [-1..10] of Boolean;
```

Array B has 12 Boolean elements, B[-1], B[0], B[1],..., B[10]. The subrange need not be integer, it can be of any enumerated type.

```
C : array [False..True] of Integer;
```

Array C has two integer elements, C[False] and C[True].

```
D : array ['A'..'Z'] of Boolean;
```

Array D has 26 Boolean elements, D['A'], D['B'],...,D]'Z'].

Each of the separate variables in an array is referred to by the array name and the subscript in brackets. The subscript can either be a constant or an expression that must evaluate to a legal subscript. The following examples all show legal subscripts.

```
var
  Num : array[1..10] of Integer;

  Num[1] := 7;
  Num[8] := Num[1] + 3;
  K := 4;
  Num[K] := 3;
  Num[K + 2] := 4;
```

Arrays and For loops are a natural combination. The For loop can be used to sequentially access all the elements of an array. Let's use a For loop to initialize all the elements in array Num to zero.

```
for I:=1 to 10 do Num[I] := 0;
```

As this For loop iterates, the assignment statement is executed with all the different values of I. Thus, each of the ten elements in Num is set to zero. Let's now write the code to place into Num the following values:

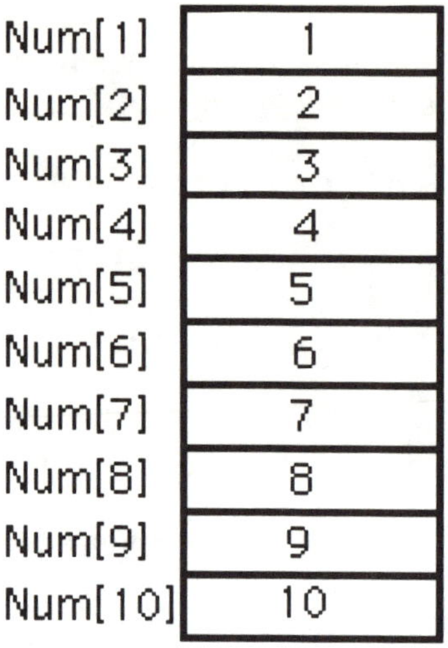

Figure 6-3. Array with Values

```
for I := 1 to 10 do
  Num[I] := I;
```

In this example, the values assigned to each element are the same as the subscript. Using an array, let's now write the 100 number average program discussed in the beginning of the chapter.

```
program Average;
 var
  Sum, I : Integer;
  Avg : Real;
  Num : array [1..100] of Integer;
 begin
  Sum := 0;
  for I := 1 to 100 do
   begin
    Writeln('Enter number', I);
    Readln(Num[I])
   end; [For loop]
    for I := 1 to 100 do
     Sum := Sum + Num[I];
    Avg := Sum / 100;
    Writeln('The average is ', Avg :6 : 2);
    Readln
   end.
```

The first For loop is used to read 100 values and place them into the array. The second For loop is used to add together all the values in the array. Finally, the average is computed. The use of the array has preserved the values entered for use in further calculations.

Two-Dimensional Arrays

Sometimes problems don't lend themselves to representation in a one-dimensional array but can more easily be represented in a two-dimensional data structure. The data type of the elements in an array can also be an array.

```
var
 A : array [1..3] of array [1..2] of Integer;
```

This creates a structure called a **two-dimensional array**. A two-dimensional array can be pictured as a matrix. Here is the array declared above:

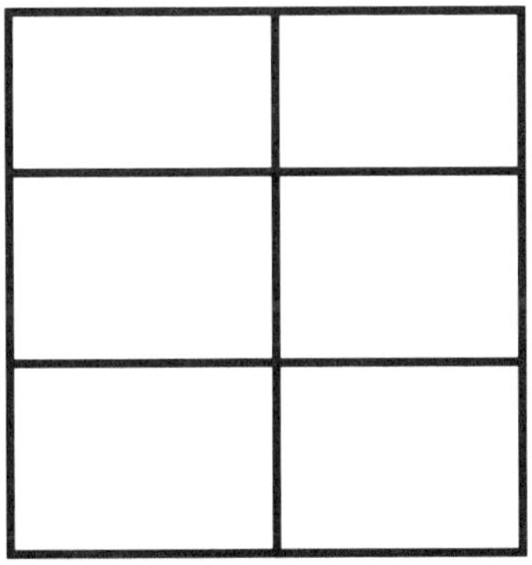

Figure 6-4. A Two-Dimensional Array

This two-dimensional array is said to have three rows and two columns. Normally, we compact the declaration of a two-dimensional array to

```
var
 A : array [1..3,1..2] of Integer;
```

The number of rows is always specified first, then the number of columns. Each element in the array has two subscripts, one for the row and one for the column. Each element is referred to as A[row,column]. Here is the same array with each element marked with its subscript.

	Column 1	Column2
Row1	A[1,1]	A[1,2]
Row2	A[2,1]	A[2,2]
Row3	A[3,1]	A[3,2]

Figure 6-5. A Two-by-Three Array

Two-dimensional arrays are used to represent data that has a row-and-column relationship. A good example of this is a tic-tac-toe board.

Let's look at some examples involving two-dimensional arrays.

```
var
  TwoD : array [1..3, 1..5] of Integer;
```

The above var section declares a two-dimensional array of three rows and five columns. Let's fill each element in this array with its column number.

```
for Row := 1 to 3 do
 for Col := 1 to 5 do
  TwoD[Row, Col] := Col;
```

The array would now appear as

1	2	3	4	5
1	2	3	4	5
1	2	3	4	5

Figure 6-6. A Three-by-Five Array

Notice that the array is filled one row at a time. That is, the value of the outer "For" control variable, Row, was 1, while the values of the inner loops control variable, Col, varied from 1 to 5. The effect was the same as if the following statements had been executed:

```
TwoD[1, 1] := 1;
TwoD[1, 2] := 2;
TwoD[1, 3] := 3;
TwoD[1, 4] := 4;
TwoD[1, 5] := 5;
```

The same thing happens in the other rows.

Now let's write the code that will add together the value in a column of the array. This is done by holding a column constant as we vary the rows. Let's first add the first column.

```
Sum := 0;
for Row := 1 to 3 do
   Sum := Sum + TwoD[Row, 1] ;
```

This loop is equivalent to the following statement:

```
Sum := TwoD[1, 1] + TwoD[2, 1] + TwoD[3, 1];
```

Notice that these are the three elements in the first column. All the columns can be added together by placing this loop into another For loop.

```
for Col := 1 to 5 do
 begin
```

```
   Sum := 0;
   for Row := 1 to 3 do
   Sum := Sum + TwoD[Row, Col] ;
   Writeln('The sum of column', Col : 2, 'is', Sum : 2)
  end;
```

The contents of a row can be added together by holding the row constant while varying the columns.

```
Sum := 0;
for Col := 1 to 5 do
 Sum := Sum + TwoD[1, Col];
```

This is equivalent to the following statement:

```
Sum := TwoD[1, 1] + TwoD[1, 2] +
    Two D[1, 3] + TwoD[1, 4] +TwoD[1, 5];
```

Now that we are familiar with using two-dimensional arrays, we can write a program that acts as a tic-tac-toe board for a game between two players. The program will keep track of the moves and inform the players of a win or tie. The tic-tac-toe board could be represented with a two-dimensional array with three rows and three columns. Each element in the array will hold an integer, 1 representing an X and 0 representing an O. Here is the declaration of the array:

```
Board : array [1..3,1..3] of Integer;
```

Let's begin by writing the pseudocode for the program.

```
while no winner do
 begin
   Get player A's move
   Mark it in the array
   Print board
   Is it a win?
   Get player B's move
   Mark it in the array
   Print board
   Is it a win?
 end
```

A second level of refinement includes some of the variable declarations, the procedure calls, and the main program.

```
program TicTacToe;
type
   Win = (Yes, No, Tie);
   Player = (X, O);
var
   Board : array [1..3,1..3] of Integer;
   CurrentPlayer : Player;
   Winner : Win;
   Sum, Total : Integer;
          .
          .
          .
begin
   Winner : No;
   InitializeArray;
   CurrentPlayer := B;
   while Winner = No do
      begin
         if CurrentPlayer = O then  {Flip
CurrentPlayer}
            CurrentPlayer := X
         else
            CurrentPlayer := O;
         GetMove;
         PrintBoard;
         WinOrTie;
         if Winner = Yes then
            Writeln('Game won by ', CurrentPlayer);
         if Winner = Tie then
            Writeln ('Game ends in a tie');
      end
end.
```

Now all that is left to do is write the procedures. The procedure InitializeArray will assign a −9 to all the elements in the array. This is done to make it easier to tell if there is a winner.

```
procedure InitializeArray;
var
   R, C : 1..3;
begin
   for C := 1 to 3 do
      for R := 1 to 3 do
```

```
            Board[R, C] := -9
end; {Initialize Board}
```

This initialization is performed with the help of two nested For loops. The loops will produce every combination of the subscripts in the following order.

Board[1, 1]

Board[2, 1]

Board[3, 1]

Board[1, 2]

Board[2, 2]

Board[3, 2]

Board[1, 3]

Board[2, 3]

Board[3, 3]

Note that the variable R is changed by the inner For loop, which iterates three times for each value of C.

The procedure GetMove will prompt the current player for his move.

```
procedure GetMove;
begin
   Writeln('Player ', PrintPlayer, ' Your Move');
   Writeln('Enter the row');
   Readln(Row);
   Writeln('Enter the column');
   Readln(Column)
end; {GetMove}
```

GetMove calls a small function, PrintPlayer, used to display the player since CurrentPlayer is a user-defined type and cannot be output by a Writeln statement.

```
function PrintPlayer : Char;
begin
  if CurrentPlayer = X
     then PrintPlayer := 'X'
  else
     PrintPlayer := 'O'
end;
```

The procedure PrintBoard writes the two-dimensional array to the console window. Two nested For loops are used for this.

```
procedure PrintBoard;
var
   R, C : 1..3;
begin
   for R := 1 to 3 do
      begin
         for C := 1 to 3 do
            Write(Board[R, C], ' ');
         Writeln
      end; {For R loop}
   Writeln
end;
```

The outer loop counts the rows, the inner loop the columns. This means the array is printed row 1 column 1, row 1 column 2, row 1 column 3, then row 2 column 1, and so forth. Note that after a complete row is printed, a Writeln is done to advance to the next line. Note also that the Writeln statement is not contained in the innermost loop.

The procedure WinOrTie is the most complex part of the program. It analyzes the board and reports back to the main program if there is a win or tie. To tell if there is a win we must check if either player has all three positions in a row, column, or diagonal of the array. Since player A's moves are marked by a 1, if any row, column, or diagonal adds up to 3 then A is the winner. If any row, column, or diagonal adds up to 0 then B is the winner. This is why the array elements were initialized to −9 rather 0: so that three empty positions added together don't add up to 0.

Listing 6-1. WinOrTie Procedure for the TicTacToe Program.

```
procedure WinOrTie;
var
 R, C : 1..3;
 Sum, Total : Integer;
begin
 Winner := No;
 if CurrentPlayer = X then {Switch current player}
    Total := 3
 else
    Total := 0;
 {Check columns}
 for C := 1 to 3 do
    begin
       Sum := 0;
       for R := 1 to 3 do
          Sum := Sum + Board[R, C];
       if Sum = Total then
          Winner := Yes
    end; {For C loop}
 {Check rows}
 if Winner = No then
    begin
       for R := 1 to 3 do
          begin
             Sum := 0;
             for C := 1 to 3 do
                Sum := Sum + Board[R, C];
             if Sum = Total then
                Winner := Yes
          end {For R loop}
    end;
 if Winner = No then
    begin
       {Check diagonals}
       Sum := 0;
       for C := 1 to 3 do
          Sum := Sum + Board[C, C];
```

```
        if Sum = Total then
           Winner := Yes
     end; {If}
 if Winner = No then
     begin
        Sum := 0;
        Winner := Tie;
        {Look for any empty position}
         for C := 1 to 3 do
            for R := 1 to 3 do
               if Board[R, C] = -9 then
                  Winner := No
      end
end;
```

The output of the routine is in the global variable Winner. Depending upon the move of the last player, Winner is set to either Yes, No, or Tie, the three possible values of the data type Win. This routine is divided into three parts. First all columns are checked. We add together the contents of each of the columns. This is done with two For loops. The column that is varied by the outer loop is held constant as the inner loop controls the rows. Once all three elements in a column are added, the sum is compared to the total, which would indicate a winning move was completed for that player. All three columns are checked even if a winner has already been determined. This is because the rows are checked with For loops, and there is no way to abort the checking even after finding the condition we want (this could have been done with a While loop). However, this is no problem since Winner is initially set to No and only set to Yes if a winning row is found. A variable used in this way is called a **toggle** or **switch**.

```
{Check columns}
for C := 1 to 3 do
   begin
      Sum := 0;
      for R := 1 to 3 do
         Sum := Sum + Board[R, C];
      if Sum = Total then
         Winner := Yes
   end; {For loop}
```

If no winning column is found, we now move on to check the rows. The rows are checked in the same manner except that the columns are kept constant as the loop adds together the contents of each row.

```
{Check rows}
for R := 1 to 3 do
   begin
      Sum := 0;
      for C := 1 to 3 do
         Sum := Sum + Board[R, C];
      if Sum = Total then
         Winner := Yes
   end {For loop}
```

The diagonals have to be checked in a different way. The major diagonal, the one that goes from the upper left-hand corner to the lower right-hand corner, consists of the elements Board[1, 1], Board[2, 2], and Board[3, 3]. Note that in each of these elements the row and column subscripts are the same. The contents of these elements can be added with one For loop using the loop control variable as both subscripts.

```
for C := 1 to 3 do
   Sum := Sum + Board[C, C];
if Sum = Total then
   Winner := Yes
```

The minor diagonal, the one that goes from the upper right-hand corner to the lower left-hand corner, contains the elements Board[1, 3], Board[2, 2], and Board[3, 1]. All these elements can be added with one For loop if the relationship between the row and column subscripts is noticed.

```
for C := 1 to 3 do
   Sum := Sum + Board[C, 4 - C];
if Sum = Total then
   Winner := Yes;
```

If no winning move was made, the array is now checked to see if there is a tie. In tic-tac-toe there is a tie if there is no place for a player to move. This would be represented in the array by no element equal to the initial value of −9. First, Winner is set to Tie and then two nested For loops are used to examine the contents of all the array elements. If any element is found to have the initial value, then there is a place to move, and Winner is toggled to No.

```
if Winner = No then
  begin
     Sum := 0;
     Winner := Tie;
     {Look for any empty position}
     for C := 1 to 3 do
        for R := 1 to 3 do
           if Board[R, C] = -9 then
              Winner := No
  end
```

PROGRAMMING EXAMPLE—THE TIC-TAC-TOE PROGRAM

Here is the TicTacToe program all together. This program has more than just entertainment value. Running the program, we help acquaint you with the row and column positions in a two-dimensional array. Worth noting in this program listing is the comment line of dashes used to separate procedures. This is done to improve the readability of the program.

Listing 6-2. The Complete TicTacToe Program.

```
program TicTacToe;
 uses
  Memtypes, QuickDraw, OSIntf, ToolIntf;
 type
  Win = (Yes, No, Tie);
  Player = (O, X);
 var
  Board : array[1..3, 1..3] of Integer;
  CurrentPlayer : Player;
  Winner : Win;
  Row, Column : 1..3;
 procedure InitializeArray;
```

```
    var
     R, C : 1..3;
    begin
    for C := 1 to 3 do
     for R := 1 to 3 do
      Board[R, C] := -9;
    end; [Initialize Board]
   {---------------------------------------------}
   function PrintPlayer : Char;
    begin
     if CurrentPlayer = X
       then PrintPlayer := 'X'
      else
       PrintPlayer := 'O'
    end;
   {---------------------------------------------}
  procedure GetMove;
   begin
    Writeln('Player ', PrintPlayer, ' Your Move');
    Writeln('Enter the row');
    Readln(Row);
    Writeln('Enter the column');
    Readln(Column)
   end; {GetMove}
   {---------------------------------------------}
   procedure PrintBoard;
    var
     R, C : 1..3;
   begin
    for R := 1 to 3 do
     begin
      for C := 1 to 3 do
       Write(Board[R, C], ' ');
      Writeln
     end; {For R loop}
    Writeln
   end;
    {--------------------------------------------}
  procedure WinOrTie;
    var
     R, C : 1..3;
     Sum, Total : Integer;
   begin
```

```
  Winner := No;
  if CurrentPlayer = X then {Switch current player}
   Total := 3
  else
   Total := 0;
{Check columns}
  for C := 1 to 3 do
   begin
    Sum := 0;
    for R := 1 to 3 do
     Sum := Sum + Board[R, C];
    if Sum = Total then
     Winner := Yes
   end; {For C loop}
  {Check rows}
  if Winner = No then
   begin
    for R := 1 to 3 do
     begin
      Sum := 0;
      for C := 1 to 3 do
       Sum := Sum + Board[R, C];
      if Sum = Total then
       Winner := Yes
     end {For R loop}
   end;
  if Winner = No then
   begin
{Check diagonals}
    Sum := 0;
    for C := 1 to 3 do
     Sum := Sum + Board[C, C];
    if Sum = Total then
     Winner := Yes
   end; {If}
  if Winner = No then
   begin
    Sum := 0;
    Winner := Tie;
{Look for any empty position}
    for C := 1 to 3 do
     for R := 1 to 3 do
      if Board[R, C] = -9 then
```

```
      Winner := No
    end
  end;
  {-----------------------------------------------------}
  function GoodMove (R, C : Integer) : Boolean;
   begin
    If Board[R,C] = -9 then
     GoodMove := True
    else
     begin
      GoodMove := False;
      SysBeep(2);
      Writeln('Invalid Move')
     end
   end;
  {-----------------------------------------------------}
 begin {Main program}
  Winner := No;
  InitializeArray;
  CurrentPlayer := O;
  while Winner = No do
   begin
    if CurrentPlayer = X then
     CurrentPlayer := O
    else
     CurrentPlayer := X;
    repeat
     GetMove;
    until GoodMove(Row, Column);
    if CurrentPlayer = X then
     Board[Row, Column] := 1
    else
     Board[Row, Column] := 0;
    PrintBoard;
    WinOrTie;
    if Winner = Yes then
     begin
      SysBeep(10);
      Writeln('Game won by ', PrintPlayer)
     end; {If}
    if Winner = Tie then
     begin
      SysBeep(10);
```

```
      Writeln('Game ends in a Tie')
     end {If}
   end; {While loop}
   Readln;
 end. {TicTacToe}
```

Do More

An interesting way to adapt the TicTacToe program is to replace the two-dimensional array of integer with a two-dimensional array of a user-defined type with three values: a value of each of the two player's moves and a third value for an unused position (initial value). Think about the changes that would be required in the WinOrTie procedure.

Reach Further

A second and more complex change in the program is to replace one of the players with the computer itself. This requires the program to identify which of the empty positions is the most advantageous and requires analysis of the strategy of the TicTacToe game. To proceed, play several games on paper and try to identify why you made each move. Then try to quantify your reasoning into an algorithm which can be programmed.

Arrays of Characters

A limitation of standard Pascal is that the type Char can only hold a single character. An array whose elements are of type Char can be used to handle a stream of character data. To read from the keyboard and store up to 80 characters, we can declare an array as follows:

```
Inchar : array [1..80] of Char;
```

The array Inchar has 80 elements, each one capable of holding 1 character. We can read characters from the keyboard and place them into Inchar with

```
I := 0;
Read(Ch);
while not (eoln) do
  begin
    I := I + 1 ;
    Inchar[I] := Ch;
    Read(Ch)
  end; {while}
```

We want this loop to keep on reading characters from the keyboard until a carriage return is entered. EOLN, which stands for End of Line, is helpful in such situations. EOLN is a Boolean function that returns a value of False if a carriage return has not been entered since EOLN was last used and True otherwise. We want the loop to continue executing when EOLN is False, but a While loop executes when the condition is True. We therefore reverse the value of EOLN with the use of a "not." When EOLN is used, the Read statement must be used instead of Readln. Using Readln will cause the program to work improperly. Note that in this loop, the characters are first read into the Char variable Ch and then placed into the array. This is done to trap the carriage return character and not place it into the array.

This loop could also be written a different way without using EOLN. We could use the While loop to check the ASCII value of the character entered.

```
I := 1;
Read(Ch);
while ORD(Ch) <> 13 do
  begin
    Inchar[I] := Ch;
    I := I + 1;
    Read(Ch)
  end; {While}
```

Note that the ASCII code for a carriage return is 13.

STRINGS

Character data is often processed by a computer. However, handling character data in an array of type Char is inefficient and awkward.

Fortunately, Turbo Pascal has available an extended data type known as string. A variable of type string can hold a sequence of from 1 to 255 characters long. A variable is declared to be a string with the following type of declaration:

```
S : string[80];
```

This declares S to be a string variable. The maximum number of characters the string can hold is called its **size** and is indicated in brackets. The default size is 255 if no size is specified. The size of S is 80, but the length of the string may vary dynamically from 0 to 80 characters at any time. We could say that a string's size is its maximum length. A value is placed in a string variable with an assignment statement.

```
S:='ABCD';
```

The string value 'ABCD' is enclosed in single quotes. The current length of string S is now 4. A string variable can be cleared by assigning to it the null string, which is a string with no contents indicated by two consecutive quotes. The length of the null string is zero.

```
S:=''; {Assign null string to S}
```

An error will occur if an attempt is made to assign a string value whose length is greater than the size of the string variable. For example, the following program segment will produce a run-time error:

```
var
 S1 : string[4];
      .
      .
 S1:='ABCDEF';
```

Arraylike Access

The individual characters in a string can be accessed as though they were elements in an array. For instance:

```
S := 'ABCD';
Write(S[1]);
```

would print 'A'. The integer in the brackets is an index to the characters in the string. An attempt to reference `S[0]` or a position greater than the current length of the string would result in a run-time error. The contents of a string can also be changed in this manner.

```
S :='HI';
S[1] := 'B';
Writeln(S);
```

The above program segment would print BI.

Reading a String

String values can be read from the keyboard using Readln.

```
Readln(S1,S2);
```

This Readln statement will read two strings, S1 and S2. A carriage return is used as a sentinel to signify the end of a string when reading it from the keyboard. The carriage return is not placed in the string.

Comparing Strings

The value of two strings can be compared in a Boolean expression. The comparison is based on the value of the ASCII codes of the characters in the strings. When two strings of different lengths are compared, each extra character in the longer string is considered to be greater than the missing characters in the shorter strings. Two strings must be of equal length to be equal.

'AB' is greater than 'AA'

'AT' is less than 'ATTACH'

'BILL' equals 'BILL'

'BILL' is not equal to 'HILL'

Numerically, the ASCII codes for uppercase letters are smaller than those for lowercase letters, so that

```
'a' is greater than 'A'
```

An array of strings can be alphabetized in this way.

THE STRING FUNCTIONS AND PROCEDURES

The arithmetic operators (+,−,/, DIV, and so on) cannot be used with string values. Operations on strings are performed with the help of a set of built-in functions and procedures.

The Length Function

```
function Length( Str : string) : Integer;
```

The Length function returns the current length of the given string. For example, the following program segment:

```
S:='GOOD';
Write(Length(S));
```

prints 4.

The Concat Function

```
function Concat(S1, S2, ... : string) : string;
```

The Concat function is used to combine any number of strings into one. For example, this statement:

```
S:=Concat('GOOD', ' ', 'MORNING');
```

produces a value of S of 'GOOD MORNING.' The length of the result should not exceed 255, or else the characters past 255 will be truncated.

The Pos Function

```
function Pos(Substr, Str : string) : string;
```

The Position function returns as an integer the position of the first occurrence of the substring in the string. The statement

```
I := Pos('CD', 'ABCD');
```

assigns 3 to I, since the substring 'CD' starts at the third position in 'ABCD.' If the substring is not present, a zero is returned.

The Copy Function

```
function Copy(String, Index, Count : string) : string;
```

The Copy function returns a string of count characters starting at String[Index]. The following statement:

```
StrgVar := Copy('ABCDE', 3, 2)
```

assigns to StrgVar

```
'CD'
```

The Delete Procedure

```
procedure Delete( var Str : string, Index, Count :
Integer);
```

The Delete procedure removes from the specified string Count number of characters starting at String[Index]. The statements

```
S:='ABCDE';
Delete(S, 3, 2);
```

results in the value of S being 'AE'. If characters outside the length of the string are referenced, it is not an error. Only the characters that lie within the range are deleted. Note that Delete is a procedure, not a function, and does not return a value.

The Insert Procedure

```
procedure Insert(var Source : string;  Destination :
string; Index : Integer);
```

The Insert procedure places the destination string into the source string at the index position. After execution of the statements

```
S := 'ABCDE';
Insert(S, 'FF', 3);
```

the value of S is now

```
ABFFCDE
```

7
More on Structures

INTRODUCTION

Because it is a sophisticated programming language Pascal has a large menu of structures. The set of structures is large enough to provide the programmer with the right tool for the right job. In this chapter we will start to complete our study of Pascal's structures by looking at the last of Pascal's loops, the Repeat loop, and several other features of the language.

THE REPEAT LOOP

The third of Pascal's loop structures is the **Repeat loop**. Repeat is a free loop (like While, unlike For) and can be roughly described as an upside-down While loop.

The form of the Repeat loop is

```
repeat
 statements
until expression is True;
```

When executed, the Repeat loop executes all the statements in the loop and then checks if the condition is True.

Repeat is very much like the While loop. There are three differences:

1) The Repeat loop checks the condition at the bottom of the loop rather than at the top, as is done in the While loop, so in the Repeat loop the body of the loop is always executed at least once. In the While loop, if the condition is initially False, the body of the loop will not be executed at all.

2) The "repeat" and "until" reserved words automatically bracket a compound statement. "Begin" and "end" are not needed.

3) The Repeat loop iterates if the condition is False, the While loop iterates when the condition is True.

Let's look at a Repeat loop side by side with a While loop.

```
I := 1;
repeat
  Writeln(I);
  I := I+1
until I  > 10;
```

```
I := 1;
while I <= 10 do
 begin
  Writeln(1);
  I := I+1
 end;
```

These loops both print the integers from 1 to 10. In examining the differences, notice where in the loop the condition is checked and how the opposite conditions are used. The Repeat loop uses the condition I > 10, and the While loop uses the condition I <= 10.

Checking Input Validity

A useful application of the Repeat loop is to check the validity of input. For example, a program that analyzed exam grades might use the following loop to make sure that the values entered as exam grades were valid:

```
repeat
 Writeln('Enter Grade');
 Readln(Grade)
until (Grade >= 0 and Grade <= 100);
```

Here the condition is a multiple test. Since we want the value entered to fall inside a range, the logical operator And is used. If the value entered does not fall within the range, the condition is not met, and the body of the loop is performed again. Think of the difference between this and declaring the variable Grade as the subrange 1 . . 100. In the case of using the subrange, if a value out of the range is entered, an error would occur while the program was executing, stopping the program. In this loop execution would not stop execution, but rather would prompt the user to enter the value a second time. This method is preferable since a major goal in programming is to prevent a program from crashing (stopping due to an error) because of run-time errors.

However, this input validity technique is useless if the user enters a noninteger that would "crash" the program (think about the example back in Chapter 2). How can we protect the program from this? The most common technique is to accept the input to the program as a string and then convert the string into an integer. This requires scanning through the string, isolating each digit in the string (which is in character form), converting it to an integer, and then creating the entire number from the individual digits. We can build a function that takes a string that represents a positive integer and returns either the integer or a negative number as an error code.

```
function StringToInt(S : string) : Integer;
var
 Sum, Num, Ct : Integer;
 Valid : Boolean
 Ch : Char;
begin
 Ct := 1;  Valid := True
 Sum := 0;
 repeat
    Ch := S[Ct];
    If not (Ch >= '0') and (Ch <= '9') then
      Valid := False;
    Num := Ord(Ch) - Ord('0');     {Convert to an integer}
    Sum := Sum * 10 + Num;  {Build the number}
    Ct := Ct + 1;
 until  (Ct > Length(S)) or (Valid = False);
 if Valid then
    StringtoNum := Num
   else
   StringtoNum := -1
end {Function}
```

The function uses the Repeat loop to iterate through the string. The condition checked is whether the last character in the string has been looked at or if an invalid character (doesn't represent a digit) has been found. This function can now be placed in a Repeat loop, which is driven by the result returned by the function

```
repeat
 Read(Grade)
until StringToInt(Grade>=0);
```

THE BUBBLE SORT

A **sort** is an algorithm used to place the values in an array in numerical order. There are many different sorting methods; the bubble sort is one of the easiest to follow and sufficiently efficient to be used in many situations. A book on data structures will explain in much more detail different sorts and the criteria used to evaluate them.

The bubble sort operates by comparing each two adjacent elements in an array. If they are out of order, they are exchanged. The comparisons run through the entire array. After a pass is complete, if any exchanges were made, the process is started again at the top. When no exchanges take place in a pass through the array, the array is sorted.

Here is the bubble sort in a procedure. The array to be sorted is passed to the procedure in a variable parameter and is of the global type ArrayType. Its elements are of the global type ElementType. The parameter NumElements is an integer containing the number of elements in the array.

```
 procedure BubbleSort(var A : ArrayType; NumElements :
 Integer);
 type
  Exch = (Yes, No);
 var
  Exchanged : Exch;
  Temp : ElementType;
  I : Integer;
begin
 repeat
   I := 1;
   Exchanged := No;
```

```
    for I := 1 to NumElements - 1 do
    if A[I] < A[I+1] then
     begin
      Exchanged := Yes;
      Temp := A[I+1];
      A[I+1] := A[I];
      A[I] := Temp
     end
    until Exchanged = No
   end;{Procedure}
```

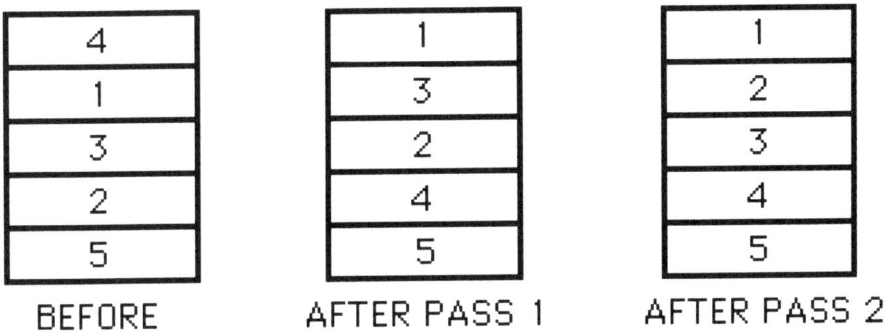

Figure 7-1. The Bubble Sort

RECORDS

One of the most important and powerful data types in Pascal are **records**. While arrays consist of variables of the same data type, a record is a collection of variables that can be of different data types and are logically related to each other. For example, a record might contain all the information about a person—name, age, sex, and so on.

A record declaration includes a name of the record and a name and type of each record element.

```
type
 PayRec = record
    ID    : Integer;
    Hours : Real;
    Rate  : Real;
    Pay   : Real
 end;{ PayRec}
```

Examining the declaration above, we see that PayRec is declared in the type section. The record type PayRec consists of four components, ID of type Integer, and Hours, Rate, and Pay of type Real.

We can now declare a variable to be of type PayRec.

```
var
 Payroll : PayRec;
```

Payroll is now of type PayRec and has four components (also called **elements** or **fields**). They are referred to as

Payroll.ID

Payroll.Hours

Payroll.Rate

Payroll.Pay

Each field (or element) is referred to by both its record name and its field name; a point or period is used to separate them. A record element can do anything that any other variable of that type can do. The only difference between a record element and any other variable of that type is that the record element is part of a larger structure. Examples of assignment statements are

Payroll.ID := 99;

Payroll.Hours := 40.0;

Payroll.Rate := 12.5;

Payroll.Pay:= Payroll.Hours * Payroll.Rate;

If more than one record is declared of the same record type such as

```
var
 DayPay,WeekPay : PayRec;
```

then an entire record can be assigned to another with a simple assignment statement.

```
WeekPay := DayPay;
```

Any operation other than simple assignment has to be performed with each separate element. For instance, to multiply all the elements of our record by 5:

```
WeekPay.ID := DayPay.ID * 5;
WeekPay.Hours := DayPay.Hours * 5;
WeekPay.Rate := DayPay.Rate * 5;
WeekPay.Pay := DayPay.Pay * 5;
```

Information in a record is written to the screen or read from the keyboard into a record by using the complete field name.

```
Writeln(PayRoll.ID);
Readln(WeekPay.Rate);
```

This is only a beginning to the use of records. Records are used extensively by the Toolbox to organize data. For instance, the definition of a Rectangle is a record defined as follows:

```
Rectangle = record
   top    : Integer;
   left   : Integer;
   bottom : Integer;
   right  : Integer
end;
```

We haven't been aware of the structure of a rectangle because the SetRect procedure has been used to fill a rectangle's structure without actually having to view the record. When records are used in conjunction with files, they provide a powerful tool for business applications and a way to save data for future use. When used with pointers they can represent myriad situations. Both files and pointers will be presented in the next few chapters.

The With Statement

When using records, it can become tedious to have to use the complete name of a record element over and over. The With statement is used to shorten the name of a record element when used in a statement.

```
with Payroll do
  Readln(ID);
```

This is the equivalent of

```
Readln(Payroll.ID);
```

The With statement automatically prefixes the field name ID with the record name Payroll to result in Payroll.ID.

The power of the With statement can be expanded by including it in a compound statement.

```
with Payroll do
 begin
  ID := 10;
  Readln(Hours,Rate);
  Pay := Hours * Rate
 end;
```

This With statement replaces

```
Payroll.ID := 10;
Readln(Payroll.Hours,Payroll.Rate);
Payroll.Pay := Payroll.Hours * Payroll.Rate;
```

Consider the following declarations:

```
type
 BirthRec = record
    Age : Integer;
    Date: String;
 end;

 AnnivRec = record
    Length : Integer;
    Date    : String
 end;

var
```

```
BirthDay     : BirthRec;
Anniversary : AnnivRec;
```

More than one record name can be included in the With statement.

```
with Birthdays, Anniversaries do
  Age := Length;
```

is equivalent to

```
Birthdays.Age := Anniversaries.Length;
```

The proper record name is found and is added to the field name. The position of the record name in the With statement is insignificant. It follows, then, that the With might have read

```
with Anniversaries, Birthdays do
 Age := Length;
```

Using either of the two With statements, this assignment statement would be ambiguous:

```
Date := Date;
```

It is impossible to tell which field is in which record, and therefore this kind of programming is considered bad practice.

Arrays of Records

We can declare an array whose elements consist of records. This is a powerful structure capable of holding a large amount of information easily. Let's design a program that keeps track of the weather over a period of a year. Here are the declaration sections:

```
type
 SkyType = (Sun, Rain, Cloudy);
 WeatherRec = record
 Temp : Integer;
 Sky  : SkyType
end;
```

```
var
 Weather : array [1..365] of WeatherRec;
```

We have set up a type, WeatherRec, as a record with two fields. An array was then declared, Weather, which has 365 elements (one for each day of the year) of type WeatherRec. Thus there are 365 records in the array. When we have an array of records, we specify a particular field in a particular record as

```
Weather[Index].Temp
```

The record name with its position in the array given as a subscript is followed by the field name. This array can be pictured as follows:

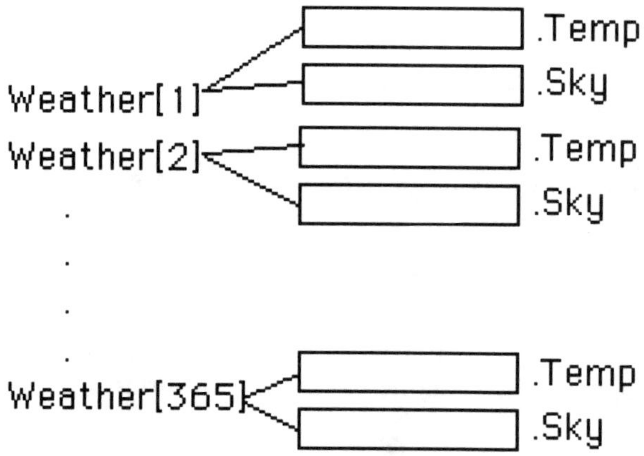

Figure 7-2. An Array of Records

Since each record is an element in the array, we always use the array name with a subscript, even when using the With statement. Here the Temp field of the first record is read

```
with Weather[1] do
  Readln(Temp);
```

Here the Temp field of the Ith record is read

```
with Weather[I] do
  Readln(Temp);
```

To continue our weather tracking program, let's read the weather for each day of last year.

```
for I := 1 to 365 do
 with Weather[I] do
 begin
  Writeln('Enter temperature for day', I);
  Readln(Temp);
  Writeln('S)un, R)ain or C)louds');
   Readln(SkyTemp);
   case SkyTemp of
    S : Sky := Sun;
    R : Sky := Rain;
    C : Sky := Clouds;
    otherwise Writeln('incorrect value')
 end; {With}
```

Because of the With statement, when Temp was used in the Readln statement it referred to Weather[I].Temp.

We can now average the daily temperatures.

```
TempSum := 0;
for I:= 1 to 365 do
 with Weather[I] do
  TempSum := TempSum + Temp;
AvgTemp := TempSum / 365;
Writeln('The average temperature was', AvgTemp : 6 : 2);
```

Here is the whole weather program together:

Listing 7-1. Weather Program.

```
program Weather;
const
   DaysInYear = 3;
type
   SkyType = (Sun, Rain, Cloudy);
   WeatherRec = record
      Temp : Integer;
      Sky  : SkyType
   end;
var
   SkyTemp : char;
```

```
   Weather : array [1..DaysInYear] of WeatherRec;
      I, TempSum : Integer;
      AvgTemp : Real;
begin {program}
   for I := 1 to DaysInYear do
      with Weather[I] do
         begin
            Writeln('Enter temperature for day', I : 2);
            Readln(Temp);
            Writeln('S)un, R)ain or C)louds');
            Readln(SkyTemp);
            case SkyTemp of
               'S' : Sky := Sun;
               'R' : Sky := Rain;
               'C' : Sky := Cloudy;
               otherwise Writeln('incorrect value')
            end
         end; {With}
   TempSum := 0;
     for I:= 1 to DaysInYear do
        with Weather[I] do
              TempSum := TempSum + Temp;
     AvgTemp := TempSum / DaysInYear;
        Writeln('The average temperature was',
          AvgTemp : 6 : 2);
     Readln
 end.{Program}
```

The obvious limitation of this program is that the data entered into the array will be lost as soon as we stop using the program. What is needed is a mechanism to save the data for further use on an external device such as the built-in disk drive. This is the role played by external files, which will be covered in Chapter 8.

Nested Records

The data type contained in a record can also be a record. This nests one record inside another. Let's examine the following type declarations:

```
type
  FileRec = record
      File1 : string[20];
```

```
      File2 : string[20];
      File3 : string[20]
 end;

  DiskRec = record
     DiskName : string[20];
     Contents : FileRec
 end;

var
     Disk1 : DiskRec;
```

We now have a record (Disk1) that has as an element a subrecord. Pictorially it looks like this:

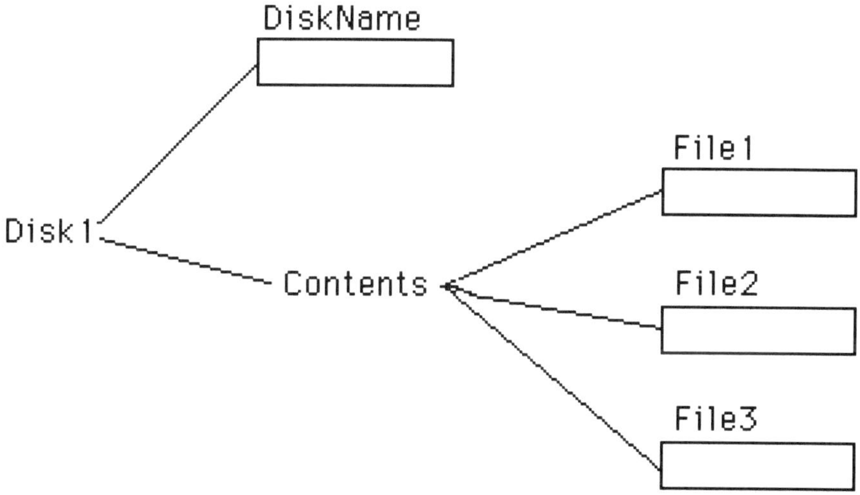

Figure 7-3. A Nested Record

The way we assign data to a field in this record will differ depending upon which level of a record the field is in. The field DiskName is in the first level, so we need to use the record and the field name

```
Disk1.DiskName := 'PaulStuff';
```

The fields File1, File2, and File3 are all in the second level of the record, and their names are composed of the record name, the sub-record name, and the field name:

```
Disk1.Contents.File1 := 'Resume';
```

A field in a record can also be an array. Let's change the declaration of FileRec to

```
FileRec = record;
   Files : Array[1..10] of String[20];
end;
```

The record Disk1 can now be pictured as

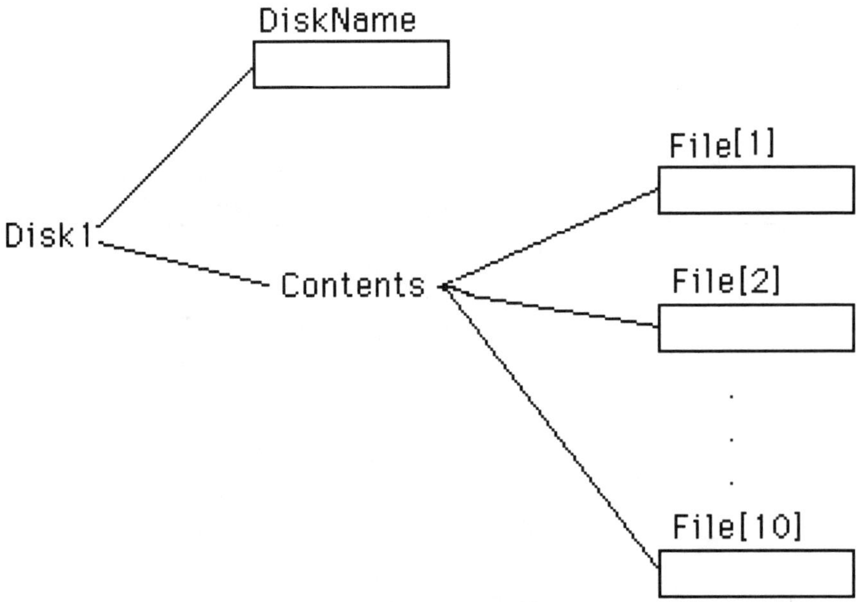

Figure 7-4. Nested Record with Array

The fields that are array elements are referred to as

```
Disk1.Contents.Files[I]
```

Notice that here the subscript is after the field name rather than after the record name, as it is when we have an array of records.

TIME AND DATE OPERATIONS

The Macintosh Toolbox contains two procedures to fetch and alter the real time clock built into the computer. To access the clock, Turbo Pascal has a built-in record type defined as

```
DateTimeRec = record
 Year,
 Month,
 Day,
 Hour,
 Minute,
 Second,
 DayOfWeek : Integer
end;
```

The meaning of most of the fields is obvious. Hour is the number of hours since midnight, sometimes referred to as the 24-hour clock. Month is the number of the month from 1 to 12. Day of the week is 1 to 7, from Sunday to Saturday.

To fetch the clock information, first declare records of type DateTimeRec and LongInt.

```
var
 Clock : DateTimeRec;
 Secs  : LongInt;
```

The clock is read by the system's GetDateTime procedure.

```
procedure GetDateTime( var Secs : LongInt);
```

The GetDateTime procedure returns the number of seconds between January 1, 1904, and the time at which the procedure was called (kudos to the reader who can figure out the last date that the clock can hold). Fortunately, you need not convert this figure into the Date-

TimeRec yourself, the built-in Secs2Date procedure will do that operation.

```
procedure Secs2Date (secs : LongInt; var date :
DateTimeRec);
```

The Secs2Date procedure takes the number of seconds elapsed since January 1, 1904, and converts that into a DateTimeRec. So in order to read the clock and make sense out of the data, we would use the two procedures together.

```
GetDateTime(Secs);
Secs2Date (Secs, Clock);
```

The fields of Clock now contain the current time and date information. Two Case statements could now be used to display the name of the month and day.

SETS

Sets are a structured data type unique to Pascal among the more popular programming languages. A set is an unordered collection of items of the same data type, called **members**. Unlike any other type in Pascal, the number of elements in a set may change dynamically. A set is indicated by enumerating members of the set inside brackets.

```
[1,3,5,9]              is the set of odd numbers from 1 to 10.
['A','E','I','O','U']  is the set of uppercase vowels.
```

A subrange can also be used to enumerate the members of a set.

```
['a'..'z']             is the set of all lowercase letters.
```

The general form for the declaration of a set is

```
var
 SetName : set of data type;
```

The data type can be any ordinal type other than real. A user-defined ordinal type can also be used.

This declaration creates a set whose members can be uppercase letters:

```
var
 Vowels : set of 'A'..'Z';
```

The declaration of a set does not place any members into it any more than declaring a variable to be an integer gives it a value. Members have to be assigned to the set. The members of a set are represented as shown before.

```
Letters := ['A','B','C'];
```

The set Letters now has three members. The order of the members of a set has no significance, nor can a set have more than one of the same member. A set with no members is called the **empty set** and is represented with two brackets next to each other [ ].

Set Operators

To perform operations on sets of the same type, there are several set operators.

+ Set Union or Addition

− Set Difference

* Set Intersection

SET UNION

Set union forms a third set made up of each of the elements in two sets. Any member appearing in both sets is only included once.

```
Expression                       Result
 [1,2,3] + [3,4]                  [1,2,3,4]
 ['A','C','E'] + ['B','D']        ['A','B','C','D','E']
```

SET DIFFERENCE

Set difference forms a third set with the members of the first set that are not in the second set.

```
Expression                              Result
 [1,2,3] - [3,4]                         [1,2]
 ['A'..'Z'] - ['A','E','I','O','U']      the set of all uppercase
                                           consonants
```

SET INTERSECTION

Set intersection forms a third set with all the members that the first and second sets have in common.

```
Expression                              Result
[1,2,3] * [2,4,6]                        [2]
['A','b','c','D'] * ['a','b','c','d']   ['b','c']
```

As shown in Table 7-1 relational operators also can be used with sets, although their meanings change slightly.

Table 7-1. Regional Operators Used With Sets

Expression	Returns True If
Set1 = Set2	Set1 and Set2 are identical.
Set1 <> Set2	The intersection of Set1 and Set2 would produce the empty set.
Set1 <= Set2	Set1 is a subset of Set2 (all the members of Set1 are in Set2).
Set1 < Set2	All the members of Set1 are in Set2, and at least one member of Set2 is not in Set1. Set1 is a strict subset of Set2.
Set1 >= Set2	Set2 is a subset of Set1 (all the members of Set2 are in Set1).
Set1 > Set2	All the members of Set2 are in Set1 and at least one member of Set1 is not in Set2. Set2 is a strict subset of Set1.
Member in Set1	Member is in Set1.

All of these operators except "in" work with two sets.

Sets are useful for input verification. Their use can simplify the type of function we wrote before. If we were writing a program that accepted student's grades of A,B,C,D, and F, we might use the following code:

```
var
 GradeSet : set of 'A' . . 'Z';
 Grade : 'A' . . 'Z';
    .
    .
 GradeSet := ['A','B','C','D','F'];
 repeat
  Writeln('Enter Grade');
       Readln(Grade);
  if Grade not in GradeSet then
       Writeln('Reenter grade');
  until Grade in GradeSet;
```

Some programs require the use of uppercase characters. To convert from upper- to lowercase, note that the ASCII codes for the lowercase letters are 32 less than the uppercase. For example:

```
'A' equals CHR(ORD('a')+32)
```

Sets can be used in a program that changes the case of a character.

```
program Convert;
type
 CharSet = set of Char;
var
 InString : string[80];
 LowerCase: CharSet;
 Ct : Integer;
 Ch : Char;
begin
 LowerCase := ['a' . . 'z'];
 Writeln('Enter a string');
 Readln(Instring);
 for Ct := 1 to Length(InString) do
   if InString[Ct] in LowerCase then
    InString[Ct] := CHR(ORD(InString[Ct] )-32);
 Writeln(InString);
```

```
 Readln
end.
```

In program Convert, a set, LowerCase, contains all the lowercase characters. A string is read and a For loop is used to see if any of the characters in the string is a member of LowerCase. If so, the character's case is converted and reassigned to the same position in the string.

A similar program can use sets to list all the characters that appear in a string. The string is entered and stored in a string variable. The individual characters in the string are examined and added to the set. The characters that are members of the set are then displayed. Note that both upper- and lowercase characters can both be set members.

```
program ExamineCharacters;
 type
  CharSet = set of char;
 var
  InString : string[80];
  LetterSet := [ 'A' .. 'z'];
  Ct : Integer;
  Ch : Char;
  begin
   Writeln('Enter a string');
   Readln(Instring);
   for I := 1 to Length(InString) do
     LetterSet := LetterSet + [InString[Ct]];
   Writeln('These are the characters');
  for Ch := 'A' to 'z' do
  if Ch in LetterSet then
   Writeln(Ch);
 end.
```

Sets are a powerful Pascal structure and can be used to replace many If and Case statements. Their use helps create elegant, well-written programs.

RECURSION

The last topic to be covered in this varied chapter is a programming technique rather than a structure, which answers the question of what happens when a subprogram calls itself. The result is not a loop but a very powerful and complicated technique called **recursion**. Recursion is one of the most puzzling and interesting aspects of Pascal.

Recursion can be easily demonstrated by writing a function that calculates the factorial of a number. The factorial of a number, denoted with a exclamation point such as N!, is that number multiplied by all its predecessors down to one. For instance, 5! is 5*4*3*2*1, which equals 120. Factorials are used extensively in statistical and probabilistic work. We can also define the factorial of a number as that number itself times the factorial of that number minus one, or 5! = 5*4!. This is a recursive definition. A recursive definition is not defined in terms of itself as it might appear, but rather as a simpler version of itself. Here is the function:

```
function Factorial(N : Integer) : Integer;
begin
 if N =0 then
  Factorial := 1
 else   Factorial := N * Factorial(N - 1)
end; {Factorial}
```

This function has just one statement. If the value of N is 0, then the function simply returns a 1 and ends. If N is greater than 1—say 5—then the Else clause is done. This is where the recursive definition takes place. N factorial is defined as N times N−1 factorial. At this point what happens tends to be confusing but need not be. The function now calls the function Factorial, which happens to be itself. The current state of the function (the value of the variables and which statement is executed in the function call) is saved, and the function is started again with the new parameter. When this second call is terminated, the original call to the function is resumed with the value returned by the second call. Where this starts to get confusing is when a second call to the function calls the function again and so on. This is similar to a busy executive on the phone. When a second call comes in, she puts the first caller on hold and attends to the second caller. When a third call comes the second caller also goes on hold. Depending upon how busy she is, this sequence of events may take place several times. Of course, in order for this not to go on forever there must be some mechanism to end a call. Eventually a conversation ends and the next to the last call is resumed (assuming, of course, that the person on the line was patient). The process repeats until she is back to the original call. This is also true of recursive functions; there must be some way for each call to the function to terminate. We call this the **stop rule**. In this procedure the stop rule may be stated as follows: After N calls to the function, the value of the parameter N will be 0. This will cause the "then" part of the If statement to execute and that call to the function to finish returning a value. If there was no mechanism for the recursive calls to end, the mechanism used to track the successive calls to the procedure would overflow memory and cause a run-time error. When that call ends the function that called it is provided with a value and can also end. Recursive calls to a function are often viewed as levels, not unlike several windows on the Macintosh's screen sitting on top of each other. When the top window closes the one under it becomes active. This diagram demonstrates the recursion process.

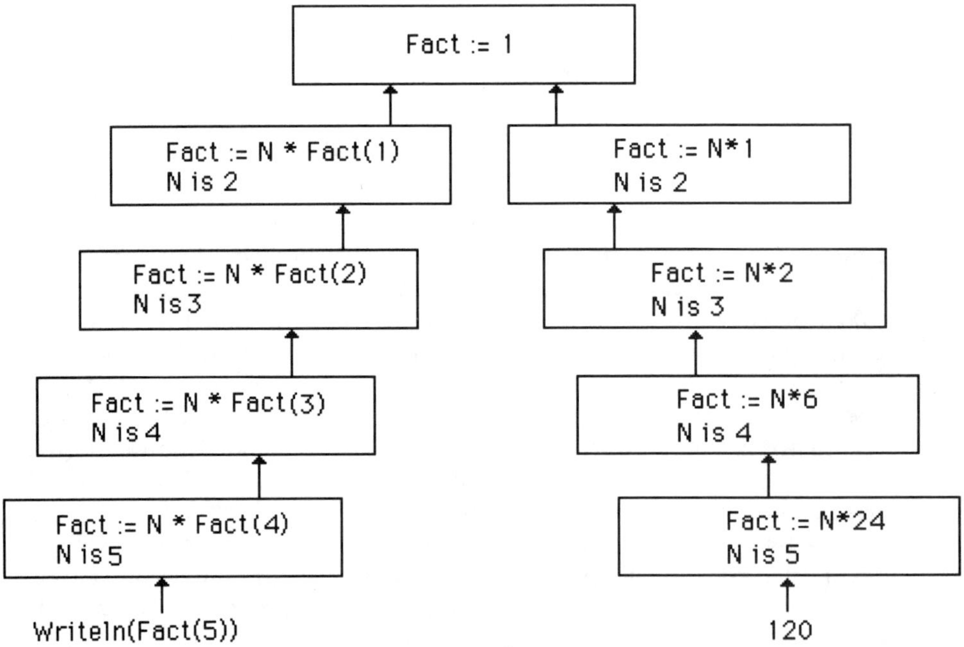

Figure 7-5. Recursion

Demonstrated are the successive calls to the function Fact with an initial value of 5. Notice that no value is returned until the fifth call to the function. At that point each previous call is evaluated and returns to the call under it.

RECURSION WITH QUICKDRAW

Graphics are a further way to help demonstrate recursion. A simple program with rectangles can help show the levels of nesting involved in recursive calls.

Enter the following program and run it:

```
program Recurse;
uses
 MemTypes, QuickDraw, OSIntF, ToolIntf;
var
 R : Rect;
procedure Box (U, D : Integer);
begin
  if (D - U) > 0 then
     begin
        SetRect(R, U, U, D, D);
        FrameRect(R);
        Box(U + 5, D - 5)  {Recursive call}
     end
end;

begin
 Box(1, 150);
 Readln
end.
```

When the program is run, 16 recursive squares will appear in the console window. A procedure is used to draw a rectangle and then recursively call itself to draw a smaller rectangle inside the one previously drawn. The stop rule will check to see that the rectangle to be drawn can't be drawn because the left and right sides of the rectangle will overlap.

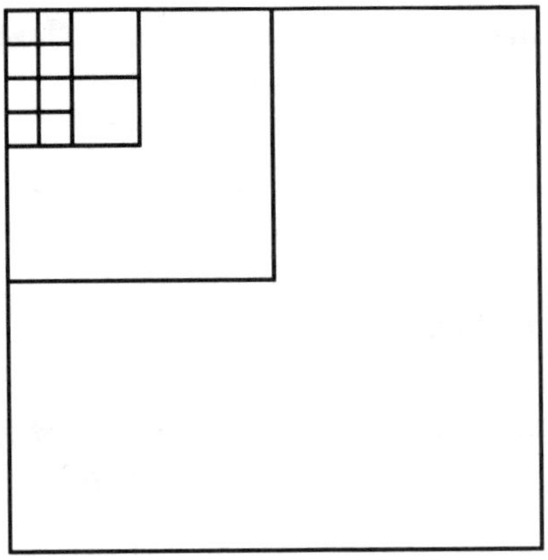

Figure 7-6. Recursive Boxes

The procedure draws a rectangle prior to a recursive call and thus draws smaller rectangles inside of the bigger one. We can reverse the drawing order (bigger outside of smaller) by moving the FrameRect statement to after the recursive procedure call. This way no rectangle is drawn until after the stop rule is reached, and therefore the smallest rectangle is drawn first. Another interesting variation in the program is to keep the FrameRect in the original position, then add an EraseRect statement after the stop rule. This will display all the rectangles prior to reaching the stop rule and erasing them after the stop rule is reached.

While the two recursion examples we have seen are interesting and intellectually stimulating, they demonstrated programs that could easily have been written without recursion (try to see if you can write them). The next two examples harness the power of recursion to simplify more complex tasks.

Let's look at a program that displays a large square and then recursively divides itself into four smaller squares. Each rectangle will continue to divide itself until the stop rule is hit. In this case, the stop rule tests to see if the width of a square is less than five points.

```
program SubDivide;
uses
 MemTypes, QuickDraw, OSIntF, ToolIntf;

procedure Box (Left, Top, Right, Bottom : Integer);
var
```

```
   Hcenter, Vcenter : Integer;
   tempRect : Rect;
begin
   if (Right - Left) >= 5 then
    begin
     SetRect(tempRect, Left, Top, Right, Bottom);
     FrameRect(tempRect);
     Hcenter := (Left + Right) div 2;
     Vcenter := (Top + Bottom) div 2;
     Box(Left, Top, Hcenter, Vcenter);
     Box(Hcenter, Top, Right, Vcenter);
     Box(Left, Vcenter, Hcenter, Bottom);
     Box(Hcenter, Vcenter, Right, Bottom)
    end
end;

begin
   Box(0, 0, 256, 256);
   readln
end.
```

This program differs from the one before because there are four recursive calls to the procedure rather than one. The original call to the procedure from the main program draws the largest box and then calls itself with the first recursive call. This new call draws a box in the upper left-hand corner of the largest box and then calls itself again. This new call draws a box in the upper left-hand corner, and the recursive calls continue until the stop rule is enacted. At this point all the upper left-hand corner boxes have been drawn, and control returns to the second recursive call, which starts drawing upper right-hand-corner boxes. Run the program and watch the order in which the boxes are drawn. Move the FrameRect statement to after the procedure call and watch the order in which the boxes will then be drawn.

Our last recursion example utilizes a procedure that draws equilateral triangles.

```
program Recursive_Triangles;
uses
   MemTypes, QuickDraw, OSIntF, ToolIntf;
procedure Tri (X, Y, Side : Real);
begin
  if Side >= 5 then
```

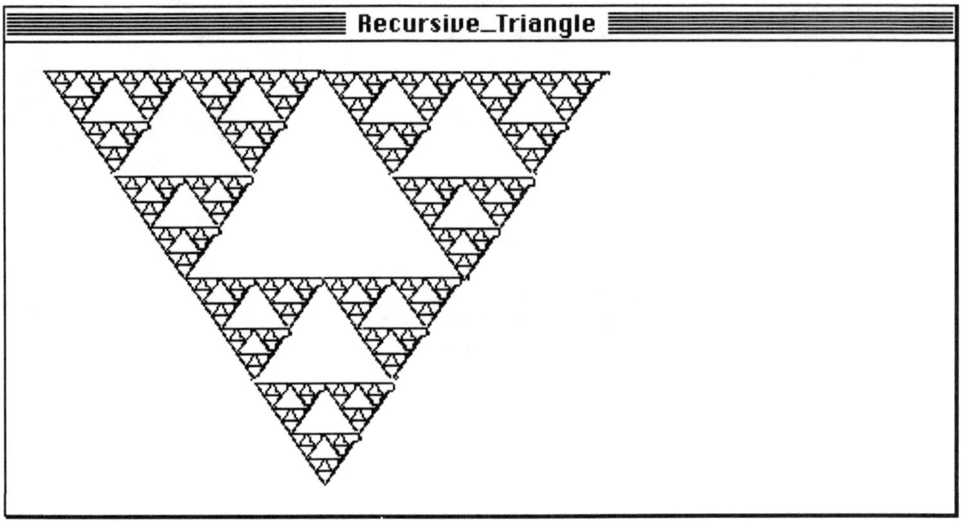

Figure 7-7. Dividing Triangles

```
      begin
         Tri(X, Y, Side / 2);
         Tri(X + Side / 2, Y, Side / 2);
         Tri(X + Side / 4, Y + Side /
           Sqrt(2) / 2, Side / 2);
         MoveTo(Round(X), Round(Y));
         LineTo(Round(X + Side), Round(Y));
         LineTo(Round(X + Side / 2),
           Round(Y + Side / Sqrt(2)));
         LineTo(Round(X), Round(Y));
      end
end;

begin
   Tri(10, 10, 300);
   readln
end.
```

This procedure differs slightly from the one written before. Real values are used instead of integers to increase accuracy. In procedures such as LineTo, which require integer parameters, the Round function is used to convert from real to integer. Run this program and observe the order in which the triangles are drawn, which is from smallest to largest. This is because the triangles are drawn after the procedure calls rather than before, as in the preceding programs.

8
A Formal Look at Graphics

INTRODUCTION

In the preceding chapters we dabbled with QuickDraw, having used "commands" that allowed us to draw graphics. As you might have guessed, these "commands" are actually functions and procedures. QuickDraw consists of these functions and procedures, along with a set of special graphics data types all stored in the ROM. While using a QuickDraw routine, you are actually executing code stored in the ROM.

Anything displayed on the screen, text or graphics, is displayed through QuickDraw, which really lives up to its name. Arguably, QuickDraw is the most important and innovative feature of the Macintosh since all features of the User Interface are implemented via QuickDraw.

In this chapter, we will take a more formal and structured look at QuickDraw, starting with its most elemental structure, the point.

POINTS

The most basic of QuickDraw's data types is the **point**. A point can be thought of as the spot where two lines on the coordinate grid intersect. A point is identified by two integers representing its X (vertical) and Y (horizontal) coordinates. We have already seen the point when using the GetMouse procedure, but we did not see that it is defined as a record.

```
type
 Point = record  of
    V : integer;
    H : integer
  end;
```

A variable of type Point is declared as follows:

```
var
 Pt : Point;
```

Here the variable Pt is of the data type Point. When we saw GetMouse, the value was placed in the record by QuickDraw. To assign a value to a record, we must access the individual fields.

```
Pt. v := 10;
Pt. h := 20;
```

Or even better:

```
with Pt do
 begin
  v := 10;
  h := 20
 end;
```

The point Pt now has a value (10, 20). Assigning a value to a point does not draw that point on the screen. It merely defines a value in the coordinate plane. Next we will see how to use points to define lines.

DRAWING LINES

In Chapter 5 we saw how to draw lines in the console window. Let's take a second look at the procedures used. Lines, like all other graphics objects, are drawn with the pen, a fictitious drawing tool used by QuickDraw. To draw a line, we position the pen to one end point of the line. This can be done with either of two procedures, one of which we have already seen.

```
procedure Moveto(X, Y : Integer);
```

The MoveTo procedure positions the pen (without drawing) at the point specified by the horizontal coordinate X and the vertical coordinate Y. Notice how the procedure was specified. In this chapter the QuickDraw procedures will be shown as they are declared in QuickDraw. This will give you an opportunity to examine the data types of the parameters used and determine whether they are variable or value parameters. Incidentally, this is the same way all ROM routines are shown in *Inside Macintosh.*

The second procedure that moves the pen is Move, which moves the pen relative to its old position.

```
procedure Move(X, Y : Integer);
```

The Move procedure adds X and Y to the current horizontal and vertical positions of the pen respectively, to yield the new current position. For example, let's examine the position of the pen after each of the following two statements are executed:

```
Moveto(3, 2);
Move(4, 2);
```

After the MoveTo statement, the pen is located at point (3, 2). After the Move statement, the pen is moved to point (7, 4), which can be thought of as point (3+4, 2+2).

To actually draw a line, there are two procedures that work in exactly the same way as Move and MoveTo (except that they draw).

```
procedure Line(X, Y : Integer);
procedure LineTo(X, Y : Integer);
```

The following program illustrates the use of the pen positioning and line-drawing procedures:

```
program Fishy;
uses
   Memtypes, QuickDraw;
```

```
var
   TempRect : Rect;
   I, J : Integer;
begin
   I := 20;
   J := 491;
   while I <= 491 do
      begin
         MoveTo(I, Round(100 * Sin(I / 120)) + 150);
         LineTo(J, -Round(100 * Sin( J / 120)) + 160);
         I := I + 5;
         J := J - 5
      end;
   Write('Press <Ret> to continue');
   readln
end.
```

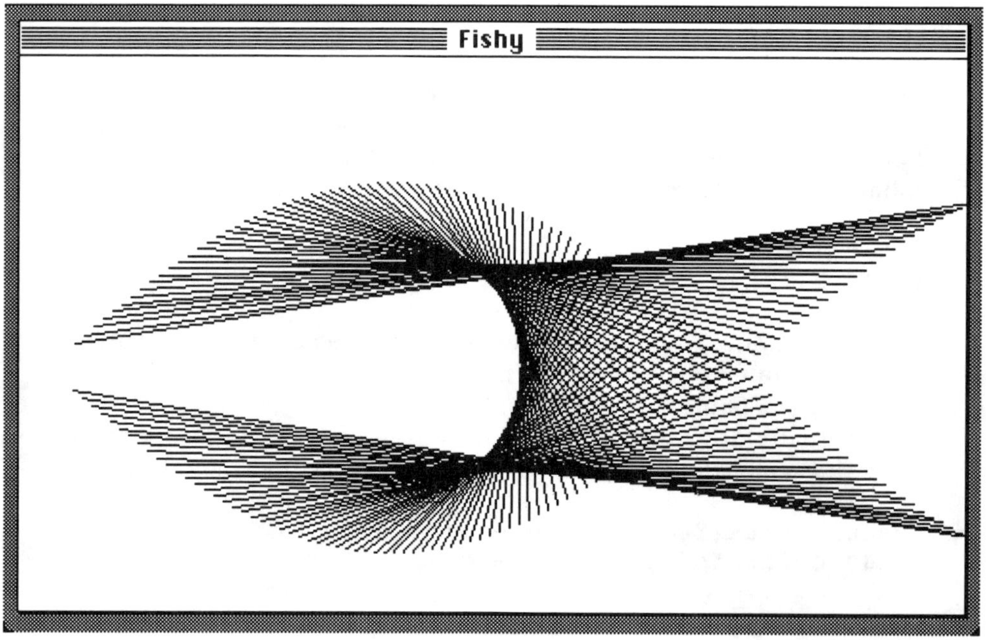

Figure 8-1. Drawing Lines

Rectangles

The first graphics data structure we saw back in Chapter 2 was the rectangle. The data type Rect, as you know, is actually defined as a record type. Let's look again at its definition.

```
type
  Rect = record of
     Top    : Integer;
     Left   : Integer;
     Bottom : Integer;
     Right  : Integer
  end;
```

Here, the fields in Rect define lines in the coordinate grid that enclose the rectangle.

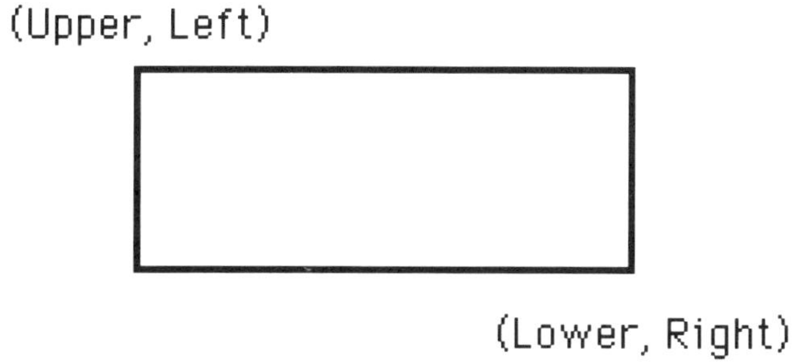

Figure 8-2. Coordinates of a Rectangle

Top and Left are the Y and X coordinates of the upper left-hand point in the rectangle and Bottom and Right are the Y and X coordinates of the lower right-hand point.

Values can be assigned to a variable of type Rect as in any record.

```
var
 TempRect : Rect;
     :
     :
 TempRect.Top := 10;
 TempRect.Left := 20;
 TempRect.Bottom := 140;
 TempRect.Right := 78;
```

As you know, we need not initialize a rectangle this way. Instead we can use the SetRect procedure to do the same thing more conveniently. Remember that defining a rectangle does not display it in the window; a second routine must be called to do that.

```
procedure SetRect(var R : Rect;Left, Top, Right, Bottom:Integer);
```

The SetRect procedure assigns to the rectangle the four boundary coordinates. The result is a rectangle with the coordinates Left, Top, Right, and Bottom. Notice that in the procedure declaration of SetRect, the lines are in the order Left, Top, Right, and Bottom, the same order as in the previous Rect declaration. The four assignment statements used before to assign values to the rectangle could be accomplished with the single statement

```
SetRect(TempRect,20,10,78,140);
```

DRAWING RECTANGLES

We have already learned how to draw rectangles and erase them with the FrameRect and EraseRect procedures. There are a total of five procedures used for drawing rectangles.

```
procedure FrameRect(R : Rect);
```

The FrameRect procedure draws a box that is enclosed by the rectangle specified by R.

```
procedure PaintRect(R : Rect);
```

The PaintRec procedure fills the rectangle specified by R in black.

```
procedure EraseRect(R : Rect);
```

The EraseRect procedure erases the rectangle indicated by R.

```
procedure InvertRect(R : Rect)
```

The InvertRect procedure inverts (white pixels made black, black pixels made white) the area enclosed by the rectangle specified by R.

```
procedure FillRect(R : Rect, Pat : Pattern);
```

The FillRect procedure draws a rectangle filled with the pattern indicated by the second parameter. The valid patterns are

White

Black

Gray

LtGray [light gray]

DkGray [dark gray]

The following program illustrates the use of FillRect:

```
program Fills;
uses
   Memtypes,QuickDraw,OSIntf,ToolIntf;
var
  Rect1, Rect2, Rect3, Rect4, Rect5 : Rect;
 begin
    InitGraf(@thePort);
    InitFonts;
    InitWindows;
    FillRect(screenBits.bounds, White);
    SetRect(Rect1, 10,30,30,50);
    SetRect(Rect2, 40,60,60,80);
    SetRect(Rect3, 70,70,100,100);
    SetRect(Rect4, 110,130,130,150);
    FillRect(Rect1, Black);
    FillRect(Rect2, Gray);
    FillRect(Rect3, ltGray);
    FillRect(Rect4, dkGray);
    Readln
 end.
```

Notice that the first four statements of this program call Toolbox routines that we have not discussed. These routines are needed because version 1.0 of Turbo Pascal does not initialize the patterns without explicitly initializing QuickDraw with the InitGraf call. The other routines, as you probably can guess from their names, initialize the systems fonts and the Toolbox's Window Manager. These additional calls are always required after QuickDraw is initialized. The rectangle screenBits.bounds covers the entire Macintosh screen. In this case we fill it completely with white to clear the screen. This rectangle is available to you whenever your programs use QuickDraw. This is a useful piece of information because it lets you know the size of the Macintosh's screen for any kind of Macintosh, be it a 512 by 342 Mac Plus, a 640 by 480 Mac II, or some future 2,048 by 2,048 giant-screen Macintosh.

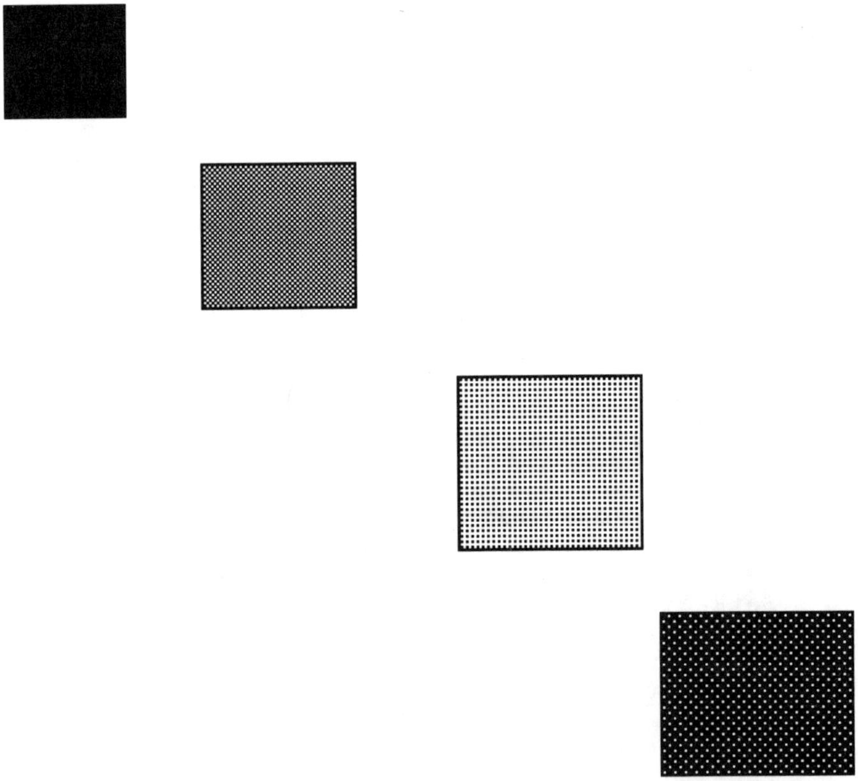

Figure 8-3. Fill Patterns

Other Shapes

Similar procedures exist for drawing ovals and round-cornered rectangles. The procedures for ovals work in exactly the same manner as those for rectangles. The size and shape of the oval is determined by the largest oval that can be inscribed in the rectangle passed to the procedure.

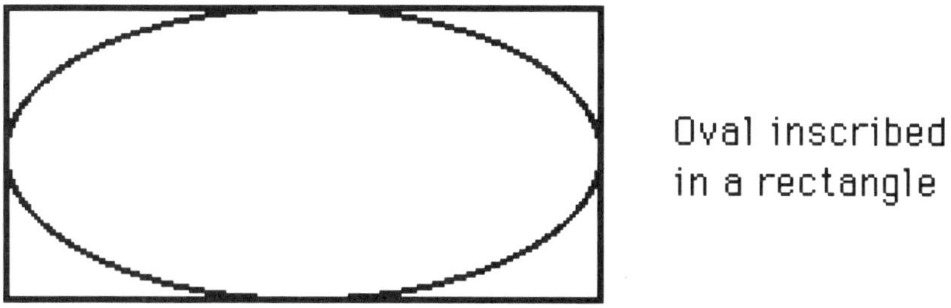

Figure 8-4. Oval Inscribed in a Rectangle

The oval drawing procedures are

```
procedure FrameOval(R : Rect);
procedure PaintOval(R : Rect);
procedure EraseOval(R : Rect);
procedure InvertOval(R : Rect);
```

There are analogous procedures for drawing round-cornered rectangles. These procedures work in the same fashion as the oval drawing procedures, except additional parameters are passed indicating the roundness of the corners. These parameters, OvalWidth and OvalHeight, specify the shape of an oval that is "fitted" into the corner of the rectangle. Figure 8-5 illustrates the distinction:

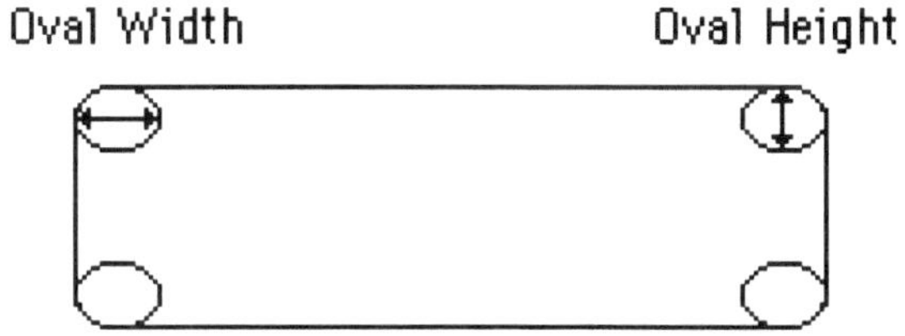

Figure 8-5. Defining a Round-Cornered Rectangle

The round-cornered rectangle procedures are

```
procedure FrameRoundRect(R : Rect;OvalWidth, OvalHeight : Integer);
procedure PaintRoundRect(R : Rect;OvalWidth, OvalHeight : Integer);
procedure EraseRoundRect(R: Rect;OvalWidth, OvalHeight : Integer);
procedure InvertRoundRect(R : Rect;OvalWidth, OvalHeight :Integer);
```

Use the **Change** feature of the Turbo editor to change the rectangles in the Fills program to ovals and round-cornered rectangles.

THE PEN

The pen is the imaginary drawing tool used by QuickDraw to draw the shapes on the screen. It's a simple concept—when the position of the pen is moved, drawing occurs on the screen. QuickDraw also has the ability to change the characteristics of the pen.

The default pen size is one pixel high by one pixel wide. To change the size of the pen, the PenSize procedure is used.

```
procedure PenSize(Width, Height : Integer);
```

Width and Height specify the size of the pen.

We can also change the pattern contained in the pen.

```
procedure PenPat(Pat : Pattern);
```

The pattern actually drawn on the screen is not necessarily the pen pattern. It is determined by three things, the pen pattern in the pen, the pattern of the pixel already on the screen, and the mode of the pen. The pen mode determines how pixels on the screen and the pattern in the pen interact to produce graphics on the screen. The pen mode can be altered by using the PenMode procedure.

```
procedure PenMode(Mode : Integer);
```

The valid values for Mode are the predeclared QuickDraw constants PatCopy, PatOr, PatXor, PatBic, NotPatCopy, NotPatOr, NotPatXor, and NotPatBic. For example, let us look at the default pen mode PatCopy. If the pen is black, then the pixel on the screen will be black no matter what it was before. If the color in the pen is white, then the pixel on the screen will end up white no matter what it was before. This is graphically represented in the following chart:

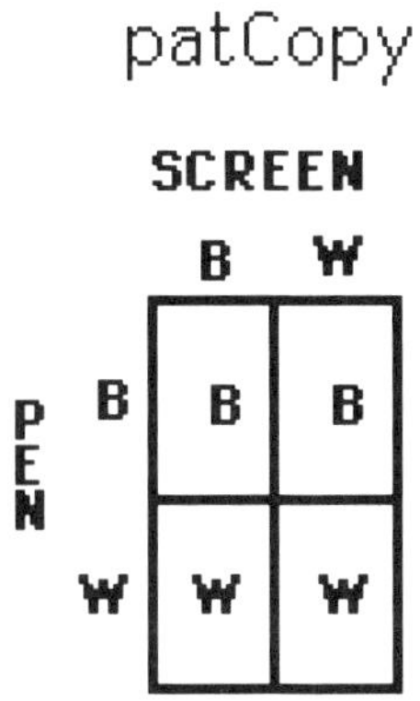

Figure 8-6. PatCopy Pen Mode

The chart is read as follows: If the pixel on the screen is black and the pen is white, the pixel on the screen shall be white; if the pixel on the screen is black and the pen is black, the pixel on the screen shall be black.

The purpose of the various pen modes is to make it possible to draw on different color backgrounds. The PatCopy pen mode corresponds to a real-life pen drawing on paper. The actions of each of the pen modes can be understood by examining the following charts:

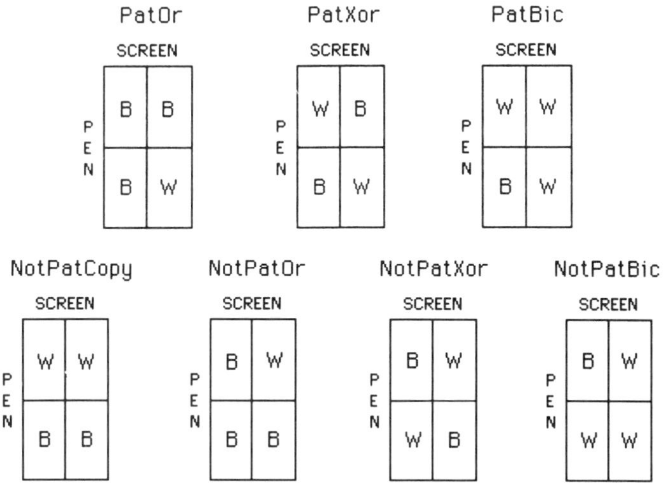

Figure 8-7. Pen Modes

Run the following program to demonstrate several of the different pen modes against different backgrounds:

Listing 8-1. Program that Demonstrates Different Pen Modes.

```
program ModeDemo;
uses
   Memtypes,QuickDraw,OSIntf,ToolIntf;
var
    tempRect    :   Rect;
begin
  InitGraf(@thePort);
  InitFonts;
  InitWindows;
  FillRect(screenBits.bounds, White);
  { Draw color bands }
  SetRect(tempRect,80,10,120,240);
  FillRect(tempRect, Black);
  SetRect(tempRect,120,10,160,240);
  FillRect(tempRect, Gray);
  SetRect(tempRect,160,10,200,240);
  FillRect(tempRect, LtGray);
  SetRect(tempRect,200,10,240,240);
  FillRect(tempRect, DkGray);
  SetRect(tempRect,240,10,280,240);
  FillRect(tempRect, White);
  SetRect(tempRect,240,10,280,240);
  FrameRect(tempRect);

  PenSize(5, 5);
  {Draw first line, default mode}
  PenPat(Black);
  Moveto(60, 20);
  Lineto(300, 20);
  {Draw second line}
  PenMode(PatCopy);
  Moveto(60, 40);
  Lineto(300, 40);
  {Draw third line}
  PenMode(PatOr);
  Moveto(60, 60);
  Lineto(300, 60);
  {Draw fourth line}
  PenMode(PatXor);
  Moveto(60, 80);
  Lineto(300, 80);
  {Draw fifth line}
```

```
  PenMode(PatBic);
  Moveto(60, 100);
  Lineto(300, 100);
  {Draw sixth line}
  PenMode(NotPatCopy);
  Moveto(60, 120);
  Lineto(300, 120);
  {Draw seventh line}
  PenMode(NotPatOr);
  Moveto(60, 140);
  Lineto(300, 140);
  {Draw eighth line}
  PenMode(NotPatXor);
  Moveto(60, 160);
  Lineto(300, 160);
  {Draw ninth line}
  PenMode(NotPatBic);
  Moveto(60, 180);
  Lineto(300, 180);
  Readln
end.
```

Displayed by this program is

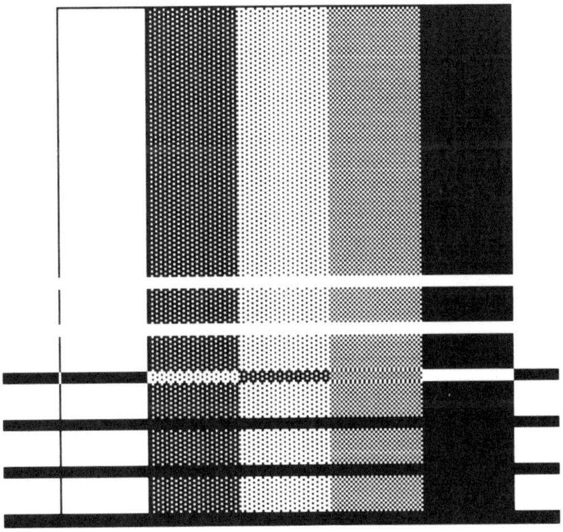

Figure 8-8. Pen Modes against different backgrounds

To get a real feel for the purpose of each pen mode, do some experimentation with each by modifying the ModeDemo program.

THE CURSOR

You have probably noticed from using the Macintosh that the cursor is always displayed on the screen—sometimes in different shapes, but always displayed. Whether it is displayed is actually controllable from a program by using two important QuickDraw routines:

```
procedure ShowCursor;
procedure HideCursor;
```

These procedures act exactly as you think they would from their names. HideCursor hides the cursor from the screen, and ShowCursor restores it. It is important to notice that when the cursor is hidden it still exists and is at some location on the screen. It is moved by the mouse even when it is hidden from view. Verify this by running the MouseDemo program again, but this time with a call to HideCursor before the While loop.

BUILDING A SKETCHPAD

Now that we have some tools to work with, let us write a simple application program that allows us to draw on the Macintosh's screen using the mouse. First let's look at some English-like pseudocode for the program.

```
repeat
 if button still down then
   draw a line from last position to current position
 otherwise if the button was pressed
    make current position the last position
    (starting position of new line)
until forever
```

This pseudocode is easily translated into the following program:

Listing 8-2. Program That Allows Drawing on the Macintosh Screen.

```
program SketchPad;
{ Make the screen a drawing pad and the mouse a
     pen }
uses
    Memtypes,QuickDraw,OSIntf,ToolIntf;

 const
  Forever = False;
 var
  Pnt       : Point;  { Holds the cursor's
    position }
  TempRect  : Rect;
  alreadyDown    : Boolean;
begin
 alreadyDown := False;
 repeat
   GetMouse(Pnt);
   if Button then
      begin
        if alreadyDown then
            LineTo(Pnt.H, Pnt.V)
        else
            MoveTo(Pnt.H, Pnt.V);
        alreadyDown := True
      end
   else
      alreadyDown := False;
 until Forever
end.
```

Figure 8-9. The SketchPad Program

This program works fine for what it is, a simple sketch program that duplicates the capabilities of a pencil and paper. The program can be improved with some more QuickDraw features, presented in the next section.

DISPLAYING TEXT

Turbo Pascal makes the display of text output very simple to do just by using the Writeln statement. This is a very convenient feature, but in some cases you will want to be able to use QuickDraw's text display capabilities directly. There are several reasons for learning to do this. First, you may display your own window in a program and thus be able to use Writeln, which works only with Turbo's console window. And second, by using QuickDraw you can control the font, size, and style of the text displayed.

Two important procedures are used for displaying text with Quick-Draw.

```
procedure DrawString(S : string);
```

The DrawString procedure displays the string constant or variable specified by S at the current pen location. The upper left-hand corner of the first character is placed exactly at the current pen location, and all subsequent characters are drawn to the right.

```
procedure DrawChar(Ch : Char);
```

The DrawChar procedure works exactly the same way as DrawString except it only displays a single character at the current pen location.

Working With Fonts

Several other QuickDraw routines allow you to change the attributes of the characters displayed on the screen.

```
procedure TextFont(Font : Integer);
```

The TextFont procedure sets the font used by QuickDraw for the text that will be displayed. The default value is 0, which will display the system font (Chicago). Each font has a unique font number. If a particular font is unavailable, the default font will be used. Experiment with other values for font to see which fonts are available on your machine.

Some of the fonts that might be available in your System File are

Chicago
Geneva
Helvetica
Monaco
Times

Figure 8-10. Fonts

```
procedure TextSize(Size : Integer);
```

The TextSize procedure determines the size in points of the characters being displayed. The default size of the system font size is 12. Examples of different font sizes are

9 points

10 points

12 points

14 points

18 points

Figure 8-11. Point Sizes

```
procedure TextFace(Face : Style);
```

The TextFace procedure selects the special characteristics of the text displayed. The parameter passed to TextFace must be of the type Style, which is defined as a set of predefined constants.

```
type
   StyleItem = (Bold, Italic, Underline, Outline,
                          Shadow, Condense, Extend);
   Style = set of StyleItem;
```

Examples of some of the different characteristics available are

Plain

Bold

Italic

Outline

Shadow

Underline

Figure 8-12. Font Styles

For example, to set the text face to italic, you could use this procedure call:

```
TextFace([Italic]);
```

Notice that "Italic" is in brackets because it is a member of a set of type Style (we told you sets would come in handy). To set the text face to both italic and underlined, you would use a set containing both:

```
TextFace([Italic, Underline]);
```

To set the text face back to normal, you would use the empty set:

```
TextFace([]);
```

CALCULATIONS WITH RECTANGLES

For our program, we will need to know if the position of the cursor is inside a rectangle on the screen or if two rectangles are touching each other. We have already worked with the PtInRect function; the other one we need is called SectRect.

```
function SectRect(FirstRect,SecondRect:Rect;
                  var ThirdRect:Rect) : Boolean;
```

The SectRect function looks at two rectangles and if they intersect returns True. It also returns as a variable parameter a new rectangle representing the intersection of the other two.

SKETCHPAD REVISITED

Let's redesign the SketchPad to be able to change the size of the pen used to draw with. We will implement this by creating two boxes on the screen. One box will have the word "Bigger" in it, and the other will have the word "Smaller" in it. When the cursor is placed inside the "Bigger" box and the button is clicked, the size of the pen will increase. When the cursor is put into the "Smaller" box, the size of the pen will decrease.

Figure 8-13. SketchPad with New Feature

Now that we have the required tools, we are ready to implement the new features into our computerized SketchPad. To implement the new features we will add several parts to our old SketchPad program.

1. We must initialize the "Bigger" and "Smaller" boxes, draw them on the screen, and label them. This will be done in the new initialization procedure.

2. Each time through the loop we must check if the user moved the mouse into (selected) the "Bigger" or "Smaller" boxes. This will be done with a call to a new function called Select, which returns True if "Bigger" or "Smaller" has been selected. To be consistent with the rest of the Macintosh environment, we will invert the box when selected and uninvert it when the mouse button is released.

3. If the box was selected, we take the appropriate action. In this case it means calling the procedure ChangePenSize to increment or decrement the size of the pen.

Listing 8-3. Program Using the ChangePenSize Procedure.

```
program SketchPad;
uses
   Memtypes, QuickDraw, OSIntf, ToolIntf;
const
   Forever = false;
var
   Pnt : Point;
   Xpen, Ypen : Integer;
   BiggerBox, SmallerBox, TempRect : Rect;
   alreadyDown    : Boolean;

 procedure Initialize;
 begin
    { Draw selection boxes on screen }
    SetRect(BiggerBox, 20, 40, 80, 60);
    SetRect(SmallerBox, 20, 60, 80, 80);
    FrameRect(BiggerBox);
    FrameRect(SmallerBox);
    Moveto(22, 54);
    DrawString('Bigger');
    Moveto(22, 74);
    DrawString('Smaller');
    { Initialize PenSize }
    Xpen := 1;
    Ypen := 1
 end;

 function Select (Box : Rect) : Boolean;
 { Returns True if Box was specified }
 begin
    Select := False;
    if PtInRect(Pnt, Box) then
       if Button then
          begin
             InvertRect(Box);
             repeat
```

```
              until not Button;
              InvertRect(Box);
              Select := True
           end
  end;

  procedure ChangePenSize (I : integer);
  begin
     Xpen := Xpen + I;
     Ypen := Ypen + I;
     PenSize(Xpen, Ypen)
  end;

begin
   Initialize;
   repeat
      GetMouse(Pnt);
      if Select(BiggerBox) then
         ChangePenSize(1)
      else if Select(SmallerBox) then
         ChangePenSize(-1);
      if Button then
         begin
            if alreadyDown then
               LineTo(Pnt.H, Pnt.V)
            else
               MoveTo(Pnt.H, Pnt.V);
            alreadyDown := True
         end
      else
         alreadyDown := False;
   until Forever
end.
```

This same technique can be used to add many other easy-to-use features to this and other programs.

Do More

Improve on SketchPad by adding features that

1. change pattern of the pen.

2. change the pen mode.

3. allow selection of different shapes, rectangles, ovals, and round-cornered rectangles. (Hint: Use the animation technique of drawing, then erasing the shapes while the mouse's button is down. Draw a final version of the shape when the button is released.)

FUN TIME WITH QUICKDRAW—THE PADDLEBALL PROGRAM

It is about time we had a bit of fun, so let's make use of our newly acquired skills in programming Pascal and QuickDraw to design and write a game. We will use a top-down approach that will allow us to develop the overall structure of the game first and develop the details as we go along.

When we were younger we spent a lot of time playing paddleball; so, in a spell of fond memories, let's write a Macintosh racket game where the player controls a racket using the mouse and attempts to hit a ball against a wall. If the ball goes by the racket, it goes out of play, and the game is over. Figure 8-14 shows a picture of the ball in play. To implement this program, we will need to develop several techniques that have yet to be used in this chapter. We will need to be able to

1. control the movement of a rectangle (the paddle) with the use of the mouse;

2. detect when the ball hits the paddle;

3. detect when the ball hits the side or front walls;

4. determine at what angle the ball hits the wall and change the ball's direction.

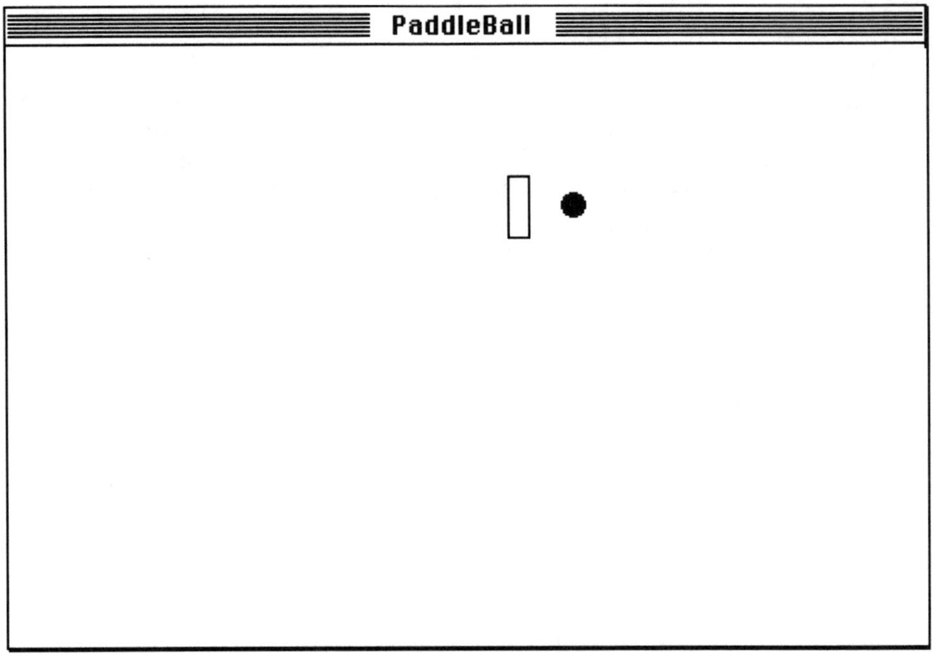

Figure 8-14. PaddleBall Program

Let us look at a very rough outline of the game.

```
program PaddleBall;
begin
  initialize;
  while not game over do
    begin
      movepaddle;
      moveball
    end
end;
```

This pseudocode can actually be used as our main program with a few additions such as variable declarations. Let's continue to develop our program by developing each of the procedures in the above program.

```
procedure initialize;
begin
  initialize score to zero
  initialize ball shape and position
  initialize ball direction
  initialize paddle shape and position
  initialize boundary walls
end;

procedure moveball;
begin
  erase ball from old location on screen
  if the ball hits right wall then
    set direction to reflect it backward
  else if the ball hits the top or bottom walls then
    set direction to reflect it vertically
  else if the ball hits the left wall then
     the game is over
  else if the ball hits the paddle then
    set direction reflect it forward
  move the ball in direction
  draw ball in new location on screen
end;

procedure movepaddle;
begin
  erase paddle from screen location
  get location of mouse controlled cursor
  draw paddle at new location
end;
```

We can achieve an animation effect in much the same way we did earlier by drawing some object on the screen, leaving it there a short period of time, erasing it, and redrawing it a short distance away. If this process is done repeatedly at high speed, the drawn object appears to move smoothly across the screen. In the pseudocode, both the paddle and the ball are animated in this way.

Now that the rough design for our game is complete, we can turn our attention to the details of how our graphics objects move and how they can be represented using the Macintosh's QuickDraw routines. First to be examined in more detail is the procedure that will move the ball around the screen. There are several factors to consider when moving the ball—the direction the ball is heading, the position of the ball, and whether or not the ball hits a wall or the paddle. We will need a variable to keep track of which horizontal direction the ball is traveling.

```
var
  Direction : (East, West);
```

When the ball moves across the screen it will travel in both horizontal and vertical directions, so in order to keep track of how many pixels the ball should travel in each direction on the screen, we will need two variables, Dh to track the number of pixels to move horizontally, and Dv to track the number of pixels to move vertically. Since screen coordinates are integer values, these variables will be integers.

The ball will travel at angles, so we need to declare a variable Slope that will hold the angle the ball is moving in. The slope will tell how many pixels the ball travels up or down for every pixel it travels sideways. For example, to move due east, the direction would be right and the slope would be 0 to represent no up or down movement, just movement to the right.

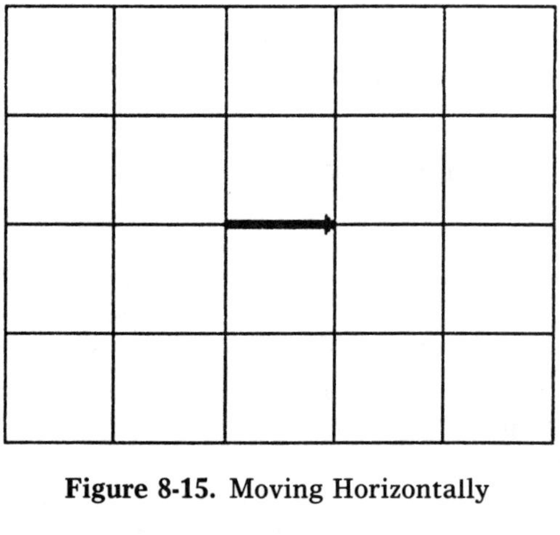

Figure 8-15. Moving Horizontally

To move the ball north-northwest, the direction would be left and the slope would be −2: 2 pixels up for every 1 pixel to the left.

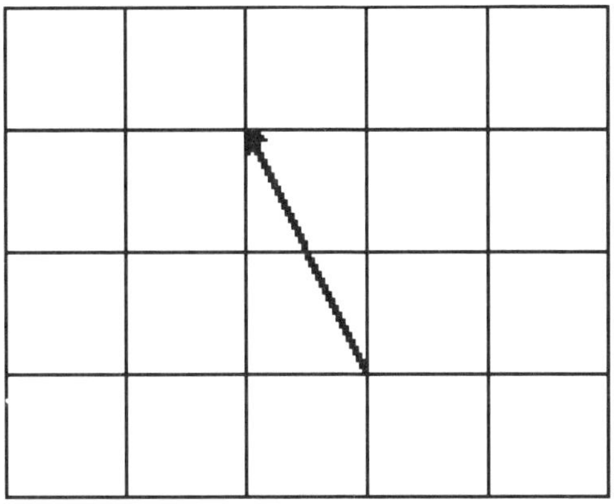

Figure 8-16. Slope

This representation of the ball's direction allows us to specify precisely every direction except for straight up and straight down. The slope for these directions would be infinity and negative infinity respectively. Since the computer cannot represent these numbers, the ball will not be able to travel in these directions. This is fine because the ball would never reach the paddle on the left side of the screen if it were to travel vertically. When the ball hits a wall or paddle, it should reflect off the wall in a natural manner.

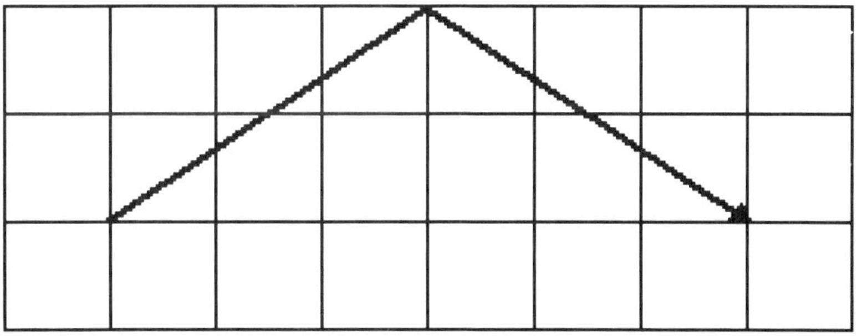

Figure 8-17. Reflecting Shot

Before the ball hits the top wall, it is traveling X pixels up for every pixel it is traveling across the screen. After bouncing off the top wall, the ball is traveling X pixels down for every pixel across. The horizontal direction of the ball does not change. Therefore only the sign of the slope changes when the ball hits the top wall. The same is true for the bottom wall. When the ball bounces off the right wall or the left side of the paddle, the slope remains the same, but the direction changes.

Well, we are now about ready to develop the entire program.

Listing 8-4. Complete PaddleBall Program.

```
program PaddleBall;
{Play a game of hit the ball off the wall, but don't
   let it get by}
uses
   Memtypes, QuickDraw, OSIntf, ToolIntf;
var
   Ball, Paddle, Top,  Bottom,
   Left, Right : Rect;
   Difficulty, XPaddle,  YPaddle, DispHoriz,
   DispVert,  Slope       : Integer;
   Gameover   : Boolean;
   Direction  : (East,West);

procedure Init;
begin
   InitGraf(@thePort);
   InitFonts;
   InitWindows;
   FillRect(screenBits.bounds, White);
   HideCursor;
   { Size of ball is 9 by 9 }
   SetRect(Ball, 0, 0, 9, 9);
   { Set the boundaries of the game }
   SetRect(Left, 0, 11, 1, 332);
   SetRect(Top, 0, 20, 502, 21);
   SetRect(Bottom, 0, 342, 511, 343);
   SetRect(Right, 511, 20, 512, 342);
   { Initial position of ball is 100,100 }
   DispHoriz := 100;
   DispVert := 100;
   { Set initial direction of ball }
   Slope := 2;
   Direction := East;
   { Set initial position of paddle }
   Difficulty := 0;
   Gameover := False
end;

{ Erase paddle and redraw at new location }
procedure MovePaddle;
```

```
var
   XMouse, YMouse : Integer;
   location       : Point;
begin
   GetMouse(location);
   XMouse := location.h;
   YMouse := location.v;
   EraseRect(Paddle);
   SetRect(Paddle, Difficulty, YMouse, Difficulty
     + 11, YMouse + 25);
   FrameRect(Paddle);
end;

{ Display ball in appropriate location on screen
taking }
{ into account reflection of the ball off the borders
}
procedure MoveBall;
var
   TempRect : Rect;
begin
   if SectRect(Right, Ball, TempRect) then
      begin
         SysBeep(1);
         Direction := West
      end
   else if SectRect(Left, Ball, TempRect) then
      Gameover := true    { Hit left wall, game over }
   else if SectRect(Top, Ball, TempRect)
                                  or
           SectRect(Bottom, Ball, TempRect) then
      begin
         SysBeep(1);
         Slope := -Slope
      end
   else if SectRect(Paddle, Ball, TempRect) and
     (Direction = West)
   then
      begin
         SysBeep(1);
         Direction := East;
         Difficulty := Difficulty + 10;
      end;
   if Direction = East then
      DispHoriz := DispHoriz + 10
   else
      DispHoriz := DispHoriz - 10;
   DispVert := DispVert + Slope;
```

```
    EraseOval(Ball);
    SetRect(Ball, DispHoriz, DispVert, DispHoriz + 9,
      DispVert + 9);
    PaintOval(Ball)
end;
begin {Main program}
    Init;
    while not Gameover do
       begin
          MoveBall;
          MovePaddle;
       end
end. {Main program}
```

Do More

Try to add the following features to the PaddleBall program:

1. Scoring

2. Obstacles on the playing field

3. Other animated objects such as another ball or other moving objects

CHAPTER SUMMARY

In this chapter we have seen several of QuickDraw's features and, more important, learned how to harness them with programming techniques. We are close to our final goal to being able to produce a true Macintosh-style application, but more still needs to be learned. In the next chapter we will learn how to store data over the long haul in files, and then we will increase our ability to work with the Toolbox by seeing how to work with the Mac's memory management techniques.

9
Files

INTRODUCTION

Computers would not be very useful if they were limited to working only with the information that could fit in their memories. Even the most formidable of Macintoshes can only store up to 16 million bytes in RAM. This would never be enough to store all the programs and data files you will use over a long period of time. To overcome this limitation, computers store information on secondary storage devices such as disk drives and retrieve this information into memory only when needed.

FILES

Information is stored on a disk in a structure called a **file**. If you are familiar with the Mac, you will probably have seen or used both a floppy disk drive (such as the one built into the machine) and a "hard" disk, a permanently sealed disk capable of holding large amounts of data. A file is a collection of components all of the same data type. This is similar to an array, but there are significant differences between files and arrays. An array is held entirely in memory and is limited to the number of elements it was declared to have. A file is maintained on a secondary storage device and has no fixed size; components can be added or deleted at any time. Because a file is kept on disk, it is in one sense independent of the program that created it. A file can continue to exist after the program that built it has terminated. A file created by a Turbo Pascal program can be seen in the Desktop with an icon and its own name.

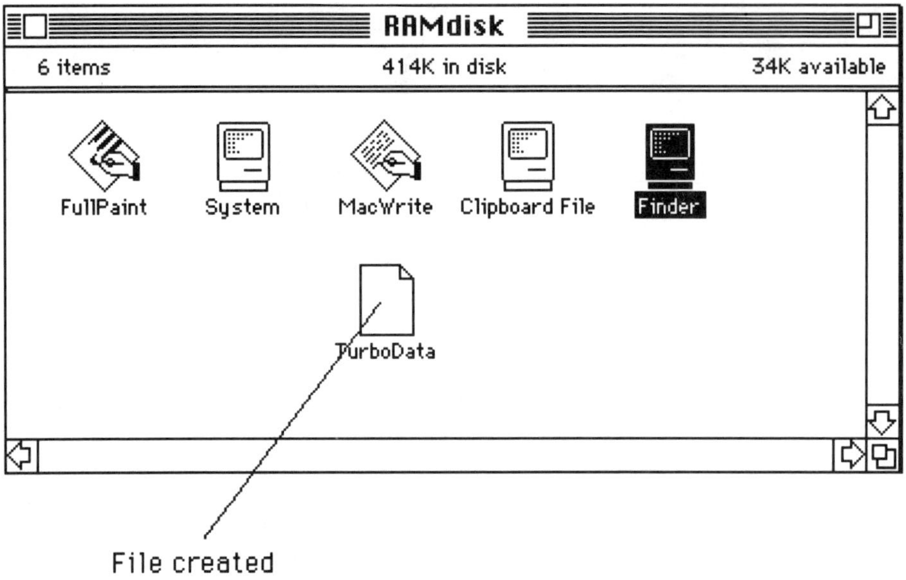

Figure 9-1. Data File on Disk

An example of a file you are already familiar with is a text file. All source codes for Turbo Pascal programs are stored in text files. As we will see, a text file is a file where all the components are of the Char data type. Of course, the components of a file could be of any declared type.

File Access

In this chapter we will be looking at the two ways to store and retrieve data in a file, sequential and random access. In a sequential file, all the file components must be accessed in the order in which they were placed into the file. This can be thought of as being similar to a cassette tape: to hear a song recorded at the end of the tape, all the songs before it must be passed over. In a random file, any particular file component can be accessed in any order. This is sometimes called **direct access** and is more like moving the tone arm of a phonograph (for the CD generation: a tone arm is an antiquated device for playing old-fashioned phonograph records) directly to the particular song you want to hear. Each component of a file, called a **record**, is numbered starting with zero. Random access is accomplished by specifying the record number of the desired component. Don't confuse this use of the term "record" with the record data type. The records in a file may contain data whose type is any valid Pascal data type.

File access is a feature of Pascal that is highly implementation dependent. By this we mean that each version of Pascal has its own system for storing and accessing data. The original description of the Pascal programming language was not very concerned with input and output, so each Pascal system included its own extensions to the language to handle files. As we will see, Turbo uses a somewhat different approach to files that varies with the most modern versions of Pascal.

Declaring a File

A file is created in the variable declaration section of a program or procedure by declaring a filename and the type of the file's components. For example:

```
type
 PersonInfo = record
     FirstName,
     LastName : string[20]
     Phone    : string[10]
 end;  { PersonInfo }
var
   People    : file of PersonInfo;
   Numbers   : file of integer;
```

This declaration creates two file variables, People and Numbers. The data type of the components of a file can be any standard Pascal type or any type created in a type declaration. Very often the component type of a file is a record. In People, the components will be of the type PersonInfo. All the components of Numbers will be integers. A file variable such as People and Numbers are different from other types of variables in that they can be used only with the file procedures that we will soon look at. No other operations such as assignment can be performed with them.

Using Files

There are three major steps in using files: opening a file, accessing a file, and closing a file. For each of these steps, Turbo Pascal provides built-in procedures.

Figure 9-2. File Processing

Opening a File

Opening a file is the first step before storing or retrieving data from that file. Associated with each file are two names. The first is the file variable, which is used in the program to refer to the file. This is sometimes called the **logical filename**. The other name is that by which the file will actually be called on the disk. This is called the **physical filename**. It is the one you can see next to the icon for the file on the Macintosh Desktop. The logical and physical filenames are linked together when you open the file in a program. We always refer to a file in a program via its logical name.

There are two procedures provided by Turbo Pascal for opening files, Rewrite and Reset.

```
Rewrite(FileVar, FileTitle)
```

Rewrite creates a file on disk with the physical filename specified by FileTitle. FileTitle may be either a string constant or a variable of type string. If a file with the name specified already exists on the device, it is destroyed and a new file with that name is created. The logical filename for the file is specified by FileVar. From this point on, all references to the file will use that logical filename. After Rewrite is executed, the current file position is positioned to record number zero of the file. The current file position points to the location in the file where the next file access will occur.

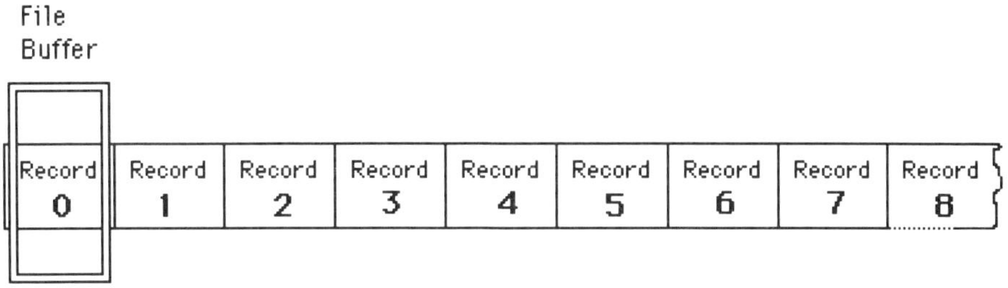

Figure 9-3. File Pointer

```
Reset(FileVar [ , FileTitle ] )
```

The second way to open a file is with the Reset procedure. Reset opens the disk file specified by the FileTitle (the brackets mean that it is optional). Reset assumes that the disk file already exists, otherwise an error condition will exist and an error message will be displayed in an alert box. Like Rewrite, the FileTitle can be either a string constant or a string variable, and the file variable FileVar is associated with the open file. After a Reset, the current file position is record number zero of the file (the first record). FileTitle is omitted if you don't want to open the file but wish to rewind the current file position to the beginning of the file (record zero).

Quick Review

Rewrite is used to create and open a new file and will destroy any file with the same filename. Reset is used to open an existing file or rewind an open file. For the record, all files created will be placed on the same disk drive that Turbo Pascal itself is placed. We can change this, as we will soon see.

Accessing a File

Data is written to a file with the Write procedure and read from a file with the Read procedure. This would seem perfectly natural to you unless you have used other versions of Pascal. Other Pascals use the standard procedures Get and Put for file access. Turbo has forsaken this standard in favor of simplicity. As you might expect, Write places information into a file, and Read retrieves it. How does the compiler know that Read does not refer to the keyboard and Write to the screen? When you are using Read and Write to refer to a file, you must use an additional parameter.

```
Write([file], var1, var2 . . . var3);
Read([file], var1, var2 . . . var3);
```

This parameter is the logical name of the file being referenced. Of course, that file needs to have been opened previously, or an error will result.

The following section of code uses the Rewrite procedure to create a file and Write to place in it the integers from 10 down to 1.

```
Rewrite(Numbers, 'Space Ship');
for Countdown := 10 downto 1 do
    Write(Numbers, Countdown)
```

The logical filename in this example is Numbers, which we have previously declared to be a file of integers. The Rewrite procedure creates a file on the disk called Space Ship and equates the logical and physical names. The For loop assigns the values to Countdown, which is used in the Write statement. After each Write or Read statement, the current file position is moved to the next component in the file.

A word about physical filenames. They do not have to follow the rules for identifiers. Physical filenames may be broken up (such as Space Ship) and may start with a number.

After this loop executes, the records of this file will contain as follows:

Record 0 contains 1

Record 1 contains 2

Record 2 contains 3

.

.

Record 9 contains 10

We can then read that information from the file with Read.

```
var
  Numbers : file of integer;
  I, Value : Integer;
          :
          :
  Reset(Numbers,'Space Ship');
  for I := 1 to 10 do
     begin
        Read(Numbers, Value);      { Read from the file   }
        Writeln(Value);            { Write to the screen }
     end;
```

Closing a File

The last part of using a file is closing it. Closing a file terminates the association between the logical file and the physical file. All subsequent attempts to access the file will produce an error because the file no longer exists as far as the program is concerned. A file must be closed before the program ends in order to save all the information placed into the file. This is easily done with the Close procedure.

```
Close(FileVar);
```

FileVar is the file's logical filename.

Random File Access

We have seen that as we read information from a file, the current file position is advanced to the next record. We have also seen how a file can be "rewound" to record number 0 with the Reset procedure. This has been an example of what is known as **sequential file access**. That is, all the information in the file is accessed in sequence. If you think about this type of access for a minute, you will quickly realize the shortcomings of such a system. For instance, how could we be able to replace the information contained in one particular record of the file? Since it is impossible to backtrack a record, we couldn't read a record, change its contents, and then rewrite it to the file. There are of course ways of doing this, but they are inefficient and slow. Two solutions to this problem come to mind. One would be to read the entire file into an array in memory (if there is enough memory space), change the record, erase the file, and then write the new file to the disk. A second way might be to keep track of the record number of the record to be replaced. Read it, rewind the file, read each record prior to the one to be replaced, then write them all to a new file and place the changed record into the new file, followed by the rest of the records from the original file. Needless to say, a program that depended heavily on the ability to change records in a file would perform poorly working in this fashion. Why is this the case? When Pascal was first developed, small, inexpensive disk drives did not exist, and large amounts of input/output processing were done with magnetic tapes, which by their very nature are sequential-access devices. The sequential file access in Pascal was designed to work with this type of storage device.

Fortunately, today we have small, inexpensive, high-density storage devices such as the Mac's microfloppy disk drive, which can access any portion of a disk directly. Turbo and other Pascals have implemented extensions to the Pascal language to work with these devices. These random-access techniques allow a record anywhere in the file to be accessed without first accessing any other records. For this reason random-access files are also sometimes known as direct-access files.

The key to random file access in Turbo Pascal is the Seek procedure.

```
Seek(File, RecordNumber)
```

Seek will advance any file to the position right before the record whose number is passed as the parameter RecordNumber. For instance, to read the tenth record of a file directly, we would use the following:

```
Seek(MyFile, 9);
Read(MyFile, MyRecord);
```

Remember, the tenth record is record number 9, since records are numbered starting with 0. The Seek positions the current file position to the desired location, and the Read gets the record.

As an example of a typical use of a Seek statement, let's go back to our file of integers and change the value of all the records we have placed in the disk file named Space Ship.

```
for RecordOfNumber := 0 to 9 do
 begin
    Seek(Numbers, RecordOfNumber);
    Read(Numbers,Value);
    {Change the value}
    Value:= Value + 1;
    Seek(Numbers, RecordOfNumber);
    { Put the changed record in Value back
        into the file }
    Write(Numbers, Value)
 end;
```

Why is the Seek procedure used twice? After the first Seek, a Read is used to get the record from the file. When performed, the Read advances the current file position to the next record so the next Read would access the subsequent record. So we must backtrack one record so that the Write replaces the correct record.

Finding the End of a File

The above program goes through a file whose size is known in advance (held in NumberOfRecords). This is not always the case. A business is not likely to know the number of customers or transactions to be stored in a file in advance. Therefore, the size of a file usually changes dynamically as needed. If a program that changes all the records in a file accesses such a file, then it is necessary to determine, while the program is running, when the end of the file has been reached. Pascal has a built-in function known as EOF for End of File, which returns True if a Read or Seek has attempted to access past the end of a file and False otherwise. EOF is a simple Boolean function of the form Eof(FileVar). We can use this to determine if the record we are attempting to read is contained in the file. Our program could be written for a file of unspecified size as follows:

```
Reset(Numbers,'Space Ship');
RecordofNumber := 0;
while not Eof(Numbers) do
   begin
      Seek(Numbers, RecordOfNumber);
      Read(Numbers, Value);
      Value := Value + 1;
      { Put the changed record in the file }
      { buffer back into the file          }
      Seek(Numbers, RecordOfNumber);
      Write(Numbers, Value);
      RecordofNumber := Recordof Number + 1
   end;
```

Since the EOF function returns False if a record exists and the While loop needs a condition of True, we must reverse the Boolean value returned by the function using a Not. The EOF function can also be used with data read from the keyboard. Holding down the Command key on the keyboard while typing the period (.) is used to signal the End of File condition.

TEXT FILES

In addition to using files to store information on secondary storage devices, files are also useful for transferring information to input/output devices. All along we have been using files for this purpose without even knowing it. Every time we have used a Write statement to display information on the screen, we have used a predeclared file called Output, which is automatically opened for writing to the console. Each time we used a Read or Readln, we read from a predeclared file called Input, which is automatically opened for reading from the keyboard. It's just that we have not been required to use the optional filename parameter since a Write is assumed to be directed to the screen and a Read to accept input from the keyboard, unless the file parameter is used to indicate otherwise. While Turbo uses Write and Read to access all types of files, these instructions behave a little differently when used with text files.

A **text file** is essentially a file of characters where each line is terminated by a carriage return character. A text file is declared as follows:

```
var
 myTextFile : Text;
```

"Text" is a Pascal reserved word.

As you can see, there is a relationship between keyboard input, screen output, and text Files. All output is sent to the console window and input read from the keyboard via a text file known as 'Console:'. This is accomplished by associating a text file with a special kind of file known as a **device**. Instead of being held on a storage media, a device is actually part of the hardware of the computer. Every Turbo Pascal program by default associates Pascal's built-in text files Input and Output with the standard Turbo device known as the **console**. The console is used by Turbo to make the Mac work like a standard terminal with a keyboard and an 80-column display on the screen (which is, of course, the console window we have been using all along). When a program starts to execute, it is as though the following two instructions were executed:

```
Reset(Input, 'Console:');
Rewrite(Output, 'Console:');
```

These establish the relationship between what is known as the 'Console:' device and the standard files Input and Output. Turbo also assumes that every Read and Readln that contains no file variable parameter by default contains a reference to the built-in text file Input. So a Readln statement such as

```
Readln(Num);
```

directed to the keyboard is the equivalent of

```
Readln(Input, Num);
```

Every Write or Writeln that contains no filename parameter contains a reference to the built-in text file Output. So a Writeln statement such as

```
Writeln('What's your name, good-looking');
```

is the equivalent of

```
Writeln(Output, 'What's your name, good-looking');
```

In addition to reading or writing to the default 'Console:' device, it is also desirable to be able to write to devices such as the printer. To send information to the printer rather than the screen, we work with the predeclared 'Printer:' device. To send all output to a printer, we simply redefine the device associated with the Output file to the printer with a Rewrite statement.

```
Rewrite(Output, 'Printer:');
```

Of course, after this all standard Write and Writeln instructions will send their output straight to a printer. When doing this, the native printing font of the printer will be used. None of the fancy printing normally associated with the Mac is done. In order to print fancy, the use of the Toolbox and QuickDraw is involved. This technique is covered in the last chapter of the book.

We could almost as easily send some output to the console window and some to the printer by creating a second text file and associating that with the printer.

```
 var
  Prnt : Text;
     :
begin
 Rewrite(Prnt, 'Printer:');
 Writeln(Prt, 'This will print on the printer');
```

In your programs, you may find it convenient to be able to direct the output from your program to either the console window or your printer. This can be done by adding to all your Write and Writeln statements an output file and then using a procedure to direct this file to the desired output device.

```
 var
  Ch : Char;
  Output : Text;
         :
procedure SelectDevice;
begin
   Writeln('Where should the output go');
   Writeln('Enter P for the printer or C for the
Console window');
   Read(Ch);
   if Ch = 'P' then
      Rewrite(Output,'Printer:');
   if Ch = 'CT' then
      Rewrite(Output, 'Console:')
end;
```

The Writeln statements in the program should then all look like

```
Writeln(Output, variable list);
```

Naturally, using the Seek makes no sense when used with a device or text file. A text file can also be stored on disk. In fact, all programs written in Pascal are stored as text files on disk. The following program prompts the user for the name of a text file (perhaps a Turbo Pascal program file) and reads the file from the disk line by line, displaying each line in the console window:

```
program DisplayText;
var
   TextFile : Text;
   FileLine, Name : string[80];
begin
   Writeln('Enter name of file');
   Readln(Name);
   Reset(TextFile, Name);
   while not Eof(TextFile) do
      begin
         Readln(TextFile, FileLine);
         Writeln(FileLine);
```

```
      end;
    Writeln;
    Writeln('Press <Ret> to continue');
    Readln
end.
```

FILE PROGRAMMING TECHNIQUES

Seeing If a File Exists

You have just seen about all there is to working with files. However, to program with files you need to know more than just how files operate; you also need some familiarity with programming techniques. One of the simplest but most important of these techniques is the ability to detect whether a file already exists on a disk or whether it must be created. This becomes important in situations where a program will read a file if it exists or build it if it doesn't. The Reset procedure will cause a run-time error if the file being opened does not exist, yet Pascal contains no way to test if a file exists prior to using Reset. Fortunately, Turbo has a way to shut off its error checking on input and output operations. This can be used to test if a file exists or not. The Turbo compiler switch {$I-} will disable all error checking during I/O operations so that if no file exists while doing a Reset, no run-time error will be triggered. Caution must be exercised when switching off error checking because many error conditions that you would like to be aware of will not be caught by the compiler. Once the error checking is disabled, we need some mechanism for checking if an I/O operation (such as Reset) was successful. For this purpose, Turbo maintains a built-in function known as IOResult, which returns a 0 if the last I/O operation was successful and a negative number otherwise.

```
{$I-}
Reset(myFile, 'file.data');
Code := IOResult
```

The preceding code segment switches off I/O error checking, performs a Reset, and then checks the error code. Depending upon that value, we can either proceed normally if the file exists or create it with Rewrite otherwise.

```
{$I-}
Reset(myFile, 'file.data');
Code := IOResult
if Code < 0 then
    Rewrite(myFile, 'file.data')
{$I+}
{Process file}
```

At the end of this program segment, the I/O error checking was restored with the compiler switch {$I+}.

Never attempt to view the result of IOResult from a Write statement for debugging purposes such as

```
Reset(myFile, 'file.data');
Write(IOResult)
```

What's the problem? This will display the result of the last I/O operation, which is the Write and not the Reset. The proper result can be achieved by first assigning the value returned by IOResult to a variable and then displaying it.

```
Reset(myFile, 'file.data');
Code := IOResult;
Write(Code);
```

A complete list of all the possible values returned by IOResult is listed in Appendix D.

Examining a File's Contents

Very often while developing a program it would be helpful to view the contents of a file being created. Turbo's schizophrenic ability to edit and run more than one program at a time is quite helpful here. It gives us the ability to keep a small file exam "utility" in one window while developing a larger system. Such a utility only needs to treat the contents of a file as characters and then display them in the console window.

```
program FileTest;
var
 f : file of Char;
 Ch : Char;
 Name : string[80];
begin
 Writeln('Examine which file?');
 Readln(Name);
 reset(f,Name);
 while not eof(f) do
  begin
   Read(f,ch);
   writeln(ch,' ', Ord(ch));
  end;
 readln;
end.
```

No matter what data type is stored in the file, each byte of the file is read by FileTest as a character and displayed on the screen along with its ASCII code. This will help identify the contents of most files as long as you understand how the information is organized when it is stored.

Pathnames

A file can be sent to a particular disk drive (floppy or hard) and into a particular directory on an HFS (hierarchical file system) disk by specifying them in the physical filename. For instance, to create a file on the volume known as PaulStuff:

```
Rewrite('ResumeFile PaulStuff:MyFile',);
```

With HFS, to do the same thing but also use the folder "Resume," you would use

```
Rewrite('ResumeFile PaulStuff:Resume:MyFile',);
```

A FILE PROCESSING APPLICATION—THE CHECKING AND SAVINGS PROGRAM

Now that you are familiar with file operations, we are ready to develop a full-scale application that utilizes file processing. This is a good exercise not only in file handling, but also in how to plan and program a significant project. The particular application we will tackle is a program that will prove useful in your banking transactions.

Overview

The Checking and Savings program will track transactions for a checking account and a savings account. These were both included because many banks now bundle a checking and savings account together. Several types of transactions can be entered for both accounts. For the checking account, the transactions that can be entered are

1. deposits;
2. checks written;
3. interest paid by the bank (for interest-paying checking accounts);
4. fees charged by the bank.

For the savings account, the transactions accepted are

1. deposits;
2. withdrawals;
3. interest paid by the bank.

For either account, a report of all the transactions can be printed with the current balance.

Data Structures

One of the first things to consider when developing any application is what data structure will be used. That is, how will the data be organized, handled, and stored? In this program we essentially have two types of information. The first is a transaction for either checking or savings. Since the transactions for both types of accounts are similar, they can both be stored in the same record structure with a field indicating which account the transaction is for. The other fields in the record are needed to keep track of the particulars of the transactions. The record structure is

```
type
 TransType = (Checking, Savings);
 TransRec = record
    CheckOrSave : TransType;
    Code        : 1..5;
    Date        : string[8];
    Amount      : Integer;
    TaxDeduct   : Char;
    CheckNumber : Integer;
    PayTo       : string[80]
 end;
```

The first four fields are needed for any type of transaction. The last three are used only for a check. After a transaction is entered, it is written to an external data file named Trans.data. The field Code is used to specify which type of transaction the record represents. The codes are shown in Table 9-1.

Table 9-1. Field Codes

Code	Checking	Savings
1	Deposit	Deposit
2	Withdrawal	Check
3	Interest	Interest
4	Fee	—

The second type of information to keep track of is the balance of both accounts. We could not include that as a field in the transaction records since the balance changes after each transaction. A separate record structure is used to hold the balances.

```
BalanceRec = record
    SavBal : Integer;
    CheckBal : Integer
end;
```

A different field in the record is used for the balance in each account. This record is updated after every transaction. At the end of the program the record is written to an external disk file named Balance.data. When the program is run subsequent times, the record is read from this file. In this way up-to-date balance information is maintained.

Development

This program differs from all others we have seen because several program options are available to the user, and none of them are done in any specific order. The options are selected by the user from a series of menus, and the selection entered controls the execution. The main menu provides the choices of a savings or checking transaction to be entered, balances to be displayed, or exiting from the program. The checking or savings choices lead to submenus that provide the choice transactions. The balance option displays the balances, and the exit option does the file housekeeping before returning control of Turbo Pascal to the user. No pull-down menus are used; chapter 11 covers that.

A first level of development for the program would produce pseudocode indicating what action will take place for each of the possible program options.

```
repeat
  Display Main Menu
  Get option
  Case option of
   1 : Savings transaction
   2 : Checking transaction
   3 : Display balances
   4 : Exit program
 until Exit option is picked
```

A second level of development will show detailed pseudocode for how each of the main menu options will be processed.

Listing 9-1. Pseudocodes for the Savings and Checking Programs.

```
SAVINGS TRANSACTIONS
  Deposit
    Get information
    Add amount to savings balance
    Place transaction in file
  Withdrawal
    Get information
    Subtract amount from savings balance
    Place transaction in file
  Interest credited
    Get information
    Add amount to savings balance
    Place transaction in file
  Report
    while not (eof(Trans.data))
      begin
        Read a transaction
        If savings transaction then Print transaction information
       end {While}
      Print balance
CHECKING TRANSACTIONS
  Deposit
    Get information
    Add amount to checking balance
    Place transaction in file
  Check
    Get information
    Subtract amount from checking balance
    Place transaction in file
  Interest credited
    Get information
    Add amount to checking balance
    Place transaction in file
  Checking fee
    Get information
    Subtract amount from checking balance
    Place transaction in file
 Report
    while not (eof(Trans.data))
        Read a transaction
        If checking transaction then Print transaction information
     Print balance
DISPLAY BALANCES
  Clear screen
  Display balances
```

```
EXIT
    Replace balance record in Balance.data
  Close all files
```

A third level of refinement will include writing the main program with the variable declarations and the procedures that implement the menu structure.

Listing 9-2. Main Savings and Checking Program.

```
program CheckingAndSavings;
type
   TransType = (Checking, Savings);
   TransRec = record
      CheckOrSave : TransType;
      Code        : 1..5;
      CheckNumber : Integer;
      PayTo       : string[60];
      Date        : string[8];
      Amount      : Real;
      TaxDeduct   : Char;
   end;

   BalanceRec = record
      SavBal      : Real;
      CheckBal    : Real
   end;
var
   Out         : Text;
   Transaction : TransRec;
   Balance     : BalanceRec;
   FourSet,
   FiveSet     : set of 1..10;
   Option      : Integer;
   TransFile   : file of TransRec;
   BalanceFile : file of BalanceRec;
   Stop        : Boolean;
   I           : Integer;
        .
        .
begin
   Stop := False;
   FourSet := [1, 2, 3, 4];
```

```
FiveSet := [1, 2, 3, 4, 5];
 {$I-}
Reset(BalanceFile, 'Balance.Data');
i := ioresult;
{$I+}
if i < 0 then
   begin
      Balance.savbal := 0 ;
      Balance.checkbal := 0;
   end
else
   begin
      Seek(BalanceFile, 0);
      Read(BalanceFile, Balance);
      close (BalanceFile);
   end;
Rewrite(out, 'Printer:');
{OpenTransaction File}
If FileSize(TransFile) = 0 then
   begin
      Rewrite(TransFile, 'Trans.data');
      Close (TransFile)
   end;
Reset(TransFile, 'Trans.data');
{Move to last position in file}
Seek(TransFile, FileSize(TransFile));
repeat {Main driver}
   DisplayMainMenu;
   InitRec;
   case option of
      1 :
         begin
            Transaction.CheckOrSave := Checking;
            CheckingMenu;
            CheckingOptions
         end;
      2 :
         begin
            SavingsMenu;
            Transaction.CheckOrSave := Savings;
            SavingsOptions
         end;
      3 :
```

```
            ShowBalances;
        4 :
            Stop := True;
      end;{Case}
   until Stop = True;
   Close(TransFile);
   Rewrite(BalanceFile,'Balance.data');
   Write(BalanceFile, Balance);
   {Replace Balance record in file}
   Close(BalanceFile);
end. {Program}
```

The main program first initializes the variables used in the program and opens the files needed. If the balance file does not exist, then the fields in its record are set to zero. The other function of the main program is to drive the program by calling a procedure to display the main menu and then calling the procedures necessary to handle the transaction to be entered. As you can notice we used that little trick for determining if a file is present on the disk. The procedures called from the main program are

DisplayMainMenu—Displays the main menu in the text window.

InitRec—Initializes the transaction record so that no information is in it from the previous transaction.

CheckingMenu—Displays the menu of checking options.

CheckingOptions—Processes the checking transactions.

SavingsMenu—Displays the menu of savings options.

SavingsOptions—Processes the savings transactions.

ShowBalances—Displays the current account balances.

The next step of the development is to write the procedures called in the main program. This set of procedures will handle all the various account transactions.

```
procedure DisplayMainMenu;
begin
    Writeln('Checking and Savings System');
    Writeln;
    Writeln(' 1. Checking Transaction');
    Writeln(' 2. Savings Transaction');
    Writeln(' 3. Show Balances');
    Writeln(' 4. Exit');
    Writeln;
    repeat
       Write('Selection ');
       Readln(Option);
    until Option in FourSet;
end; {DisplayMainMenu}
```

This procedure displays the main menu. The user's selection is returned to the main program in the global variable Option. Notice the input verification done in the Repeat loop utilizing sets.

```
procedure CheckingMenu;
begin
   Writeln('Checking System');
   Writeln;
   Writeln('1. Enter a Deposit');
   Writeln('2. Enter a Check');
   Writeln('3. Enter Interest');
   Writeln('4. Checking Fees');
   Writeln('5. Checking Report');
   repeat
      Writeln;
      Write('Selection ');
      Read(Option)
   until Option in FiveSet;
end; {CheckingMenu}

procedure SavingsMenu;
begin
   Writeln('Savings System');
   Writeln;
   Writeln('1. Enter a Deposit');
   Writeln('2. Enter a withdrawal');
   Writeln('3. Enter Interest');
   Writeln('4. Savings Report');
```

```
    repeat
      Write('Selection ');
      Read(Option)
    until Option in FourSet;
  end; {SavingsMenu}
```

The procedures CheckingMenu and SavingsMenu are very similar. They both display the possible account transaction and send the selected option back to the main program in the global variable Option.

Listing 9-3. Procedures That Handle Savings and Checking Transaction.

```
procedure SavingsOptions;
begin
   case Option of
      1 :
         begin
            EnterDeposit;
            Balance.SavBal := Balance.SavBal + Transaction.Amount;
            WriteTransaction
         end;
      2 :
         begin
            Enterwithdrawal;
            Balance.SavBal := Balance.SavBal - Transaction.Amount;
            WriteTransaction
         end;
      3 :
         begin
            EnterInterest;
            Balance.SavBal := Balance.SavBal + Transaction.Amount;
            WriteTransaction
         end;
      4 :
         PrintSavingReport;
   end {Case}
end; {SavingsOptions}

procedure CheckingOptions;
begin
   case Option of
     1 :
       begin
         EnterDeposit;
         Balance.CheckBal := Balance.CheckBal + Transaction.Amount;
         WriteTransaction
       end;
     2 :
```

```
      begin
        EnterCheck;
        Balance.CheckBal := Balance.CheckBal - Transaction.Amount;
        WriteTransaction
      end;
    3 :
      begin
        EnterInterest;
        Balance.CheckBal := Balance.CheckBal + Transaction.Amount;
        WriteTransaction
      end;
    4 :
      begin
        EnterFee;
        Balance.CheckBal := Balance.CheckBal - Transaction.Amount;
        WriteTransaction
      end;
    5 :
      PrintCheckingReport;
  end {Case}
end;{CheckingOptions}
```

The procedures SavingsOptions and CheckingOptions handle the account transactions. The selection entered to CheckingMenu or SavingsMenu is used as the selector in a Case statement. Several more procedures are called that accept the transaction data. The balance is then calculated and the transaction written to the file.

EnterDeposit—Prompts the user for deposit information.

EnterWithdrawal—Prompts the user for withdrawal information.

EnterInterest—Prompts the user for interest information.

EnterFee—Prompts the user for fee information.

EnterCheck—Prompts the user for check information.

WriteTransaction—Write the transaction record to the file.

PrintCheckingReport—Prints the report for the checking account.

PrintSavingsAccount—Prints the report for the savings account.

The next step in the development is to write this set of procedures.

Listing 9-4. Procedures That Accept the Savings and Checking Transactions Data.

```
procedure EnterCheck;
begin
  with Transaction do
    begin
      Writeln('Enter a Check');
      Writeln;
      Write('Check Number:');
      Readln(CheckNumber);
      Write('Paid to:');
      Readln(PayTo);
      GetAmount;
      Write('Tax Deductible(Y/N):');
      Read(TaxDeduct);
      Writeln;
      Code := 2;
      Write('Enter Date MM/DD/YY: ');
      Readln(Date);
    end
end; {EnterCheck}

procedure EnterDeposit;
begin
  with Transaction do
    begin
      Writeln('Enter a Deposit to ', Transaction.CheckOrSave);
      Writeln;
      GetAmount;
      Write('Enter Date MM/DD/YY: ');
      Readln(Date);
      Code := 1;
    end {With}
end; {EnterDeposit}

procedure EnterInterest;
begin
  Writeln(' Enter Interest to ', Transaction.CheckOrSave);
  Writeln;
  with Transaction do
    begin
      GetAmount;
      Code := 3;
      Write('Enter Date MM/DD/YY: ');
```

```
        Readln(Date);
      end {With}
end; {EnterInterest}

procedure EnterFee;
begin
   with Transaction do
      begin
        Writeln('Enter a Fee');
        Writeln;
        GetAmount;
        Write('Enter Date MM/DD/YY: ');
        Readln(Date);
        Code := 4;
     end
end; {EnterFee}

procedure EnterInterest;
begin
    Writeln(' Enter Interest to ', Transaction.CheckOrSave);
    Writeln;
    with Transaction do
       begin
         GetAmount;
         Code := 3;
         Write('Enter Date MM/DD/YY: ');
         Readln(Date);
       end {With}
end; {EnterInterest}

procedure EnterFee;
 begin
   with Transaction do
     begin
       Writeln('Enter a Fee');
       Writeln;
       GetAmount;
       Write('Enter Date MM/DD/YY: ');
       Readln(Date);
       Code := 4;
     end
end; {EnterFee}

procedure EnterWithdrawal;
begin
   with Transaction do
      begin
        Writeln('Enter a Withdrawal to ', CheckOrSave);
```

```
        Writeln;
        GetAmount;
        Code := 2;
        Write('Enter Date MM/DD/YY: ');
        Readln(Date)
      end {With}
end; {EnterWithdrawal}
```

All of these procedures are similar, prompting the user for transaction information and assigning it into the Transaction record. Because of the similarity between the two accounts, the procedures EnterDeposit and EnterInterest are used for both checking and savings.

Listing 9-5. Procedures That Print the Savings and Checking Transaction Reports.

```
procedure PrintCheckingReport;
begin
  PrinterMessage;
  Writeln(Out, 'Checking Report');
  Seek(TransFile, 0);
  Read(TransFile,Transaction) ;
  while not (eof(TransFile)) do
     begin
        if Transaction.CheckorSave = Checking then
           with Transaction do
              begin
                 Write(Out, Date);
                 case code of
                    1 :
                       Write(Out, 'Deposit');
                    2 :
                       begin
                          Writeln(Out, 'Check number ',
                             CheckNumber, ' ' :10, 'Deductible');
                          Write(Out, 'Paid to:', PayTO)
                       end;
                    3 :
                       Write(Out, 'Interest ');
                    4 :
                       Write(Out, 'Fee');
                 end; {Case}

                 Writeln(Out, Amount : 7 : 2);
     end; {With}
  Read(TransFile,Transaction)
```

```
 Read(TransFile,Transaction)
    end; {While}
    Writeln(Out);
    Writeln(Out, 'Balance ', Balance.CheckBal : 7 : 2)
 end; {PrintCheckingReport}

procedure PrintSavingReport;
 begin
    PrinterMessage;
    Writeln(Out, 'Savings Report');
    Seek(TransFile, 0);
    Read(TransFile, Transaction);
    while not (eof(transfile)) do
       begin
          if Transaction.CheckorSave = Savings then
          with Transaction do
             begin
                Write(Out, Date);
                case Code of
                   1 :
                      Write(Out, 'Deposit');
                   2 :
                      Write(Out, 'Withdrawal');
                   3 :
                      Write(Out, 'Interest ')
                end; {Case}
                Writeln(Out, Amount : 7 : 2);
             end; {With}
          Read(TransFile, Transaction);
       end; {While}
    Writeln(Out);
    Writeln(Out, 'Balance ', Balance.SavBal : 7 : 2)
end; {PrintSavingsReport}
```

Both of the report procedures read the transaction file starting at the first record. A Seek is used to position the file pointer to the zero record. Subsequent records are read until the end of the file is reached. The CheckOrSave field in the record is examined; if the record is the proper type of transaction, then the information is sent to the printer. A last set of procedures is called by this set.

GetAmount—Prompts the user for the amount of the transaction. This is needed in enough places to justify making it a procedure all its own.

```
procedure GetAmount;
begin
  Write('Amount: $');
  Readln(Transaction.Amount)
end; {GetAmount}

procedure PrinterMessage;
begin
  Writeln('Set up printer');
  Writeln('Then press the mouse button');
  repeat
   {Do nothing loop}
  until button
end; {PrinterMessage}
```

The only lines of interest in these two procedures is the Repeat loop in PrinterMessage. This loop is used to freeze the menu on the screen until the user presses the mouse button. This causes the built-in Boolean function Button to return True and the loop to end. You could also use the function KeyPress for this.

Here is the entire program together.

Listing 9-6. The Complete Savings and Checking Program.

```
program CheckingAndSavings;
uses
   Memtypes, QuickDraw, OSIntf, ToolIntf, PasPrinter;
type
   TransType = (Checking, Savings);
   TransRec = record
      CheckOrSave : TransType;
      Code : 1..5;
      CheckNumber : Integer;
      PayTo : string[60];
      Date : string[8];
      Amount : Real;
      TaxDeduct : Char;
   end;
   BalanceRec = record
      SavBal : Real;
      CheckBal : Real
   end;

var
   Out         : Text;
```

```
   Transaction : TransRec;
   Balance     : BalanceRec;
   FourSet,
   FiveSet     : set of 1..10;
   Option      : Integer;
   TransFile   : file of TransRec;
   BalanceFile : file of BalanceRec;
   Stop        : Boolean;
   I           : Integer;

procedure DisplayMainMenu;
begin
   Writeln('Checking and Savings System');
   Writeln;
   Writeln(' 1. Checking Transaction');
   Writeln(' 2. Savings Transaction');
   Writeln(' 3. Show Balances');
   Writeln(' 4. Exit');
   Writeln;
   repeat
      Write('Selection ');
      Readln(Option);
   until Option in FourSet
end; {DisplayMainMenu}

procedure CheckingMenu;
begin
   Writeln('Checking System');
   Writeln;
   Writeln('1. Enter a Deposit');
   Writeln('2. Enter a Check');
   Writeln('3. Enter Interest');
   Writeln('4. Checking Fees');
   Writeln('5. Checking Report');
   repeat
      Writeln;
      Write('Selection ');
      Read(Option)
   until Option in FiveSet
end; {CheckingMenu}

procedure SavingsMenu;
begin
   Writeln('Savings System');
   Writeln;
   Writeln('1. Enter a Deposit');
   Writeln('2. Enter a Withdrawal');
   Writeln('3. Enter Interest');
   Writeln('4. Savings Report');
   repeat
      Write('Selection ');
      Read(Option)
   until Option in FourSet
```

```
end; {SavingsMenu}

procedure InitRec;
begin
   with Transaction do
      begin
         CheckNumber := 0;
         PayTo := '';
         Amount := 0;
         TaxDeduct := ' ';
         Date := ''
      end
end;{InitRec}

procedure WriteTransaction;
begin
   Write(TransFile,Transaction);
end; {WriteTransaction}

procedure GetAmount;
begin
   Write('Amount: $');
   Readln(Transaction.Amount)
end; {GetAmount}

procedure PrinterMessage;
begin
   Writeln('Set up printer');
   Writeln('Then press the mouse button');
   repeat
      {Do nothing loop}
   until button
end; {PrinterMessage}

procedure ShowBalances;
begin
   with Balance do
      begin
         Writeln('Checking: ', CheckBal : 7 : 2);
         Writeln('Savings: ', SavBal : 7 : 2);
         Writeln;
      end;
   Writeln('Hit the mouse button to continue');
   repeat
   until button
end;

procedure EnterCheck;
begin
   with Transaction do
      begin
         Writeln('Enter a Check');
         Writeln;
```

```
            Write('Check Number:');
            Readln(CheckNumber);
            Write('Paid to:');
            Readln(PayTo);
            GetAmount;
            Write('Tax Deductible(Y/N):');
            Read(TaxDeduct);
            Writeln;
            Code := 2;
            Write('Enter Date MM/DD/YY: ');
            Readln(Date)
         end
end; {EnterCheck}

procedure EnterDeposit;
begin
   with Transaction do
      begin
         Write('Enter a Deposit to ');
         if Transaction.CheckOrSave = Checking then
            Writeln('Checking')
         else
            Writeln('Savings');
         Writeln;
         GetAmount;
         Write('Enter Date MM/DD/YY: ');
         Readln(Date);
         Code := 1;
      end {With}
end; {EnterDeposit}

procedure EnterInterest;
begin
   Writeln(' Enter Interest to ');
   if Transaction.CheckOrSave = Checking then
      Writeln('Checking')
   else
      Writeln('Savings');
   Writeln;
   with Transaction do
      begin
         GetAmount;
         Code := 3;
         Write('Enter Date MM/DD/YY: ');
         Readln(Date);
      end {With}
end; {EnterInterest}

procedure EnterFee;
begin
   with Transaction do
      begin
         Writeln('Enter a Fee');
```

```
         Writeln;
         GetAmount;
         Write('Enter Date MM/DD/YY: ');
         Readln(Date);
         Code := 4;
      end
end; {EnterFee}

procedure EnterWithdrawal;
begin
   with Transaction do
      begin
         Writeln('Enter a Withdrawal to ');
         if CheckOrSave = Checking then
            Writeln('Checking')
         else
            Writeln('Savings');
         Writeln;
         GetAmount;
         Code := 2;
         Write('Enter Date MM/DD/YY: ');
         Readln(Date)
      end {With}
end; {EnterWithdrawal}

procedure PrintCheckingReport;
begin
   PrinterMessage;
   Writeln(Out, 'Checking Report');
   Seek(TransFile, 0);
   Read(TransFile,Transaction) ;
   while not (eof(TransFile)) do
      begin
         if Transaction.CheckorSave = Checking then
            with Transaction do
               begin
                  Write(Out, Date);
                  case code of
                     1 :
                      Write(Out, 'Deposit');
                     2 :
                      begin
                         Writeln(Out,'Check number ',
                            CheckNumber,' ' :10,
                              'Deductible ');
                         Write(Out, 'Paid to:', PayTO)
                      end;
                     3 :
                      Write(Out, 'Interest ');
                     4 :
                      Write(Out, 'Fee');
                  end; {Case}
                  Writeln(Out, Amount : 7 : 2);
```

```
               end; {With}
            Read(TransFile,Transaction)
         end; {While}
      Writeln(Out);
      Writeln(Out, 'Balance ', Balance.CheckBal : 7 : 2)
   end; {PrintCheckingReport}

   procedure PrintSavingReport;
   begin
      PrinterMessage;
      Writeln(Out, 'Savings Report');
      Seek(TransFile, 0);
      Read(TransFile, Transaction);
      while not (eof(transfile)) do
         begin
            if Transaction.CheckorSave = Savings then
            with Transaction do
               begin
                  Write(Out, Date);
                  case Code of
                     1 :
                        Write(Out, 'Deposit');
                     2 :
                        Write(Out, 'Withdrawal');
                     3 :
                        Write(Out, 'Interest ')
                  end; {Case}
                  Writeln(Out, Amount : 7 : 2);
               end; {With}
            Read(TransFile, Transaction);
         end; {While}
      Writeln(Out);
      Writeln(Out, 'Balance ', Balance.SavBal : 7 : 2)
   end; {PrintSavingsReport}

   procedure SavingsOptions;
      begin
         case Option of
            1 :
               begin
                  EnterDeposit;
                  Balance.SavBal := Balance.SavBal
                    + Transaction.Amount;
                  WriteTransaction
               end;
            2 :
               begin
                  EnterWithdrawal;
                  Balance.SavBal := Balance.SavBal
                    - Transaction.Amount;
                  WriteTransaction
               end;
            3 :
```

```
            begin
               EnterInterest;
               Balance.SavBal := Balance.SavBal
                 + Transaction.Amount;
               WriteTransaction
            end;
         4 :
            PrintSavingReport;
      end {Case}
end; {SavingsOptions}

procedure CheckingOptions;
begin
   case Option of
      1 :
         begin
            EnterDeposit;
            Balance.CheckBal := Balance.CheckBal
              + Transaction.Amount;
            WriteTransaction
         end;
      2 :
         begin
            EnterCheck;
            Balance.CheckBal := Balance.CheckBal
              - Transaction.Amount;
            WriteTransaction
         end;
      3 :
         begin
            EnterInterest;
            Balance.CheckBal := Balance.CheckBal
              + Transaction.Amount;
            WriteTransaction
         end;
      4 :
         begin
            EnterFee;
            Balance.CheckBal := Balance.CheckBal
              - Transaction.Amount;
            WriteTransaction
         end;
      5 :
         PrintCheckingReport;
   end {case}
end;{CheckingOptions}

begin
   Stop := False;
   FourSet := [1, 2, 3, 4];
   FiveSet := [1, 2, 3, 4, 5];
   {$I-}
   Reset(BalanceFile, 'Balance.Data');
   i := ioresult;
```

```
    {$I+}
    if i < 0 then
       begin
          Balance.savbal := 0 ;
          Balance.checkbal := 0
       end
    else
       begin
          Seek(BalanceFile, 0);
          Read(BalanceFile, Balance);
          close (BalanceFile)
       end;
    Rewrite(out, 'Printer:');
   {OpenTransaction File}
   If FileSize(TransFile) = 0 then
      begin
         Rewrite(TransFile, 'Trans.data');
         Close (TransFile)
      end;
   Reset(TransFile, 'Trans.data');
   Seek(TransFile, FileSize(TransFile)); {Move to last
     position in file}
   repeat {Main driver}
      DisplayMainMenu;
      InitRec;
      case option of
         1 :
            begin
               Transaction.CheckOrSave := Checking;
               CheckingMenu;
               CheckingOptions
            end;
         2 :
            begin
               SavingsMenu;
               Transaction.CheckOrSave := Savings;
               SavingsOptions
            end;
         3 :
            ShowBalances;
         4 :
            Stop := True;
       end;{Case}
    until Stop = True;
    Close(TransFile);
    Rewrite(BalanceFile,'Balance.data');
    Write(BalanceFile, Balance);
   {Replace Balance record in file}
    Close(BalanceFile);
 end. {Program}
```

Do More

The Checking and Savings program provides a strong framework from which many features can be added by writing new procedures. Consider some of the following:

1. Adapt the report procedures to print only transactions after a given date.

2. Add a field to the transaction record to note if a check has cleared, and then add a procedure to reconcile the checking account.

3. Adapt the checking report to allow it only to print out tax-deductible expenses.

CHAPTER SUMMARY

This chapter introduced file concepts and then quickly integrated them with sophisticated programming techniques. Also presented was the longest application program yet. In the next chapter we will examine the final Pascal topics not yet covered, and then we will have the background necessary to move into some sophisticated uses of the Toolbox and QuickDraw.

10
Variant Records, Pointers, and Handles

INTRODUCTION

In this chapter we will discuss three of the more sophisticated and useful features in Pascal. Variant records are an extension of the concept of records, as already seen. Pointers are a data type totally different from any other we have seen so far in Pascal. Handles, which are based upon pointers, are a data type used extensively in implementing the Macintosh's User Interface. All three structures play important roles when using the Toolbox since many of the Toolbox's data structures are defined as records are and accessed via pointers and handles. For instance, all access to pull-down menus, as we will see in Chapter 11, are done through handles.

VARIANT RECORDS

In some situations, records that differ only slightly in structure are required. For example, suppose we want to represent information about all the people who are on a college campus. We would like to keep each person's name, address, and identification number. But depending upon whether the individual was a student or a faculty member, we would want to maintain different information. For students we want class standing, but for members of the faculty we would want job title and department worked for. To represent this information using the record structure with which we are already familiar would require these two separate records:

```
type
   Person = (Student, Faculty);

   StudentInfo = record
      Name         : string[20];
      IDNum        : string[9];
      Occupation   : Person;
      Standing     : 1..4;
   end;

   FacultyInfo = record
      Name          : string[20];
      IDNum         : string[9];
      Occupation    : Person;
      Description   : string[20];
      Department    : string[20]
   end;
```

By using **variant records**, this different information can be represented in a single record structure. A variant record allows the value of one field in the record to determine the type of information that can be stored in other fields.

```
type
   Person = (Student, Faculty);

   InfoRec = record
      Name          :    string[20];
      IDNum         :    string[9];
      case Occupation : Person of
         Student  :    (Standing : 1..4);
         Faculty  :    (Description : string[20];
                         Department : string[20])
   end; {InfoRec}
```

The declaration of a variant record differs from the standard record declaration because a Case clause is included. The Case clause must be the last part in the declaration, and the fields listed above it are handled just like a standard record declaration. The purpose of the Case clause is to show that this record may hold different kinds of information at different times. The field after the reserved word "case" (in this example Occupation : People) is called the **tag field**; it determines which of the variants in the Case clause are to be used. When the field Occupation has the value Student, the record will contain the field Standing. When the field Occupation has the value Faculty, this record will hold the Description and Department fields. The tag field Occupation is present in both variations of the record. Notice that there is no "end" used for the Case statement. Let's now declare two records to be of type InfoRec and examine them more closely.

```
var
 Person1, Person2 : InfoRec;
      .
      .
 Person1.Name := 'Marian';
 Person1.IDNum := '12355321';
 Person1.Occupation := Student;
 Person1.Standing := 4;
```

In the record Person1 the tag field Occupation is set to Student. The appropriate variant field to use is Standing.

```
Person2.Name := 'Alan';
Person2.IDNum := '12351234';
Person2.Occupation := Faculty;

Person2.Description := 'Assistant Professor';
Person2.Department := 'Computer Science';
```

In the record Person2 the tag field is set to Faculty. The variant fields that should be used are Description and Department.

Which fields in the variant part of a record to access (Standing or Department and Description) is a decision that should be made dynamically in the program by testing the tag field (in this case Occupation) and making a decision based on its value. The following example shows a procedure that can be used to display a record of type InfoRec:

```
procedure DisplayInfo(theRec : InfoRec);
begin
   { Display field common to both variants }
   Writeln('Name      : ', theRec.Name);
   Writeln('ID Number: ', theRec.IDNum);
   case theRec.Occupation of
      Faculty :  { Display information unique to faculty }
         begin
            Writeln('Occupation : Student');
            Writeln('Standing    : ', theRec.Standing);
         end
      Student :  { Display information unique to students }
         begin
            Writeln('Occupation : Faculty');
            Writeln('Department : ', theRec.Department);
            Writeln('Description: ', theRec.Description)
         end
   end
end;
```

Notice that the number of fields in the different variant parts do not have to be the same. Variant parts could also be declared containing no fields at all. It is not uncommon for a Pascal programmer to use a variant record without a tag field. This is perfectly legal. Instead of the tag field, just a tag type is used in the Case statement.

```
TestRec = record case Boolean of
   True : (Int : Integer);
   False : (Ch : Char)
  end; {Record}
```

This technique can only be used when the programmer knows which fields to use from the context of the program. An example of this would be when a programmer knows that all even records in a file will contain a number and all odd records will contain a character, or any other similar scheme. In this example, we used the type Boolean in the tag part of the Case clause to represent two variants; if we wanted to have more than two variants and still not use a tag field, we could use the type Char or Integer in the case because they have more than two possible values.

Why Use Variant Records?

Variant records are a space saver. The previous example about faculty and students could have been accomplished without variant records by including all three fields (Standing, Department, and Description) into our record. Since we know the fields Standing, Department, and Description would never be used at the same time, the variant record allows us to use the same space for both alternatives. If you were to write a program that stored 50,000 of these records on a disk, the space saving could be significant. The space taken up by variant records is the space needed to hold the largest variant (in our example Department, Description uses more space than Standing). Because of this, all variants of a record are the same size. This means a single type of file can hold the different kinds of information.

Since different variants occupy the same portion of memory, tricks can be done to circumvent Pascal's type checking. It is recommended that you not use this technique unless you are familiar with the way Turbo Pascal represents data internally.

Variants In The Toolbox

Many of the data structures used by the Toolbox and QuickDraw are declared as variant records. One example of this is the definition of a Point. We have already looked at the way a point is defined, but that definition was slightly simplified for instructional purposes. Now let's see the actual definition.

```
Point = record case Integer of
   0 : (v : Integer;
        h : Integer);
   1 : (vh : array[vhSelect] of Integer)
 end;
```

Here, vhSelect is defined as a user-defined type as follows:

```
vhSelect = (v,h);
```

As you can see, the true declaration of a point is a variant record that has no tag field. Essentially, a point is represented in memory by two consecutive integers. The objective is to allow the programmer to access the same information in whichever way is more convenient. Because of the variant definition of a point, these two groups of assignment statements have the same effect.

```
Pt.v := 10
Pt.h := 20;
```

and

```
Pt.vh[v] := 10;
Pt.vh[h] := 20;
```

Use whichever is more convenient in the program—in fact, both forms can be intermixed.

POINTERS

All the variables we have seen so far have been static variables. This meant that the variables were declared in the var section of a program, and memory space for the variable was allocated when the program started to execute. When we use static variables we must know in advance how much data we will need to store. For example, if we use an array to keep track of all the students in a university, we would have to know the maximum number of students who may register and then declare that many elements in the array. If half the students decided to drop out after taking Computer Science 101 last semester, then half the array would be wasted. On the other hand, if more people enrolled than anticipated, the array would be smaller than required, and the program would not work.

In Pascal, we have a way of creating new variables dynamically as they are required during program execution. These dynamic variables are not accessed the way static variables are, but rather through other variables known as **pointers**. To show how pointers work, let's look at a simple example of a dynamic integer and a pointer to it.

```
var
 P : ^Integer;
```

This declares P as a pointer to an integer variable. Notice that a pointer is declared with an up arrow ^ (Shift-6 key on Macintosh) preceding the data type of the variable it will point to. This declaration declares only the pointer, not the variable. We create the variable that P will point to dynamically with the New procedure.

```
New(P);
```

This procedure creates an integer variable that is not named but can be referenced though the pointer P. The variable P points to can be accessed with P^.

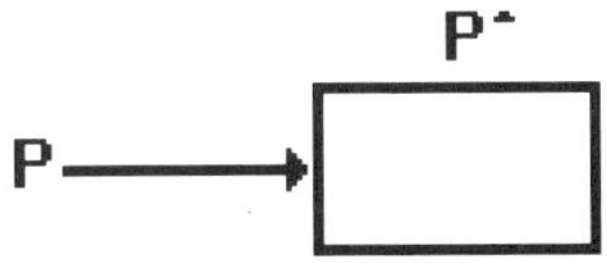

Figure 10-1. Pointer P

P The pointer

P^ How we reference the variable P points to

When a dynamic variable is created, its value is unitialized. A value can be placed in the newly created variable with

```
P^ := 26;
```

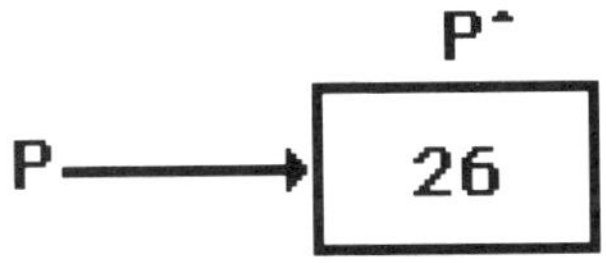

Figure 10-2. Assigning a Value

P^ refers to the variable and can be used like any other integer variable. The statement

```
P := 26;
```

has no meaning and will cause an error since P is a pointer to an integer and can't contain a value itself. If a second pointer to an integer Q were declared, we could make it point to the same variable that P does with

```
P := Q;
```

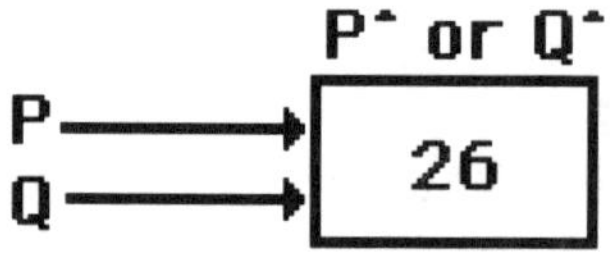

Figure 10-3. Assigning a Pointer

Q now points to the same variable P does.

An assignment statement with pointers takes on a slightly different meaning from any other type of variable. The pointer on the left side of the assignment operator is made to point to the same variable as the one on the right side. We can access the variable we created with either of the two pointers that point to it, Q or P.

```
Q^ := 4;
Write(P^);
```

This prints the value of P^, which is 4.

When a variable created dynamically is no longer needed, we can dispose of it and liberate the memory space it occupied with the Dispose procedure.

```
Dispose(P);
```

This destroys the variable that P pointed to. When a pointer doesn't point to anything, it is said to point to Nil, a predeclared constant. The link between a pointer and its variable can be destroyed by assigning Nil to it.

```
P := NIL;
```

So far, what we have seen as the use of pointers has no advantage over the use of static variables since we must declare a pointer for every dynamic variable used. Hence we are in the same boat as before, having to know the number of variables to be created prior to program execution. The advantage to using pointers can be seen when a dynamic variable contains a pointer to another dynamic variable. This can be done with the help of records.

```
type
  Dynamic : record
    Data : Integer;
    Link :  ^Dynamic
  end;
```

The declared record type has two fields: Data, which will contain an integer; and Link, which is a pointer to the type Dynamic (the record type itself). Now let's declare two records of type Dynamic.

```
var
 P, Q : ^Dynamic;
```

P and Q are both pointers to the record type Dynamic. Notice that no records actually exist at this time, only pointers to records. We can create a record dynamically with

```
New(P);
```

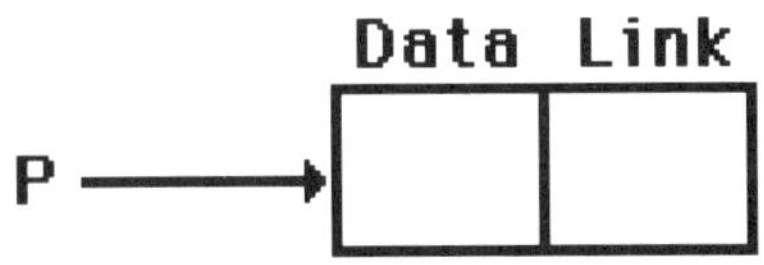

Figure 10-4. A Dynamic Record

A record now exists, and P points to it. A second record can be created with

```
New(Q);
```

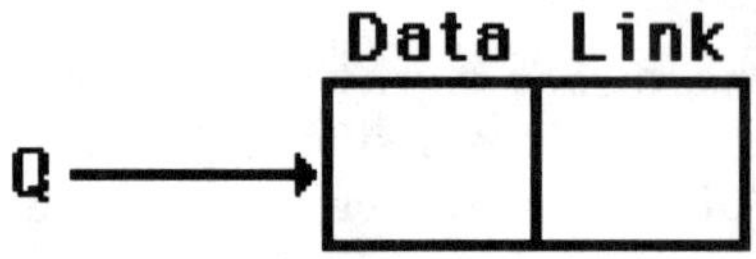

Figure 10-5. A Second Record

We now have two dynamic records pointed to by P and Q. These two records can be linked together by connecting the pointer field (P^.Link) of the first record to the second record. This is done by making it point to the same thing Q does.

```
P^.Link := Q;
```

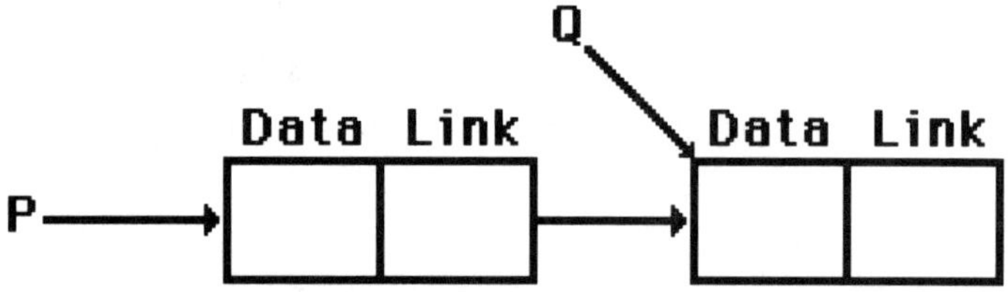

Figure 10-6. Connecting the Records

A third record can be added to our chain of records by creating a new record that Q points to and then linking it to the second record.

```
New(Q);
P^.Link^.Link := Q;
```

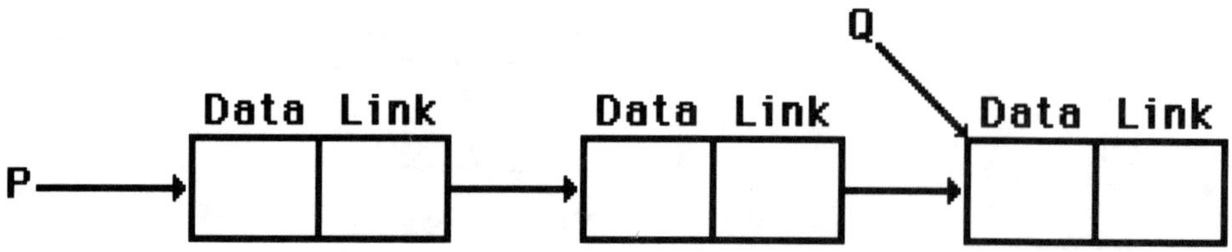

Figure 10-7. A Third Record

We were able to use Q to create a new record even though it already pointed to something. The link to what it previously pointed to is lost, and Q will point to a newly created record. The complicated

P^.Link^.Link refers to the field Link of the second record. This is like an expression evaluating to a field. It is evaluated left to right.

P^.Link	Refers to the Link field of the first record, the one that P points to.
P^.Link^	Refers to what the Link field of the first record points to, the second record.
P^.Link^.Link	Refers to the Link field of the second record.

A chain of records linked together like this is called a **linked list**. A linked list is a dynamic data structure that has similar uses to arrays. The disadvantage of using a link list is that records in the list cannot be accessed without tracing through the list. It is essentially a sequential access structure. A quicker and more efficient way to create a linked list uses a For loop and three pointers.

```
var
   P, Q, R : ^Dynamic;
     .
     .
New(P);
R := P;
for I := 1 to 3 do
   begin
      New(Q);
      R^.Link := Q;
      R := Q
   end
end;
```

In the earlier example, two pointers were used, one to point to the first record in the list and the second to create new dynamic records. When using the For loop, we need three pointers, one to point to the first record (P), one to create new dynamic records (Q), and a third to point to the last record in the list (R). The use of the third pointer alleviates the need to spell out the name of the Link field in the last record, as we had to do in the other example. Instead, since R points to the last record, R^.Link refers to the pointer we must link to the newest record.

Let us now look at a real application for pointers. Suppose we wanted to create a program similar to the program DisplayText in Chapter 9. Unlike DisplayText, which printed a file from beginning to end, the new program, ReverseText, will display the file backward from end to beginning. Since the file we wish to print is a text file, it can only be accessed sequentially. We will have to read the entire file into memory before we can start printing it out in reverse order. We do not know the size of the file to be reversed in advance, so we will use a dynamic variable to hold each line of the file as it is read in.

The variable that holds each line of text to be read in will be the record LineRec, which contains two fields. The field TextLine is a string that holds a line of text read, and the other field, Previous, is a pointer that points to another record of the same type (the record it points to holds the previous line of text read).

```
type
   LinePtr = ^LineRec;
   LineRec = record
      TextLine : string[80];     { Hold a line of text }
      Previous : LinePtr         { Pointer to the previous line }
   end;
```

Notice that the type LinePtr is declared to be a pointer to the type LineRec, which has not yet been declared. This is the only situation in Pascal where an identifier can be referenced before it has been declared.

Listing 10-1. Program That Displays a File from End to Beginning.

```
program ReverseText;
{ Program to reverse a textfile of arbitrary size
    using pointers }
type
   LinePtr = ^LineRec;
   LineRec = record
      TextLine : string[80];     { Hold a line of text }
      Previous : LinePtr         { Pointer to the previous line }
   end;
var
   TextFile : Text;
   filename : string;
   LineBefore, NewLine : LinePtr;
begin
   Write('Enter filename : ');
```

```
   Readln(filename);
   Reset(TextFile, filename);
   LineBefore := NIL;
   while not Eof(TextFile) do
      begin
         New(NewLine);
         Readln(TextFile, NewLine^.TextLine);
         NewLine^.Previous := LineBefore;
         LineBefore := NewLine
      end;
   { Trace through linked list in reverse order
      printing lines }
   while LineBefore <> NIL do
      begin
         Writeln(LineBefore^.TextLine);
         LineBefore := LineBefore^.Previous
      end;
   Writeln;
   Write('Press <Ret> to continue : ');
   Readln
end.
```

The program works by reading the first line into a newly created dynamic variable. Since there is no previously read in line for the previous field to point to, we make it point to Nil. We then continue to read lines from the file into dynamically created variables, making each previous pointer point to the previous line read in. When there are no more lines to be read, we can trace through the linked list created in the reverse order, by using the pointer to the previous line, and print out each line.

THE MEMORY MANAGER

In the previous section we saw how memory can be allocated dynamically using pointers and the standard Pascal routines New and Dispose. There are some programming situations, however, where this method of memory allocation is inadequate. For these situations we will use handles and the Macintosh's Memory Manager routines.

Memory in a computer is a valuable resource that is available only in limited quantities and so must be managed very carefully. The Macintosh on which you are running Turbo Pascal has a certain fixed amount of memory, be it 128K, 512K, a megabyte, or more. Parts of this memory are allocated for different purposes. Suppose you are programming on a Macintosh with 1 megabyte of memory (1024k bytes). For illustrative purposes, let us assume the memory in your machine is partitioned as follows:

Macintosh's operating system = 200k

Turbo Pascal = 200k

source code of your program = 150k

object code of your program = 100k

stack space used during execution of your program = 74k

free memory available for use by the program called the Heap = 300k

Total memory in the system = 1024k

Let's take a closer look at what happens to the 300k bytes of free memory when you run your program. Suppose we ran the following program, which allocates memory dynamically using New and Dispose:

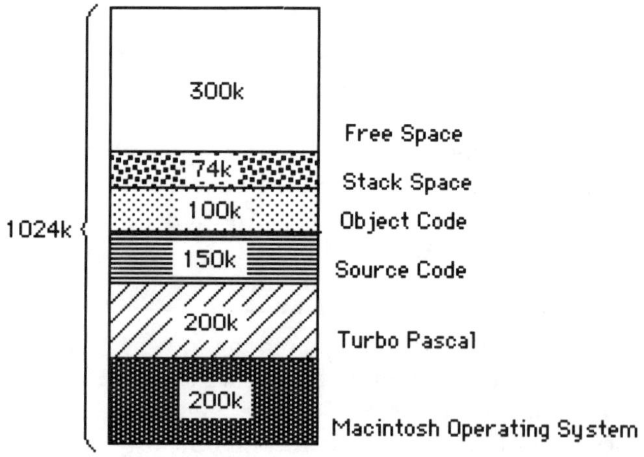

Figure 10-8. Memory Map

```
program ProveAPoint;
type
    KiloByte    = packed array[1..1024] of char;  { 1k of memory }
    SmallChunk  = array[1..50] of KiloByte;
    MediumChunk = array[1..75] of KiloByte;
    LargeChunk  = array[1..200] of KiloByte;
var
    SmallPtr  :  ^SmallChunk;
    MediumPtr :  ^MediumChunk;
    LargePtr  :  ^LargeChunk;

begin
    New(SmallPtr);     {Step 1: Allocate 50k bytes of memory }
    New(LargePtr);     {Step 2: Allocate 200k bytes of memory}
    Dispose(SmallPtr);{Step 3: Release the 50k allocated in Step 1}
    New(MediumPtr)     { Step 4: Allocate 75k bytes of memory}
end.
```

The following chart shows the state of memory after each statement in the program is executed.

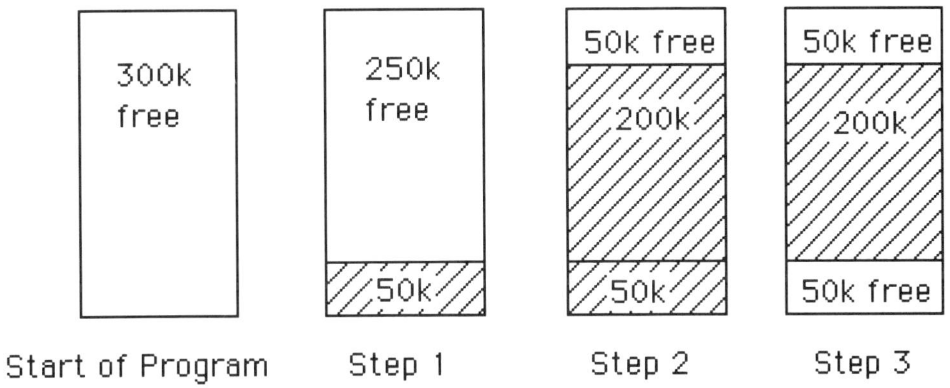

Figure 10-9. Memory Allocation

At the time we are going to perform step 4, there are 100k unallocated bytes of memory, but they are in two separate 50k-byte sections, neither of which is big enough to satisfy our 75k-byte request. The New procedure would fail to get the required amount of memory at step 4 and would place the predeclared constant Nil into MediumPtr, indicating failure to allocate memory. This situation of having enough memory but not being able to use it is called **fragmentation**. It is a shame to terminate a program when there really is enough free memory (100k bytes) to satisfy our request. A possible solution is to compact the memory by rearranging it so that all free memory is together. The problem with this solution is that any pointers used will then point to the wrong location since the data will have been relocated to a different area in memory. This situation is known as a **dangling pointer**. The chart that follows illustrates the dangling pointer problem and shows that after compaction the pointer no long points to the start of the 200k-byte block of memory. Using a dangling pointer to access the memory would then yield unexpected results. For this reason the Macintosh will not relocate memory that has been allocated using the New procedure.

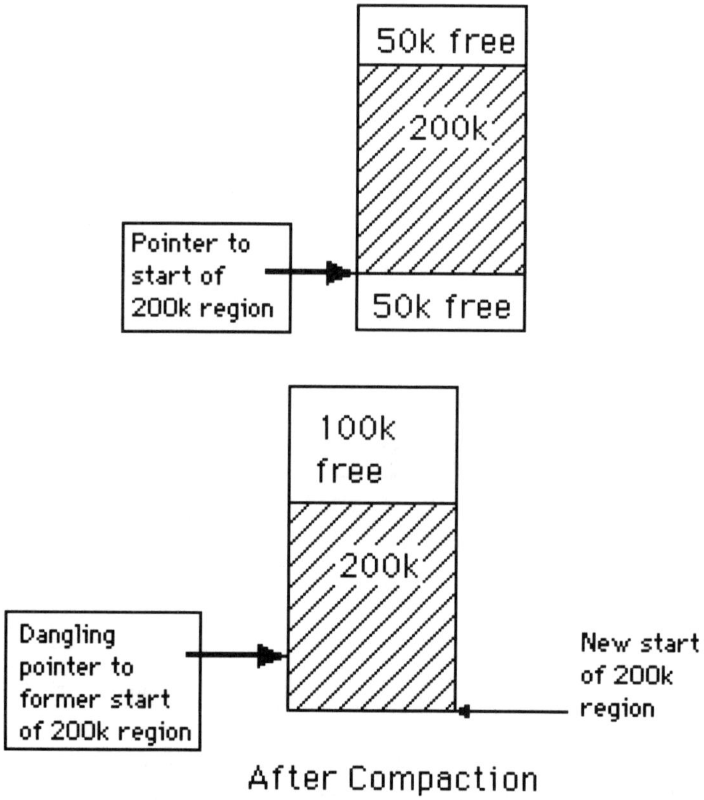

Figure 10-10. Compacting Memory

Fortunately, the Macintosh has a Memory Manager that is designed to allow the most efficient use of memory. How does it do this and avoid the infamous dangling pointer problem? If the pointer to a block of memory could automatically change to point to the memory's new location, then the data would still be accessible after compaction. The Memory Manager provides a simple and elegant scheme for accomplishing this, the **handle** data structure.

Handles

A handle is simply a pointer to a pointer.

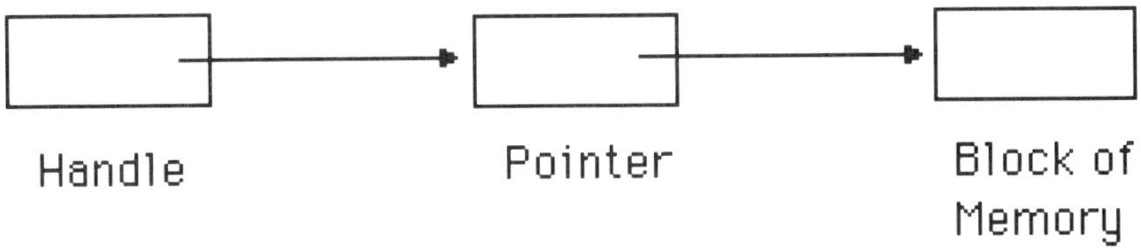

Figure 10-11. A Handle

With this scheme an extra step has been added to the process of accessing memory. The handle leads to a pointer, which in turn leads to a certain block of memory. The Macintosh's Memory Manager routines allow the handle to point to a special kind of pointer called a Master Pointer. The Master Pointer points to the dynamically allocated block of memory. If the block of memory is relocated, the Macintosh's Memory Manager automatically updates the Master Pointer to point to the block's new location. Now, no matter where in memory our block winds up we can still access it through the handle. This concept is illustrated in the figure below.

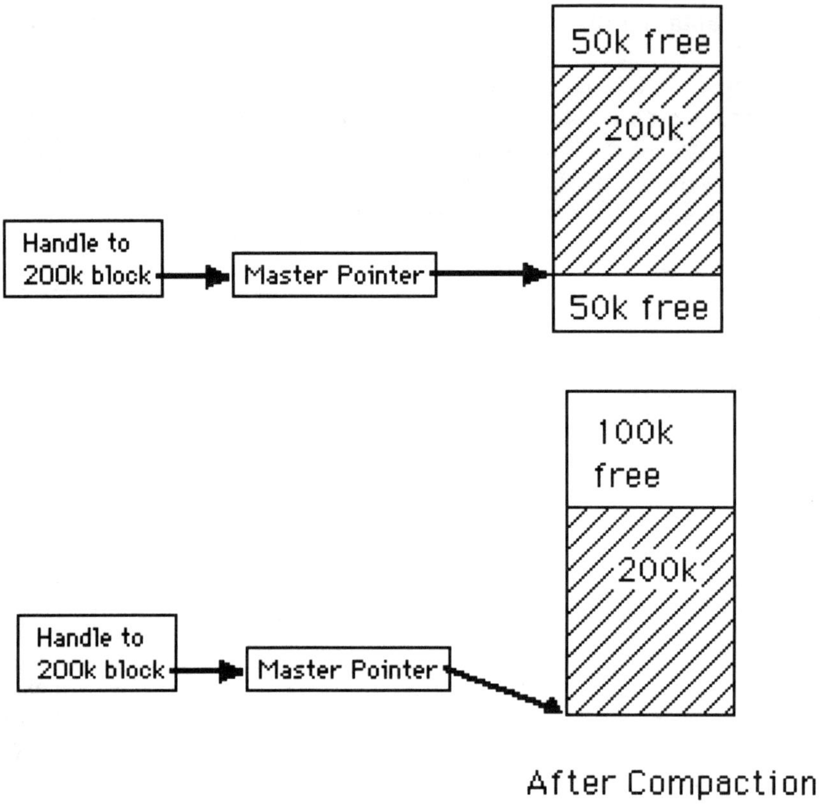

Figure 10-12. A Master Pointer

Since a handle is a pointer to a pointer, we can declare it that way. Suppose we wanted to declare a handle to an integer. First we would declare the type IntPointer to be a pointer to an integer. Then we would declare the type IntHandle to be a pointer to type IntPointer. Finally we could create a variable of type IntHandle.

```
type
       IntPointer   = ^Integer;
       IntHandle    = ^IntPointer;
var
       myHandle     : IntHandle;
```

To use a handle variable, we must make it point to something. This is done using the NewHandle function. The declaration for NewHandle function is

```
function NewHandle(Size : LongInt) : Handle;
```

where Handle is defined as follows:

```
type
    SignedByte      =  -128..127;
    Ptr             = ^SignedByte;
    Handle          = ^Ptr;
```

NewHandle allocates Size bytes of memory on the heap and makes a Master Pointer point to the allocated memory. It then returns a pointer to that Master Pointer. The returned value can be thought of as a handle to the memory that has been allocated. This value should then be assigned to a handle variable. If NewHandle cannot immediately find enough memory to satisfy the request, it will compact the heap and try again to allocate the memory. If it still is unable to find the required memory, it will return Nil. There are two minor complications in using the NewHandle routine. First, how do we know how much memory to allocate for a variable? Pascal provides us with a built-in function called SizeOf, which returns the number of bytes a variable or type occupies in memory. For example:

SizeOf(Integer) returns 2

SizeOf (LongInt) returns 4

SizeOf (Char) returns 1

You can also use an actual variable as an argument to SizeOf. In the following example, assume Num is declared as an integer and BigNum as a LongInt.

SizeOf (num) returns 2

SizeOf (bignum) returns 4

The second problem is that NewHandle returns something of type Handle, which is a generic type of handle and is probably different from the data type we will be working with. If we are working with handles to integers, for example, we must force the handle returned by NewHandle to that data type. As you remember, Pascal is very strict about not being able to assign values of one type to variables of another type (type checking). Fortunately, Turbo Pascal has a method around this problem. The solution is called **type coercion**, or **type casting.** To cast an expression of one type to another type, simply put the expression you wish to cast in parentheses and precede it by the new type. For example, if Num is of type Integer and Ch is of type Character, we could assign Ch to Num by using the following statement:

```
Num := Integer (Ch);
```

What we would get in Num is the ASCII value of Ch.

Putting it all together, we can allocate the block of memory for an integer.

```
myHandle := IntHandle (NewHandle(sizeof(Integer)));
```

If we wish to release the memory allocated with NewHandle, we use the procedure DisposHandle:

```
DisposHandle(Handle(myHandle))
```

DisposHandle expects a parameter of type Handle to be passed to it. Since we are working with handles to other types of data, we must cast myHandle to type Handle, which DisposHandle expects.

Now that we have dynamically allocated memory, we must be able to use it. We access memory through handles in a way that is analogous to the method used for pointers. When using a pointer, if we want to reference the variable pointed to by myPointer, we would use myPointer^. Since a handle is a pointer to a pointer, we can reference memory associated with myHandle by using myHandle^^. If myHandle is a handle to an integer, then myHandle^^ could treated exactly as any other integer. The result of executing the statement

```
myHandle^^ := 23;
```

could be presented graphically in the figure below.

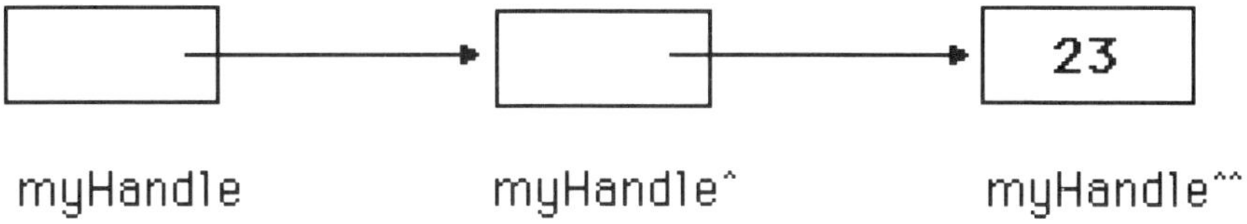

Figure 10-13. Using Handles

Here is a simple program that uses a handle:

```
program HandleDemo;
uses
   MemTypes, QuickDraw, OsIntf;
type
   IntPointer  = ^Integer;
   IntHandle   = ^IntPointer;
var
   myHandle    : IntHandle;
begin
   myHandle := IntHandle (NewHandle(sizeof(Integer)));
   myHandle^^ := 23;
   write('myHandle^^ = ',myHandle^^);
   DisposHandle(Handle(myHandle));
   Writeln;
   Writeln('Press <Ret> to continue : ');
   Readln;
end.
```

This program, as expected, prints out the number 23. There is, however, an additional point worth noting about this program. To use the Macintosh Memory Manager routines, we must include the Uses statement in the second line of the program. The unit OsIntf contains the declaration for Memory Manager routines such as NewHandle and DisposHandle. We must also use MemTypes and QuickDraw because routines in OsIntf refer to declarations in those units.

WHY BOTHER, WHO CARES?

You may ask yourself: Why should I bother learning all this Memory Manager and handle stuff? (What is the beautiful house, etc?) The answer is a simple one. Nearly every feature that makes the Macintosh such a unique computer, such as pull-down menus, windows, QuickDraw graphics, and so on, uses the Memory Manager's handle routines to implement these features. The reason? It takes a significant amount of memory to implement a feature such as a window. Why preallocate space for a large amount of windows before a program starts? If some of those windows are never used, that vital memory space will be wasted. Dynamic allocations allow the amount of memory needed to be used.

If you intend to write programs that take advantage of these features, you should use memory management techniques that can coexist peacefully with those used by the system. If you write programs that dynamically allocate a lot of memory using pointers rather than handles, you will quickly fragment your memory into unusable portions and not be able to have applications that fully use the capability of your machine.

Only a small part of the Macintosh's Memory Manager is explored in this chapter. A detailed discussion of all memory management techniques is beyond the scope of this book. For more detail, read the Memory Manager chapter of *Inside Macintosh* or one of the other books on advanced Macintosh programming mentioned in the Bibliography.

11
Events and Event Handling

INTRODUCTION

Designers of programming languages have a particularly difficult task in implementing a language on the Macintosh. This difficulty is caused by the need to interact with the Mac's sophisticated operating environment. Some programming languages have thrown the programmers to the wolves, letting them struggle with the difficult Toolbox functions by themselves. For instance, to run even a short program, the programmer would have to learn how to open a window and how to send data to that window; a formidable task even for experienced programmers. On the other end of the spectrum are languages that superimpose a new environment on top of the Mac's. These systems have two drawbacks. First, they are implemented via interpreters, which run relatively slowly as compared with compiled languages. Second, these languages provide no way to create a double-clickable application, since the interpreter's environment is needed to run a program. Turbo Pascal finds a happy medium between these two ends of this spectrum. Turbo allows the programmer to easily produce a double-clickable application and provides the convenient console window to use with that application. For those developing true Macintosh applications, Turbo provides easy access to the Toolbox routines needed.

This chapter will lead you on the long road of producing true Macintosh applications by covering the fundamentals of producing a Macintosh application and by introducing the use of pull-down menus.

EVENTS

Question: What do the following things have in common—the 1984 Summer Olympics in Los Angeles, the fifth game of the American League Playoffs in 1976 between the Yankees and the Kansas City Royals, and the last click of the mouse button on your Macintosh? The answer: They were all great events. An *event* is the term used for any external stimulus to which a program might wish to respond. Examples of events include clicking the mouse button, typing a key, and inserting a disk into the disk drive. One of the most basic features of a Macintosh application is that it is event driven—that is, the program's main task is to wait for an event to happen and then respond to it. In a sense, this is what programs that run on a brand X computer do also, except there are differences. A brand X computer is designed only to accept one type of input, typing on a keyboard. Its hardware doesn't support a mouse, can't tell if a disk has been placed in a disk drive, and certainly doesn't support windowing. However, on the Mac several different types of input can be accepted simultaneously. Macintosh programs had to be designed differently from programs on other computers, and the way programs would be designed needed to be considered before the hardware was built so that the hardware could support the software and not the other way around.

THE TOOLBOX MANAGERS

The Macintosh's User Interface Toolbox contains the routines necessary to implement all the features of the Macintosh you have no doubt already become aware of. All that is necessary to implement menus, fonts, windows, text editing, dialog boxes, and the like is available for the programmer's use. The Toolbox is logically divided into a series of managers, with each manager containing a set of routines that work in concert to implement a particular feature. Windows are implemented with the Window Manager, menus with the Menu Manager, and so on. Together, all the managers interact with each other to produce a Macintosh application. The key that ties all the User Interface features together is the Event Manager, which contains the routines necessary for the handling of events. Luckily, all the Toolbox routines were designed in Pascal (although they were later rewritten in 68000 assembly language), so access to them from Turbo is straightforward. This is not the case with both other Pascal systems and the C programming language.

To help understand what events are and what their significance is to Macintosh programming, consider the following transcript of a lesson overheard between a master Macintosh teacher and his neophyte student.

Teacher: Now, my student, you have read the Event Manager section of *Inside Macintosh*, have you not?

Student : Yes, I have.

Teacher : Good, now we can proceed with this most important lesson. What is an event?

Student : An event is a certain type of external happening that the Macintosh responds to.

Teacher : What type of happening do you mean?

Student : Most anything that a user might do.

Teacher : Most anything?

Student : Most anything at the Macintosh, depressing the mouse button, releasing the mouse button, inserting a disk, clicking on a window.

Teacher : How about the keyboard?

Student : Yes, I was just getting to that, hitting a key on the keyboard and releasing that, too.

Teacher : How does a program know that an event has happened?

Student : The Mac maintains a long chain of events that have occurred.

Teacher : Then let's start at the beginning of that chain.

Student : This is a very hard lesson, my teacher.

Teacher : The most important lessons are the hardest to learn, my son. Go on.

Student : When the event happens, the Macintosh's hardware is the first to know about it. It senses it electronically and then sends a message to the operating system, which then responds.

Teacher : I see, go on.

Student : The operating system then collects all the important information about the state of the machine at the time of the event and prepares that in a form the program that is running can use.

Teacher : So you are saying that when the program is running, the operating system is also running?

Student : I think so, I think that it is hanging out in a waiting state until an event happens, and then it suspends the program that is running for a very small fraction of a second to handle the event. I'm not sure, but I think that this is what is called an interrupt on other computers.

Teacher : Yes, you are correct, this is what is called an interrupt, and the process you described is what is known as interrupt handling. Now, what is it that is done with this information collected about the event; how is the program notified about the occurrence of the event?

Student : I'm not quite sure that I understand that correctly, I just read it last night, and *Inside Macintosh* is a hard book to understand.

Teacher : Well, my student, where are we right now?

Student : We are sitting under a tree here on the Queens College campus.

Teacher : And what time is it?

Student : I don't know. I will have to check my watch.

(The student, knowing the ways of the master teacher, does not check his watch until he is told to, for he already knows that's where the lesson will lie.)

Teacher : Have things happened in the world since we have been sitting under this old oak?

Student : They surely have.

Teacher : Have wars continued to be fought, have politicians made great speeches, have the Mets scored runs?

Student : I don't know, I would have to look at a newspaper or turn on the radio.

Teacher : So although these events have occurred, we cannot know about them until we inquire about them.

Student : This is correct.

(The student now realizes his watch had nothing to do with this lesson, and he feels badly that once again he did not fully understand the ways of the master. Still, he has come very far.)

Teacher : Now, what does this remind you of?

Student : Of course, the events continue to happen and the operating system continues to line up the information about them until the program requests that information.

Teacher : Very good, my student, you have learned this lesson well.

This dialogue might help to provide some of the conceptual framework for events and event handling. Let's run through the chain of events that occurs when an event happens.

The Macintosh actually contains two different Event Managers, the low-level Operating System Event Manager, which handles the interaction with the hardware and posts the event on an event queue, and the Toolbox Event Manager, which interfaces with programs.

Let's follow the sequence of event handling.

1. The user causes an event to occur by depressing the mouse button.

2. The Operating System (low-level) Event Manager learns of the event through the hardware and springs into action. It collects the pertinent information associated with the event, such as the position of the mouse, the time the event happened, and other event-specific information, and posts this on a list of events that have already occurred, called the *event queue.*

3. The program, via the Toolbox Event Manager, requests information about events that have occurred and then processes those events.

EVENT TYPES

There are several categories of events that can occur on the Macintosh.

Mouse—There are separate events generated when the mouse button is depressed and when the button is released. Just moving the mouse around does not generate an event.

Keyboard—There are separate events generated when a key is pressed, when it is released, and when a key is held down for a period of time, indicating an auto repeat is desired for that key.

Disk—An event is generated when a disk is inserted into a disk drive.

Network—A network event can be generated via AppleTalk.

Window—There are events generated when a window is made active and when it needs to be updated.

Application—There are four event types reserved for programmers to define their own categories of events, although the Toolbox does little to help with the management of these events.

Each type of event has its own event code (Table 11-1).

Table 11-1. Event Codes

Event Type	Event Code
nullEvent	0
mouseDown	1
mouseUp	2
keyDown	3
keyUp	4
autoKey	5
updateEvt	6
diskEvt	7
activateEvt	8
networkEvt	10
driverEvt	11
app1Evt	12
app3Evt	13
app3Evt	14
app4Evt	15

These values are used so often that they have been predefined as constants and can be used in your program as though you included the following Const definition in your program:

```
const
  nullEvent = 0;
  mouseDown = 1;
  mouseUp = 2;
  keyDown = 3;
  keyUp = 4;
  autoKey = 5;
  updateEvt = 6;
  diskEvt = 7;
  activateEvt = 8;
  networkEvt = 10;
```

```
driverEvt = 11;
app1Evt = 12;
app3Evt = 13;
app3Evt = 14;
app4Evt = 15;
```

The Event Queue

The event queue is a list of events maintained by the Operating System Event Manager. When an event occurs the event record is posted on the event queue. Programs can then use the routines provided by the Toolbox Event Manager to check the queue and remove certain events.

Figure 11-1. The Event Queue

Event Records

For each event that occurs, a record is posted to the event queue containing information on the event. The type of the event records is predefined as:

```
type
 EventRecord = record
   What : Integer;
   Message : LongInt;
   When : LongInt;
   Where : Point;
   Modifiers : Integer
  end;
```

Each field of an event record has the following meaning:

What—The What field contains the event code for the event as defined above.

Message—The Message field contains an event-specific event message, which differs for each type of event (Table 11-2).

Table 11-2. Event-Specific Messages

Event Type	Event Message
Keyboard	The character code and key code of the key
Activate, update	Pointer to the window
Mouse-up, Mouse-down and null	No meaning
Application	Whatever you desire

The event codes will be looked at in more detail when we analyze keyboard events.

When—The When field contains a LongInt representing the time the event occurred, expressed in ticks since system start-up.

Where—The Where field contains the mouse position at the time of the event, expressed as a point in global coordinates.

Modifiers—The Modifiers field contains information regarding the state of the Options, Caps Lock, Shift, and Command keys at the time of the event, as well as whether the mouse button was up or down. This will be looked at further when we analyze keyboard events in detail.

Mouse Events and an Event Loop

Now we are finally ready to develop a short event-driven program. As was noted before, there are two type of mouse events: buttonDown and buttonUp. Each time the mouse button is clicked, two events are generated and their event records placed on the event queue. Events are removed from the event queue with the GetNextEvent function from the Toolbox Event Manager. GetNextEvent is defined as follows:

```
    function GetNextEvent(eventMask : Integer; var
theEvent : EventRecord) : Boolean;
```

GetNextEvent searches the event queue for any events matching the event mask passed as a parameter; if one exists, it returns that event record as a variable parameter. The value of the function itself is a Boolean, True if an event of the type desired is found, False otherwise. If an event is found, it is removed from the event queue.

Event Masks

Each type of event has a specific mask assigned to it for use in GetNextEvent. The event masks are shown in Table 11-3.

Table 11-3. Event Masks

Event Type	Event Mask
mouseDown	2
mouseUp	4
keyDown	8
keyUp	16
autoKey	32
updateEvt	64
diskEvt	128
activateEvt	256
networkEvt	1024
driverEvt	2048
app1Evt	4096
app3Evt	8192
app3Evt	16384
app4Evt	-32768

The masks have also been predefined as constants and can be used in your program as though they were defined as

```
const
 MDownMask = 2;
 mouseUp = 4;
 keyDown = 8;
 keyUp = 16;
 autoKey = 32;
 updateEvt = 64;
 diskEvt = 128;
 activateEvt = 256;
 networkEvt = 1024;
 driverEvt = 2048;
```

```
 app1Evt = 4096;
 app2Evt = 8192;
 app3Evt = 16384;
 app4Evt = -32768;
```

There is also a constant declared for all events:

```
const
 everyEvent = -1;
```

Notice that all the constants are a power of two, arranged so that two of the constant values can be added together to produce a unique mask. To find the proper mask, you can add together the masks for the desired event types. For example, to trap all the keyboard events, you can use

```
keyDownMask+keyUpMask+autoKeyMask
```

To trap all events except mouse events, you could use

```
everyEvent - mDownMask - mUpMask
```

To trap the mouseDown and mouseUp events, we need to add both of these mask values together. This can be represented in decimal as 6, or as the sum of the two constants mDownMask + mUpMask. We are now ready to build our first event loop. An event loop, which in this case will be built with a While, continually calls GetNextEvent until a mouse event is detected.

```
program MouseEventDemo1;
uses MemTypes, QuickDraw,OSIntF,ToolIntF;
var
 myEvent : EventRecord;
begin
 while not(GetNextEvent(mDownMask+mUpMask,myEvent)) do
  Writeln('Waiting for a mouse event...');
 Readln
end.
```

MouseDemo1 is probably the simplest event-driven program you can write, yet conceptually it may be the most sophisticated program presented in this book so far. The only variable declared in the program is myEvent, an EventRecord. Note that there is no need to define the type EventRecord; this is included in the ToolIntF unit. The While loop will continually print the 'Waiting for a mouse event . . . ' message until the button is either pressed or released. At that point, the GetNextEvent will find the mouse event posted in the event queue and return it in myEvent. The program ends with our standard Readln.

We can develop this program slightly by adding a procedure that will analyze the type of mouse event that occurred.

```
program MouseEventDemo2;
uses MemTypes, QuickDraw,OSIntF,ToolIntF;
var
 myEvent : EventRecord;
procedure DoMouseEvent;
begin
 case myEvent.What of
  1: Writeln('A mouse down');
  2 : Writeln('A mouse up')
 end
end;
begin {Main program}
 while not(GetNextEvent(mDownMask+mUpMask,myEvent)) do
  Writeln('Waiting for a mouse event . . . ');
 DoMouseEvent;
 Readln
end.
```

Now, when the mouse event happens, a call is made to DoMouseEvent, which uses a Case statement to determine which of the two types of mouse events has taken place. Notice that the labels used in the Case statement are event types, not the event mask. We could replace these with constants to make the program more self-explanatory.

```
program MouseEventDemo3;
uses MemTypes, QuickDraw,OSIntF,ToolIntF;
var
 myEvent : EventRecord;
procedure DoMouseEvent;
begin
 case myEvent.What of
  mouseDown: Writeln('A mouse down');
  mouseUp : Writeln('A mouse up')
 end
```

```
end;
begin {Main program}
 while not(GetNextEvent(mDownMask+mUpMask,myEvent)) do
  Writeln('Waiting for a mouse event...');
 DoMouseEvent;
 Readln
end.
```

One last version of the program can be used to display the information in the event record by printing it in the DoMouseEvent procedure.

```
program MouseEventDemo4;
uses MemTypes, QuickDraw,OSIntF,ToolIntF;
var
 myEvent : EventRecord;
procedure DoMouseEvent;
begin
 case myEvent.What of
  mouseDown: Writeln('A mouse down');
  mouseUp : Writeln('A mouse up')
 end;
 with myEvent do
 begin
  writeln(What);
  writeln(Where.h:4, where.v:4);
  writeln(When)
 end;
end;
begin
 while not(GetNextEvent(mDownMask+MUpMask,myEvent)) do
  Writeln('Waiting for a mouse event...');
 DoMouseEvent;
Readln
end.
```

Keyboard Events

The next set of events to examine in detail are the keyboard events. As you can recall, there are three different keyboard events: keyUp, keyDown, and autoKey. The keyboard events are slightly more complex to process since there are so many keys on the keyboard compared to the one lonely mouse button. The information regarding which key has been pressed is in the Message field of the event record. We may also be interested in the Modifier field, which will tell us about the state of the modifier keys at the time of the event.

The Message field of the event record is a LongInt that encodes two separate pieces of information regarding which key caused the event.

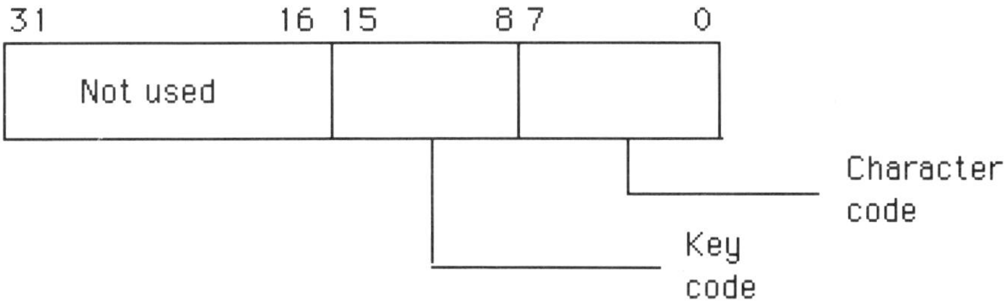

Figure 11-2. Event Messages for Keyboard Events

As you can see from Figure 11-2, the leftmost 16-bit word of the LongInt contains no information at all. The rightmost word holds both the key code for the key and the character code for the key. The key code is an integer representing the key on the keyboard that was pressed or released. The key code for each of the keys on the keyboard and the numeric key pad are as follows:

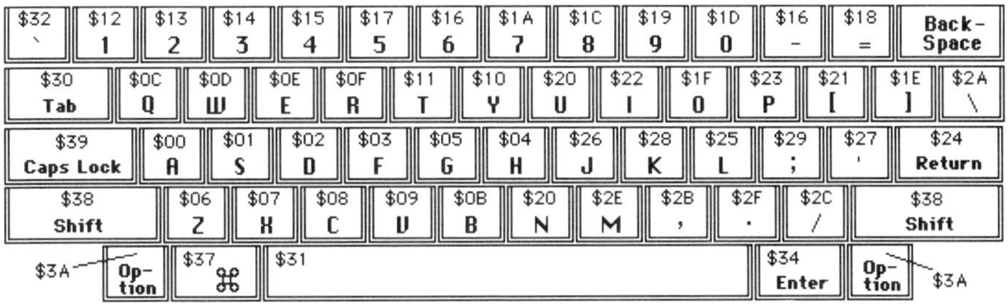

Figure 11-3. Key Codes

The key Codes for a key remain the same even if a modifier key such as the Shift key is used. This is designed for use in programs where the keyboard is logically redefined for such use as a muscial keyboard, video game controls, or Dvorak keyboard.

The character code is the Extended ASCII code for the character. The ASCII codes for all the characters are listed in Appendix J.

If the key code and character code are held in two bytes of the same word, how do you differentiate them? The easiest way to accomplish this is to use Turbo's built-in functions Hi, Lo, HiWord, and LoWord. The Hi function returns the value of the rightmost byte of an integer, and the Lo function returns the value of the leftmost byte. All we have to do is isolate the leftmost word of the LongInt and then apply the Hi and Lo function to it. The HiWord and LoWord functions are analogous to Hi and Lo, except that they operate on a LongInt and return the value of the leftmost and rightmost word. Table 11-4 is a summary:

Table 11-4. Summary of Built-In Key Code Functions

Function	Argument	Returns
HiWord	LongInt	The leftmost word of the LongInt
LoWord	LongInt	The rightmost word of the LongInt
Hi	Integer	The leftmost byte of the integer
Lo	Integer	The rightmost byte of the integer

To find the key code, we isolate the rightmost word and then the leftmost byte of that word.

```
Hi(LoWord(myEvent.Message))
```

The character code can be found in a similar fashion.

```
Lo(HiWord(myEvent.Message))
```

Now that we know how to trap key events and how to determine what key has been used, we can adapt the event-driven program to find and remove key events from the event queue, as well as the mouse events.

Listing 11-1. Program That Finds Key Events.

```
program EventDemo5;
uses MemTypes, QuickDraw,OSIntF,ToolIntF;
var
```

```
  myEvent : EventRecord;
  Mask : Integer;
 procedure DoEvent;
 begin
  case myEvent.What of
   mouseDown: Writeln('A mouse down');
   mouseUp : Writeln('A mouse up');
   keyDown : Writeln('A key down');
   keyUp : Writeln('A key up');
   autoKey : Writeln('An auto key')
  end;
  with myEvent do
  begin
   writeln(What);
   writeln(Where.h:4, where.v:4);
   writeln(When);
   writeln(LoWord(Hi(Message)):4,LoWord(Lo(Message)):4)
  end;
 end;
 begin
  Mask := mDownMask+mUpMask+keyDownMask+keyUpMask
    +autoKeyMask;
  while not(GetNextEvent(Mask,myEvent)) do
   Writeln('Waiting for a mouse event...');
 DoEvent;
 Readln
 end.
```

This program is essentially the same as the earlier versions except that the Message field information is also displayed.

Listing 11-2. Program That Displays Message Events

```
 program EventDemo5;
 uses MemTypes, QuickDraw,OSIntF,ToolIntF;
 var
  myEvent : EventRecord;
  Mask : Integer;
  StopRect : Rect;
  StopFlag : Boolean;
 procedure DoEvent;
 begin
  case myEvent.What of
   mouseDown:
    begin
     GlobaltoLocal(myEvent.Where);
     if ptinRect(myEvent.Where,StopRect)
```

```
      then StopFlag := True
    end;
   mouseUp : Writeln('A mouse up');
   keyDown : Writeln('A key down');
   keyUp : Writeln('A key up');
   autoKey : Writeln('An auto key');
  end;
  with myEvent do
  begin
   writeln(What);
   writeln(Where.h:4, where.v:4);
   writeln(When);
   writeln(LoWord(Hi(Message)):4,LoWord(Lo(Message)):4)
  end;
 end;
 begin
  StopFlag := False;
  SetRect(StopRect, 40,40,70,70);
  FrameRect(StopRect);
  Mask := mDownMask+mUpMask+keyDownMask+keyUpMask
    +autoKeyMask;
  repeat
   if GetNextEvent(Mask,myEvent) then DoEvent;
  until StopFlag;
 end.
```

Our new version of the program has some major structural changes in it. First, the While loop has been replaced by a Repeat loop terminating when a Boolean, StopFlag, becomes True. The Boolean is set when the mouse is clicked inside a rectangle, StopRect, displayed on the screen. All events returned by GetNextEvent are sent to the procedure DoEvent for processing. When a mouseDown is uncovered, the procedure checks the location of the mouse to see if it is in the rectangle.

```
case myEvent.What of
mouseDown:
 begin
  GlobaltoLocal(myEvent.Where);
  if ptinRect(myEvent.Where,StopRect)
   then StopFlag := True
 end;
```

Note that the ptinRect function needs a point specified in local coordinates so that the call to GlobaltoLocal is necessitated.

Listing 11-3. New Version of the Program in Listing 11-1.

```
program EventDemo7;
uses MemTypes, QuickDraw,OSIntF,ToolIntF;
var
 myEvent : EventRecord;
 Mask : Integer;
 StopRect : Rect;
 StopFlag : Boolean;
 Str : string;
 Ch : Char;
procedure DoEvent;
begin
 case myEvent.What of
 mouseDown:
 begin
  GlobaltoLocal(myEvent.Where);
  if ptinRect(myEvent.Where,StopRect)
   then StopFlag := True
  end;
 keyDown :
  begin
   Ch := Chr(Lo(LoWord(myEvent.Message)));
   Str := Str + Ch;
  end
 end
end;
{---------------------}
begin
 StopFlag := False;
 SetRect(StopRect, 40,40,70,70);
 FrameRect(StopRect);
 Mask := mDownMask+mUpMask+keyDownMask+keyUpMask
   +autoKeyMask;
 repeat
  if GetNextEvent(Mask,myEvent) then DoEvent;
 until StopFlag;
 Write('The string is ',str);
 Readln
end.
```

Keyboard Modifiers

The Modifier field of the event record indicates the state of the keyboard's modifier keys (Shift, Option, Command) at the time of the event. This can be used, for instance, to check if the Shift key is held down during a mouse click. Figure 11-4 diagrams the modifier flags.

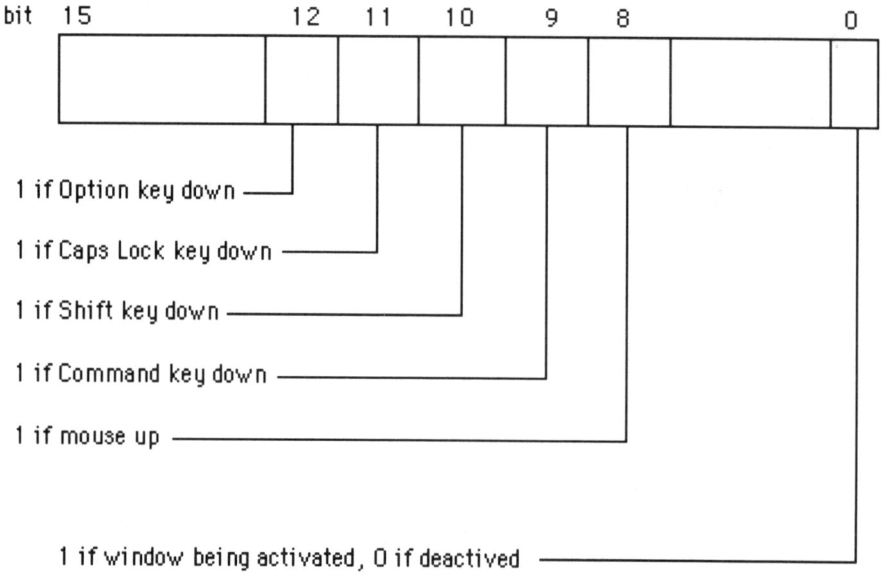

Figure 11-4. Modifier Keys

The following predefined constants can be helpful for determining the state of the modifier flags.

```
const
 activeFlag = -1 ; {Set if window is active}
 btnState = 128; {Set if mouse button is up}
 cmdKey = 256; {Set if Command key down}
 shiftKey = 512; {Set if Shift key down}
 alphaLock = 1024; {Set if Caps Lock key down}
 optionKey = 2048; {Set if Option key down}
```

These masks can be used with the And operator to determine the state of the keys you are interested in and the way event masks where checked.

PULL-DOWN MENUS

Now that we have some sense of how events operate, we can turn to the Menu Manager to implement a program using pull-down menus. The Menu Manager contains around 30 procedures and functions used to initialize, display, alter menus, and handle menu selection by the user. But before we can start implementing a program using menus, we must first examine the basic components of menus.

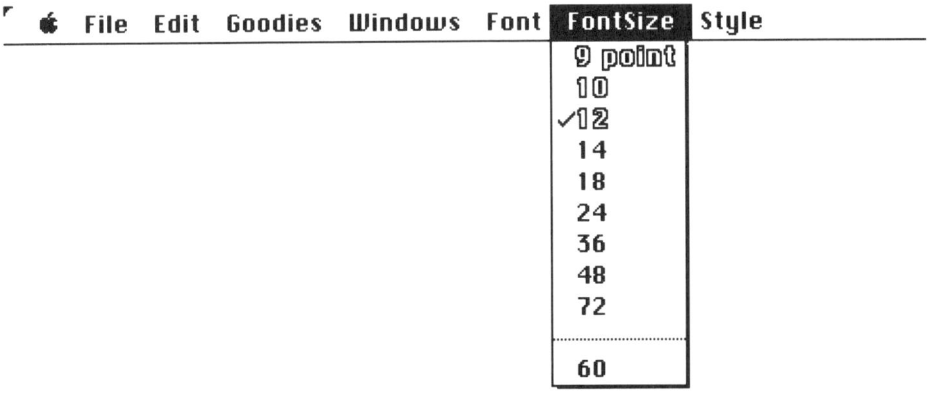

Figure 11-5. The Menu Bar and a Menu

Each menu title indicates a separate menu, and a program will usually have several menus simultaneously. These are grouped together in the menu bar, which is displayed across the top 20 pixels of the screen. This is a reserved area of the screen, and nothing but the cursor can appear in it. The menu titles are always displayed in the standard systems font and size (Chicago 12). In case you have ever wondered, the maximum number of menu titles that can be displayed at any one time is 16. When a menu is pulled down, the menu items are revealed. These items can be shown as either active or inactive, indicated by a "dimming" of the item.

Each of the menus in the menu bar is represented by a record containing the pertinent information about that menu. Fortunately, the Menu Manager creates and maintains these records so that there is no need to worry about them. All the menu records of a menu bar are held in a linked list called the **menu list**.

When a Turbo program starts, there is no active menu bar, just a blank area over the console window. A program can easily create its own menu lists and work with them. When a program run from memory is terminated, it branches back to the Turbo Pascal environment, which restores its familiar menu list.

Creating Menus

The initialization and display of a menu list is done with several Menu Manager routines.

```
procedure InitMenus;
```

This procedure initializes the Menu Manager and frees space in memory for the Menu Manager to maintain the menu list. A call to this routine does not appear to be necessary if a program is run from memory (probably because Turbo previously called it), but it should be called by a program saved to disk. After a call to InitMenu, the menu list is empty.

```
function NewMenu (menuID:Integer; menuTitle:string):
        MenuHandle;
```

The NewMenu function allocates space for a new menu and returns a handle to it. All access to a menu is done through its handle; it should never be done directly even if you could figure out how. The type MenuHandle is predefined and can be used in your program as though you have included the following type definition.

```
type
 MenuPtr = ^MenuInfo
 MenuHandle = ^MenuPtr;
```

The type MenuInfo is the record holding the information about a menu referred to before.

The parameters used with a call to NewMenu are the ID number of that menu and the name of the menu. The ID number used for a menu can only be a positive number greater than zero. Negative numbers are reserved for desk accessories, which sometimes have their own menus. The menu's title is declared in a string. A typical declaration of a menu might look like this:

```
var
 Menu1 : MenuHandle;
   •
   •
 Menu1 := NewMenu(10, 'Options');
```

We have declared a variable Menu1 as a MenuHandle and then created a menu that would be titled Options. The menu Options is both empty and not yet displayed in the menu bar.

```
procedure AppendMenu (theMenu:Menuhandle; data:String);
```

The AppendMenu procedure is used to place menu items in a menu. The theMenu parameter is the handle to the menu being worked with. The data parameter contains the menu item or items to be added to the menu. To add a single item to a menu, that item is placed in a string.

```
AppendMenu(Menu2,'End');
```

Several items can be added to a menu by separating them with a semicolon in the string.

```
AppendMenu(Menu1,'Option1;Option2');
```

A dotted line can be added to separate the two items by using one of the special metacharacters available for this purpose. To create the dotted line, a single hypen (-) is used. Any text after the hypen will be ignored.

```
AppendMenu(Menu1,'Option1;-;Option2');
```

The other metacharacters used to control the appearance of the menu items are shown in Table 11-5.

Table 11-5. Metacharacters Used to Control Menu Items

Metacharacter	Meaning
!	This item has a checkmark
<	This item has a special style
/	This item has a keyboard equivalent
(	This item is diplayed disabled

Generally, menu items are displayed in the system font. This cannot be changed. However, you can vary the style the item is displayed in by using the < metacharacter along with a second code as follows:

<B	Bold
<I	Italic
<U	Underline
<O	Outline
<S	Shadow

A good example of the attributes is the MacWrite Style menu, which displays the items representing the style attributes in those attributes.

Figure 11-6. MacWrite Style Menu

```
procedure Insertmenu( theMenu : menuHandle; beforeID :
                      Integer);
```

The InsertMenu procedure takes the menu record and moves it into the menu list. All this is done by the Menu Manager; all the programmer needs to do is call the routine. The parameters are the menu to be added to the list (of course) and the menu ID of the menu in the list that this menu will be placed in front of. A menu ID value of zero will place the menu at the rightmost position in the menu list. The menu added is not shown on the screen until the menu bar is updated.

```
procedure DrawMenuBar;
```

The DrawMenuBar procedure redraws the menu bar on the screen according to the current contents of the menu list.

As an example, let's start by creating two small menus and displaying them.

```
program MenuDemo;
uses MemTypes,QuickDraw,OSIntF,ToolIntF;
var
 Menu1, Menu2 : MenuHandle;
begin
 InitMenus;
 Menu1 := NewMenu(10, 'Options');
 Menu2 := NewMenu(20, 'Stop');
 AppendMenu(Menu1,'Option1;-;Option2');
 AppendMenu(Menu2,'End');
 InsertMenu(Menu1, 0);
 InsertMenu(Menu2, 0);
 DrawMenuBar;
 Readln
end.
```

This short program declares two menus pointed to by the handles Menu1 and Menu2. Items are appended to them, they are inserted into the blank menu list (which Turbo has left empty for you), and then the program draws the menu bar.

Figure 11-7. Menu Bar Displayed by MenuDemo

If you run this program, you will see the menus we defined, but you will be disappointed. The menus will not respond to the mouse clicks. This is because we have not included in the program the mechanism to identify a mouse click in the menu bar and then respond to it. This is the next enhancement to our program.

We now need to do several tasks. First, we must be able to identify when a mouseDown event occurs in the menu bar. Once we know that a mouseDown has occurred, the Menu Manager contains a mechanism for tracking the mouse and returning a code indicating which menu item has been selected by the user.

In order to help process a mouse down event and determine whether it was in the menu bar, the Toolbox contains a function that determines in relative terms where the cursor was located at the time of the event.

```
function FindWindow(thePt:Point; Var whichWindow:
                    WindowPtr):Integer;
```

The FindWindow function takes one parameter, thePt, which is the location of the cursor at the time of the event (taken from the event record). It then returns a code based upon the location of the cursor. For instance, it returns 1 if the location was in the menu bar, 2 if it was in a system window (desk accessory), and so on. If the cursor was in a window, the pointer to that window will be passed in the whichWindow parameter, which as you can see is a variable parameter used in a function (a rarity in Pascal).

We need not have used FindWindow for this task. We could also have defined a rectangle that coincides with the menu bar and then used ptinRect to check the location of the mouse click.

If the mouseDown event occurred in the menu bar, it must then be tracked with the MenuSelect function.

```
function MenuSelect (startPt : Point) : LongInt;
```

The MenuSelect function does most of the work of handling menus. Once the function is called with the position of the mouse down event, it keeps control of the program until the mouse button is released. This means that the function pulls down the menu and highlights the options as the mouse is moved. When the mouse button is released, MenuSelect returns a LongInt holding both the menu ID and the item number of the menu item selected. The menu ID is in the high order of the LongInt and the item number is in the low-order word. If the mouse button was not released over an enables menu item, zero is returned.

To implement our new features to the MenuDemo program, we need to change the program to use an event loop. For clarity's sake, the menu initialization routines have been moved into a procedure. When a menu item is selected, the program returns the menu ID and the menu item's number.

Listing 11-4. Menu Demo Program That Uses an Event Loop.

```
program MenuDemo2;
uses MemTypes, QuickDraw,OSIntF,ToolIntF;
var
 Menu1, Menu2 : MenuHandle;
 myEvent : EventRecord;
 WhereClick : Integer;
 whichWindow : windowPtr;
 doneFlag : Boolean;
 Choosen : LongInt;
procedure InitMyMenus;
 begin
  InitMenus;
  Menu1 := NewMenu(10, 'Options');
  Menu2 := NewMenu(20, 'Stop');
  AppendMenu(Menu1,'Option1;-;Option2');
  AppendMenu(Menu2,'End');
  InsertMenu(Menu1, 0);
  InsertMenu(Menu2, 0);
  DrawMenuBar
 end;
begin
 InitMyMenus;
 doneFlag := False;
 repeat
  if GetNextEvent(everyEvent,myEvent) then
  case myEvent.what of
  mouseDown :
   begin
    WhereClick := FindWindow(myEvent.where,
      whichWindow);
    if WhereClick = 1 then
    begin
     Choosen := MenuSelect(myEvent.where);
```

```
      writeln('Menu ID',HiWord(Choosen):4,
        'Item number'
      LoWord(Choosen):4);
      doneFlag := True;
     end;
    end
   end;
  until doneFlag;
 Readln
 end.
```

We can now jazz up our program a bit by adding some functionality behind the menu option. The following program works as a calculator with two functions, addition and subtraction, listed as items on one menu and the "end" option in the second menu. The program is structured in a way more similar to most Macintosh applications. When an event occurs, it is checked to see if it is a mouse down. FindWindow is then called to see if the event is in the menu bar, and then, finally, MenuSelect is called to track the event. The value returned by MenuSelect is passed as a parameter to a procedure that processes the particular menu options. As you can see, the size of a program using any of the User Interface features grows very quickly.

Listing 11-5. Program That Works As a Calculator.

```
 program MenuCalculator;
 uses MemTypes, QuickDraw,OSIntF,ToolIntF;
 var
  Menu1, Menu2 : MenuHandle;
  myEvent : EventRecord;
  WhereClick, Sum, Num : Integer;
  whichWindow : windowPtr;
  doneFlag : Boolean;
  Choosen : LongInt;
 procedure InitMyMenus;
  begin
   InitMenus;
   Menu1 := NewMenu(10, 'Options');
   Menu2 := NewMenu(20, 'Stop');
   AppendMenu(Menu1,'Add;-;Subtract');
   AppendMenu(Menu2,'End');
   InsertMenu(Menu1, 0);
   InsertMenu(Menu2, 0);
   DrawMenuBar
  end;
```

```
 procedure DoCommand(Command : LongInt);
 var
  Menu, Item : Integer;
 begin
  Menu := Hiword(Command);
  Item := Loword(Command);
  case Menu of
   10 : begin
          if Item = 1 then
           begin
            Write('Enter value -->');
            Readln(Num);
            Sum := Sum + Num;
            Writeln('The current sum is', Sum:4)
           end;
          if Item = 3 then
           begin
            Write('Enter value -->');
            Readln(Num);
            Sum := Sum - Num;
            Writeln('The current sum is', Sum:4)
          end;
        end;
  20 :begin
       Write('The sum is', sum:6);
       doneFlag := True
      end
    end
  end ;
begin
 InitMyMenus;
 FlushEvents(everyEvent,0);
 doneFlag := False;
 Sum := 0;
 Writeln('Macintosh Calculator');
 Writeln;
 Write('Enter value -->');
 Readln(Num);
 Sum := Num;
 repeat
  if GetNextEvent(everyEvent,myEvent) then
   case myEvent.what of
   mouseDown :
    begin
     WhereClick := FindWindow(myEvent.where,
       whichWindow);
     if WhereClick = 1 then
      begin
```

```
         Choosen := MenuSelect(myEvent.where);
         DoCommand(Choosen);
        end
    end
  end;
until doneFlag;
Readln
end.
```

After running this program, you may notice that the title of the menu selected stays highlighted until another menu is selected. It is up to the programmer to cancel the highlighting with the HiLiteMenu procedure.

```
procedure HiLiteMenu (menuID : Integer);
```

The HiLiteMenu procedure highlights the title of the menu whose ID is passed as a parameter. If a menu ID of 0 is used, HiLiteMenu unhighlights any currently highlighted menu.

SWAPPING MENU BARS

Occasionally you will create programs that will use two or more different menu bars. This can be easily accomplished with the help of a few of the Menu Manager's routines.

```
function GetMenuBar : Handle;
```

The GetMenuBar function creates a copy of the current menu bar and then returns a handle to it.

```
procedure SetMenuBar (menuList : Handle);
```

The SetMenuBar procedure copies the menu list pointed to by the handle given to the current menu list.

```
procedure ClearMenuBar;
```

The ClearMenuBar procedure removes all menus from the menu list so that a new menu can be started.

These three routines, along with DrawMenuBar, are used to swap the menu displayed. The program SwapMenus presented next starts by initializing two menu lists. This is a tricky technique because only one menu list can be built at any one time. Once the first menu list is built with NewMenu, AppendMenu, and InsertMenu, a handle to a copy of that menu list is created with GetMenuBar. The menu list is then cleared and the second list created and saved in the same way. The menu list is then cleared once more and the original list reinstated with SetMenuBar.

The program itself is very simple. Each menu list contains two menus. The first is used to swap to the other menu list and the second to terminate the program. The program keeps track of which menu list is displayed with the variable Which, which has a value of 1 if the first menu list is displayed and 2 if the second menu list is displayed.

Listing 11-6. Program That Swaps Menus.

```
program SwapMenus;
uses MemTypes, QuickDraw,OSIntF,ToolIntF;
var
 MenHand1, MenHand2 : Handle;
 Menu1, Menu2,Menu3, Menu4 : MenuHandle;
 myEvent : EventRecord;
 WhereClick, Which : Integer;
 whichWindow : windowPtr;
 doneFlag : Boolean;
 Choosen : LongInt;
procedure InitMyMenus;
 begin
  InitMenus; {First menu list}
  Menu1 := NewMenu(10, 'Menus');
  Menu2 := NewMenu(20, 'Stop');
  AppendMenu(Menu1,'Menu2');
  AppendMenu(Menu2,'End');
  InsertMenu(Menu1, 0);
  InsertMenu(Menu2, 0);
  MenHand1 := GetMenuBar; {Save reference to it}
  ClearMenuBar;
  Menu3 := NewMenu(10, 'Different Menus'); {Second
    menu list}
  Menu4 := NewMenu(20, 'Stop');
  AppendMenu(Menu3,'Menu1');
  AppendMenu(Menu4,'End');
  InsertMenu(Menu3, 0);
```

```
  InsertMenu(Menu4, 0);
  MenHand2 := GetMenuBar; {Save reference to it}
  ClearMenuBar;
  SetMenuBar(MenHand1); {Restore first menu list}
  DrawMenuBar
 end;
 procedure DoCommand(Command : LongInt);
 var
  Menu, Item : Integer;
 begin
  Menu := Hiword(Command);
  Item := Loword(Command);
  case Menu of
  10 : begin
        if Which = 1 then
         begin
           SetMenuBar(MenHand2);
           Which := 2
         end
         else
          begin
           SetMenuBar(MenHand1);
           Which := 1
          end;
        DrawMenuBar
       end;
  20 :begin
       doneFlag := True;
      end
   end;
   HiLiteMenu(0);
  end ;
 begin
  InitMyMenus;
  FlushEvents(everyEvent,0);
  doneFlag := False;
  Which := 1;
  repeat
   if GetNextEvent(everyEvent,myEvent) then
    case myEvent.what of
     mouseDown :
      begin
       WhereClick := FindWindow(myEvent.where,
         whichWindow);
       if WhereClick = 1 then
       begin
        Choosen := MenuSelect(myEvent.where);
        DoCommand(Choosen);
```

```
      end
    end
  end;
until doneFlag;
end.
```

DISPLAYING THE APPLE MENU

If you run the menu programs we have been developing, one thing might strike you as missing—that is, the apple (p) menu that lists the desk accessories. It is quite simple to interface with desk accessories so that they are available for use in any program you are developing. There are two steps to displaying the apple (p) menu. The first is the creation of a menu with the apple symbol as its title. This is quite simple. The ASCII code for the apple symbol is 14, although we can used the predefined constant appleMark instead. This code must be placed in a string. One might think that the following would work correctly, but it won't:

```
Menu1 := NewMenu(10, Chr(appleMark));
```

This won't work because it passes a single character instead of a string of length one. What's the difference? Remember that a string is stored as a record with the number of characters in the string in its first byte. The NewMenu function is looking for the string in that position, so a character will just not do. The simplest way to accomplish this is to declare a string of size 1.

```
AppTitle : string[1];
```

Assign a single blank to it and then place the appleMark in the first (and only) position of the following string:

```
AppTitle := ' ';
AppTitle[1] := chr(appleMark);
```

Finally, declare the following menu.

```
Menu1 := NewMenu(10, AppTitle);
```

Now that the menu title is set up, the more interesting question is, how do you get the names of the available desk accessories into the menu? Where do they come from? Although it might sound difficult to do this, it is really quite easily performed. As you probably know from using the FontMover utility, desk accessories are stored as resources in the System File. A Menu Manager routine is used to look in the System File, find the available desk accessories, and insert them in the menu.

```
procedure AddResMenu (theMenu : MenuHandle; theType :
                      ResType);
```

The AddResMenu procedure searches the System File (and other open resource files) for resources of type theType and appends any found to the given menu. Desk accessories are stored with a ResType of 'DRVR.' The following procedure call sets up the apple menu:

```
AddResMenu(Menu1, 'DRVR');
```

The following program displays the DA menu along with our Stop menu:

Listing 11-7. Program That Displays DA Menu and Stop Menu.

```
program DADemo1;
uses MemTypes, QuickDraw,OSIntF,ToolIntF;
var
 Menu1,Menu2 : MenuHandle;
 myEvent : EventRecord;
 WhereClick: Integer;
 whichWindow : windowPtr;
 doneFlag : Boolean;
 Choosen : LongInt;
procedure InitMyMenus;
var
 AppTitle : string[1];
 begin
  InitMenus;
  AppTitle := ' ';
  AppTitle[1] := chr(appleMark);
  Menu1 := NewMenu(10, AppTitle);
  Menu2 := NewMenu(20, 'Stop');
```

```
  AddResMenu(Menu1, 'DRVR');
  AppendMenu(Menu2,'End');
  InsertMenu(Menu1, 0);
  InsertMenu(Menu2, 0);
  DrawMenuBar
 end;
 procedure DoCommand(Command : LongInt);
 var
  Menu, Item : Integer;
 begin
  Menu := Hiword(Command);
  Item := Loword(Command);
  case Menu of
   10 : begin
        end;
   20 : begin
         doneFlag := True;
         end
 end;
   HiLiteMenu(0);
 end ;
begin
 InitMyMenus;
 FlushEvents(everyEvent,0);
 doneFlag := False;
 repeat
  if GetNextEvent(everyEvent,myEvent) then
   case myEvent.what of
    mouseDown :
     begin
      WhereClick := FindWindow(myEvent.where,
        whichWindow);
      if WhereClick = 1 then
       begin
        Choosen := MenuSelect(myEvent.where);
        DoCommand(Choosen);
       end
     end
   end;
until doneFlag;
end.
```

If you run this program, you can see the list of desk accessories up on the apple menu but can't use them. It will take some more effort to be able to do this. We must be able to identify which desk accessory has been called, invoking the desk accessory, and passing mouse clicks to the DA.

When a DA has been selected from the apple menu, the program can easily find the menu and item number but needs the actual text of the item name to call the DA. This is not a problem when a program sets up the menu, but the program does not know which DAs are in the System File. Fortunately, the Toolbox contains a routine for this task.

```
procedure GetItem (theMenu : MenuHandle; item :
                   Integer; v itemString);
```

The GetItem procedure returns as a variable parameter the text of the menu item described by theMenu and item.

Once the text of the item has been found, it can be used to call the desk accessory.

```
function OpenDeskAcc (theAcc : string) : Integer;
```

The OpenDeskAcc function reads the desk accessory having the name given in theAcc and displays it as the active window.

Once the DA is opened, mouse clicks must be passed down to it. When a mouse down occurs in a window belonging to a DA (called the system window), the FindWindow function will return the appropriate code. At that point a call should be made to SystemClick.

```
procedure SystemClick (theEvent : EventRecord;
                       theWindow : WindowPtr);
```

The SystemClick procedure is part of the Desk Manager, which is responsible for handling desk accessories. SystemClick sends the mouse down event to the DA if the system window is active or makes it the active window if it isn't.

THE SYSTEM TASK PROCEDURE

```
procedure SystemTask;
```

The SystemTask procedure causes each open desk accessory to perform any periodic action it was designed to do, such as update a clock. The SystemTask procedure needs to be called at least every 1/60 of a second. This is best done by placing it in the main event loop of the program.

Here is the DADemo program fully able to activate desk accessories. It still has some shortcomings, however. For instance, it doesn't support cut and paste operations. The structure of the program is substantially similar to the earlier version except that a second Case statement has been added to work with the results of FindWindow.

Listing 11-8. Program That Activates Desk Accessories.

```
program DADemo2;
 uses MemTypes, QuickDraw,OSIntF,ToolIntF;
var
 Menu1,Menu2 : MenuHandle;
 myEvent : EventRecord;
 WhereClick: Integer;
 whichWindow : windowPtr;
 doneFlag : Boolean;
 Choosen : LongInt;
 DAName : string;
procedure InitMyMenus;
var
 AppTitle : string[1];
 begin
  InitMenus;
  AppTitle := ' ';
  AppTitle[1] := chr(appleMark);
  Menu1 := NewMenu(10, AppTitle);
  Menu2 := NewMenu(20, 'Stop');
  AddresMenu(Menu1, 'DRVR');
  AppendMenu(Menu2,'End');
  InsertMenu(Menu1, 0);
  InsertMenu(Menu2, 0);
  DrawMenuBar
 end;
 procedure DoCommand(Command : LongInt);
 var
  Menu, Item, Temp : Integer;
 begin
  Menu := Hiword(Command);
  Item := Loword(Command);
  case Menu of
   10 : begin
          GetItem(Menu1,Item,DAName);
```

```
          Temp := OpenDeskAcc(DAName);
        end;
   20 : doneFlag := True;
  end; {Case}
   HiLiteMenu(0);
  end ;
 begin
  InitMyMenus;
  FlushEvents(everyEvent,0);
  doneFlag := False;
  repeat
   SystemTask;
   if GetNextEvent(everyEvent,myEvent) then
    case myEvent.what of
     mouseDown :
      begin
       WhereClick := FindWindow(myEvent.where,
         whichWindow);
       case WhereClick of
        inMenuBar:
         begin
          Choosen := MenuSelect(myEvent.where);
          DoCommand(Chosen);
         end;
        inSysWindow :
          SystemClick(myEvent, whichWindow);
       end {Case}
     end {Case}
  end; {If}
 until doneFlag;
 end.
```

MISCELLANEOUS MENU ROUTINES

Following are a number of additional Menu Manager routines that can be used to embellish your programs. Each is relatively straightforward if you have followed the previous examples.

```
procedure DisposeMenu (theMenu : MenuHandle);
```

The DisposeMenu procedure is used to release the memory allocated by a call to NewMenu. It should be used to discard temporary menus not being used since the memory allocated is being wasted.

```
procedure DeleteMenu (menuID : Integer);
```

The DeleteMenu procedure deletes a menu from the menu list but does not release the memory it occupied. If there is no menu with the given menu ID, DeleteMenu has no effect.

```
procedure SetItem (theMenu : MenuHandle; item : Integer;
                   itemString : string);
```

The SetItem procedure changes the text of the given menu item to itemString. The procedure does not recognize the metacharacters used in AppendMenu. This procedure is useful to swap between two alternative menu choices such as Show Window and Hide Window.

```
procedure DisableItem (theMenu : MenuHandle; item :
                       Integer);
```

The DisableItem procedure dims the given menu item so that it cannot be selected by the user. To disable an entire menu, pass a value of zero for the item.

```
procedure EnableItem (theMenu : MenuHandle; item :
                      Integer);
```

The EnableItem procedure performs the opposite function to DiableItem, enabling the given menu item. To enable an entire diabled menu, pass a value of 0 for the item.

```
procedure CheckItem (theMenu : MenuHandle; item :
                     Integer; checked : Boolean);
```

The CheckItem procedure places or removes a checkmark at the left of the given menu. After a call to CheckItem with checked=True, a checkmark will appear each subsequent time the menu is pulled down. A value of False removes the checkmark.

```
procedure SetItemMark (theMenu : MenuHandle; item :
                       Integer; markChar : Char);
```

The SetItemMark procedure works with CheckItem by describing what to display left of the menu item. Any character in the system font can be used. The following predefined values are useful as parameters to SetItemMark:

```
const
 noMark = 0 ; {NUL character, to remove a mark}
 commandMark = $11; {Command key symbol}
 checkMark = $12; {The checkmark}
 diamondMark = $13; {Diamond symbol}
 appleMark = $14; {Apple symbol}
```

```
procedure GetItemMark (theMenu : MenuHandle; item :
                      Integer; var markChar : Char);
```

The GetItemMark procedure is the reciprocal of SetItemMark, returning the current checkmark in the variable parameter markChar.

```
procedure SetItemStyle (theMenu : MenuHandle; item :
                       Integer; chStyle : Style);
```

The SetItemStyle procedure changes the character style of the given menu item to chStyle. The character style is passed as a set of members of the set Style. For example, the [bold, outline] procedure has a similar effect to the use of metacharacters in AppendMenu.

```
procedure GetItemStyle (theMenu : MenuHandle; item :
                       Integer; var chStyle : Style);
```

The GetItemStyle procedure is the complement of SetItemStyle, returning the style of the menu item as a variable parameter.

```
function CountMItems (theMenu : MenuHandle) : Integer;
```

The CountMItems function returns the number of menu items in the given menu.

```
function GetMHandle (menuID : Integer) : MenuHandle;
```

The GetMHandle function returns a handle to the menu whose menu ID is given.

```
procedure FlashMenuBar (menuID : Integer);
```

The FlashMenuBar procedure inverts the title of the given menu or, if a menu ID of zero is given, the entire menu bar. Many programs use this as a visual warning to the users should the sound be turned down.

12
A Complete Macintosh Application—The TurboDraw Program

INTRODUCTION

We have reached the final chapter of the book and now are ready to drive at full speed. As a graduation present we present not a diploma, but the design and implementetion of an entire Macintosh-style application. The program, monikered "TurboDraw," is an object-oriented drawing program. In order to develop it we will introduce some new Macintosh Toolbox routines and explore some new programming techniques.

In order to develop TurboDraw we will need to combine many of the topics covered in the book. Since this will present a Macintosh-style User Intjrface, the program will implement event handling with an event loop in the main program. We will need most of our knowledge of QuickDraw to draw the various shapes and lines used by the program and will need a sophisticated data structure such as a linked list to represent the data used. The program will need to save and load data from a disk file, a concept already covered, and print graphics, a concept presented.

DRAWING PROGRAMS

There are two basic types of drawing programs, object-oriented and bit-mapped. You have probably already encountered both. To illustrate the difference between the two, think about the task of arranging furniture in a room. It is obviously easier and less tiring to move furniture around on paper than to actually carry the furniture. One possible way to model a room on paper is to draw a picture of the room and each piece of furniture in it. With this approach, if you wanted to move a desk from one wall to another, you would have to erase the desk and then redraw it someplace else on the paper. Another approach is to cut out pieces of paper the size and shape of each piece of furniture and place them into a box that models the shape of the room. Now if you wanted to move a desk from one place to another, you simply move the piece of paper representing the desk.

The first method corresponds to the bit-mapped approach to drawing. The information contained in the picture is stored in the pixels (bits) of the drawing surface. The user creates or modifies the picture by turning each pixel either on or off (black or white). The program presented in chapter 8 used this approach, as does MacPaint. Bit-mapped drawing is best used for drawing pictures and artwork.

The second method corresponds to the object-oriented approach to drawing. The information is separate from the drawing surface. The user manipulates objects such as lines, rectangles, circles, or pieces of furniture as units rather than manipulating the pixels that make up the object. This approach is used by MacDraw and is best for modeling things in the real world and representing abstract concepts graphically.

TURBODRAW

The TurboDraw program can be used for creating many different kinds of charts, including syntax diagrams, flow charts, data flow diagrams, structure charts, organizational charts, and many others. Let's start the design process by listing what we want it to do.

1. The program will be able to represent three kind of objects, rectangles, ovals, and round-cornered rectangles, to be called **nodes**.

2. The user will be able to determine the size and shape of the nodes when they are created.

3. The user will be able to create any number of nodes.

4. The user will be able to move nodes around on the screen.

5. Relationships between two nodes can be represented by a straight line connecting the two objects, called an **edge**.

6. Graphics created by the program can be printed on the printer.

7. A diagram created by the program can be saved to and loaded from disk.

The following figure shows what a chart created by the program might look like:

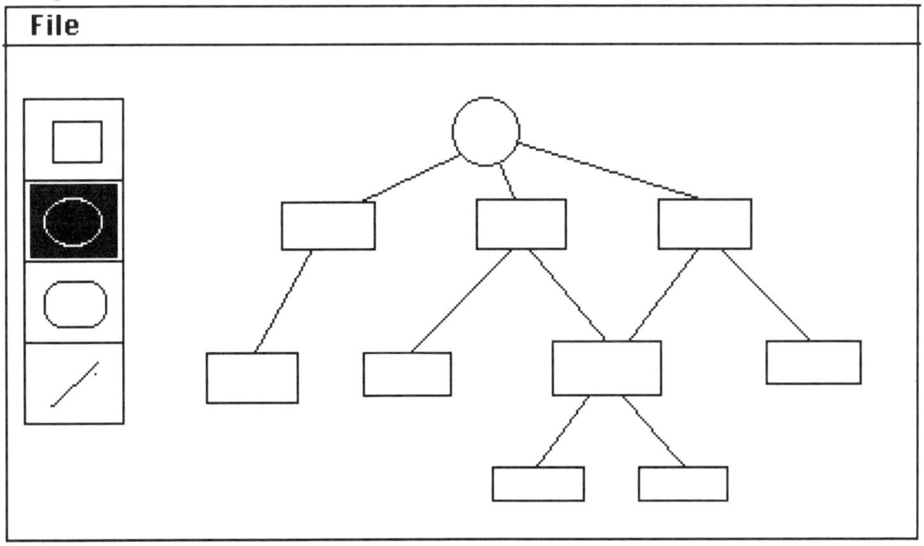

Figure 12-1. The TurboDraw User Interface

The User Interface

Now that we know what the program is going to accomplish, we must determine how the user will control the program and tell it what to do.

The program will be modeled on a metaphor of a painter's palette. On the left side of the screen there will be a palette containing the tools for drawing, each tool represented by a picture of the tool inside a rectangle. The rest of the screen will be used as the drawing surface.

The program will have eight different actions the user can take. The rules for each are as follows:

1. Select a tool.

   a. A tool can be selected by clicking in its box.

   b. When a tool is selected it will be inverted.

   c. Only one tool may be selected at any time.

   d. When a tool is selected, all other tools are unselected.

   e. When a tool is unselected its box is uninverted.

   f. Clicking on a tool that is selected unselects it.

2. Draw a node.

   a. A node can be drawn when the box, oval, or round-cornered box tools are selected.

   b. To draw a node, click on the drawing surface and hold the button down while moving the mouse until the node is the desired size. Then release the button.

3. Connect nodes.

   a. Nodes can be connected if the line tool is selected.

b. To connect two nodes, click in the first node and hold the button down while moving the mouse until the cursor is in the second node. Then release the button.

c. When two nodes are connected there will be a line drawn between them.

4. Move nodes.

a. A node can be moved when no tools are currently selected.

b. To move a node, click inside the node, then drag the node to the desired position and release the button.

c. After a node has been moved, the node and all connections at the node's previous location are erased, and the connections are redrawn at the new position.

d. If the new position of the node overlaps another node, then the node will be put back in its original position.

5. Save diagram.

a. Choose "Save" from the File menu.

b. Enter the name of the file in the standard Macintosh save dialog box.

6. Load diagram.

a. Choose "Load" from the File menu.

b. Select the name of the file to load from the standard Macintosh load dialog box.

7. Print diagram.

a. Choose "Print" from the File menu.

b. Fill out the standard Macintosh print dialog box.

8. Quit program.

   a. Choose "Quit" from the File menu.

The Data Structure

Perhaps the most important decision in program design is what data structure will be used to represent the information manipulated by the program. The choice of a data structure will impact upon every other stage of the program, and an improper selection might send you back to the drawing board. Several different kinds of objects must be represented by TurboDraw, including nodes (rectangle, oval, round-cornered rect) and edges. The program should allow any number of nodes to be drawn. This suggests the use of dynamic memory allocation and linked lists. [Since we are going to use Macintosh-like interface features (menu bar), we will also use Macintosh-like memory management, that is, handles.]

NODES

We will represent a node by storing a rectangle and a user-defined scalar type. The rectangle will specify the size and position of the node and the user-defined type will specify the shape of the node. To make each node part of a linked list, each node must also contain a link to the next node. The following is the data structure of a node :

```
ToolType = ( NoTool, RectTool, OvalTool, RndRectTool, LineTool);
NodePtr   = ^Node;
NodeHndl  = ^NodePtr;
Node = record
   Shape  : Rect;
   kind   : Integer;
   link   : NodeHndl
end;
```

This linked list data structure will be used extensively throughout the program. The list will contain a handle that always points to the first node in the list (NodeList in the next example). The list's final node will always have NIL in the link field of the last node. If the list is empty, the handle to the first node will contain NIL. Let us examine a code fragment that is used to examine each node in a linked list.

```
var
   CurrNode  : NodeHdnl;  { Handle to the current node }
begin
 CurrNode := NodeList;    { Make first node current }
 while CurrNode <> NIL do { Do as long as there
  begin                          are more nodes }
              { Do what must be done to the node }
    CurrNode := CurrNode^^.link  { Move to next node }
  end
end;
```

Note how this link list program using handles has almost the exact same structure as the one used in Chapter 10 using pointers.

EDGES

Like nodes, there can be an arbitrary number of edges. This also suggests a data structure using a dynamically allocated link list. Each edge connects two nodes, therefore each edge will contain links to two nodes and a link to the next edge :

```
EdgePtr    =   ^Edge;
EdgeHndl   =   ^EdgePtr;

Edge = record
   node1   :   NodeHndl;
   node2   :   NodeHndl;
   link    :   EdgeHndl
end;
```

The code for traversing the edge linked list structure is analogous to that for traversing the node linked list.

The following two figures show a labeled diagram drawn by TurboDraw and a conceptual picture of how the two data structures would be represented internally.

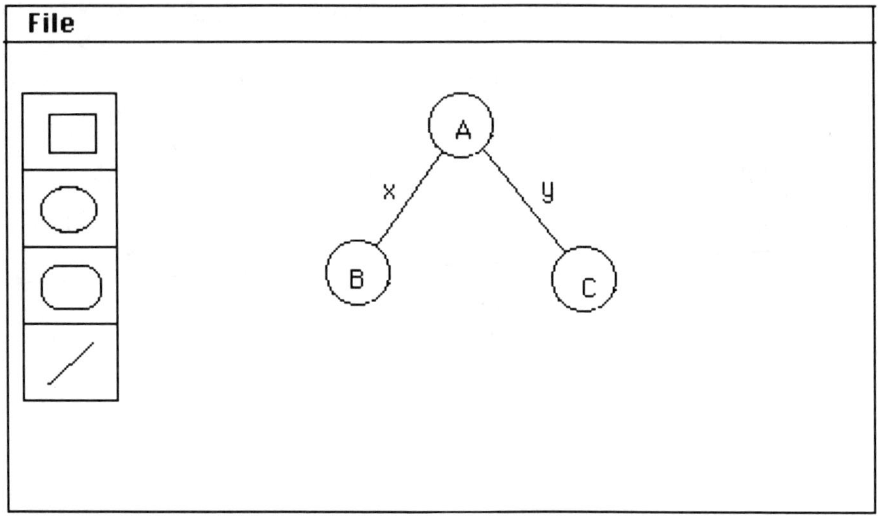

Figure 12-2. A Flow Chart

Note the letter used to label the nodes and edges above are not part of the diagram and are just used to label different components.

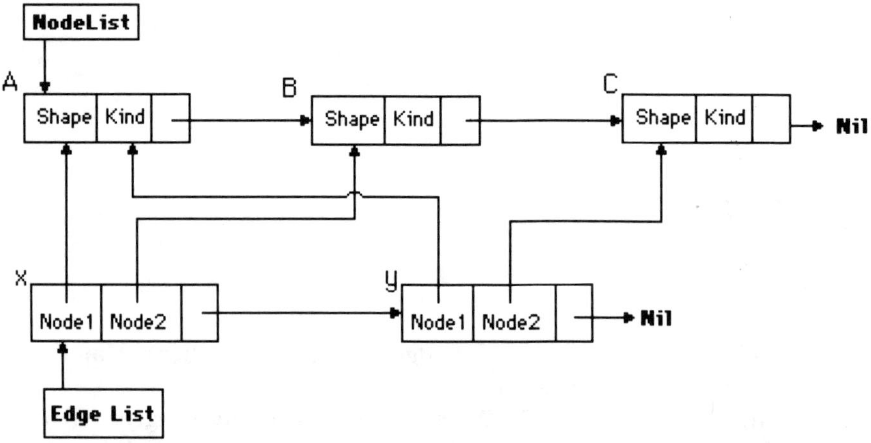

Figure 12-3. The Data Structure

Designing TurboDraw

The program will be designed in a top-down fashion using pseudocode. Details will be refined as we proceed. Let's start by looking at the main program, which like all Macintosh-style applications will use an event loop.

```
program TurboDraw
begin
   Initialize everything
   repeat
      if there is an event
         HandleEvent
   until done
end
```

The initialization routine will set all the various data structures to their initial state.

```
procedure Initialize
begin
    Initialize the menus
    Start with empty NodeList and EdgeList
    Draw the Tool Palette
    Set to not done program
    Set default name of file
end
```

The heart of the program is the HandleEvent procedure; it will process all events received. The following pseudocode shows some of the structure of that procedure.

```
procedure HandleEvent
begin
    if click outside of any window
         Let the system take care of it
    else if click in menu bar
         if save file selected then
            DoSave
         if load file selected then
            DoLoad
```

```
        if print file selected then
           DoSave
        if quit then
           set done to true
   else if click on drawing surface
        if there is a current tool
           if tool is a line
              DrawEdge
           else
              DrawNode
        else
           if click was in a node
               MoveNode
end
```

We could continue decomposing the program into smaller pieces to expose further detail. For example, let's look at the MoveNode procedure described above:

```
procedure MoveNode
begin
   get starting mouse position
   while the button is still being pressed do
       get mouse position
       draw temporary node at new position
       undraw temporary node
   if node doesn't overlap another node then
      erase edges connecting to node at old location
      erase node at old location
      draw node at new location
      draw edges connecting to node at new location
end
```

When decomposing a program with pseudocode, you should continue breaking it down until you can easily translate each pseudocode statement into Pascal. If a statement cannot be easily translated, it should be decomposed further.

Because of the size and complexity of TurboDraw, we will only examine in detail those parts of the program that introduce new concepts, new features of the Macintosh not already covered or that require more explanation than the comments can provide.

CONNECTING THE NODES WITH EDGES

One of the most interesting problems posed in the program is how to draw an edge between two nodes without having the line go inside the nodes. Let's say we want to connect two nodes that are oval in shape. It is simple to find the center point of the rectangle that defines the oval nodes and draw a line connecting them, as figure 12-4 shows.

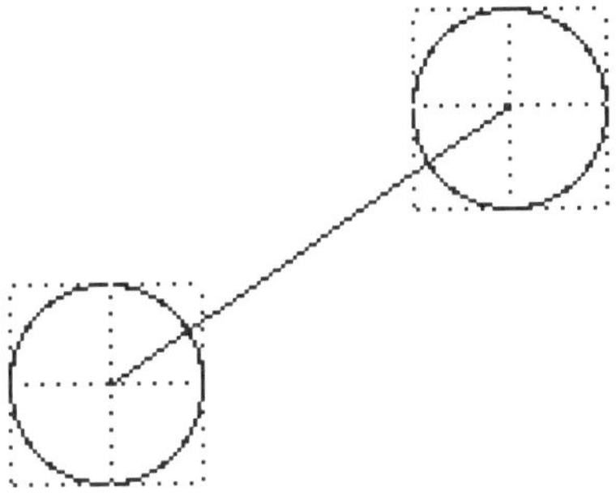

Figure 12-4. Connecting Nodes

The dotted lines indicate the edge drawn from the center of one node's rectangle to the center of the other nodes rectangle.

However, we would prefer it if the diagram looked like figure 12-5, with the edges stopping at the circumference of the node.

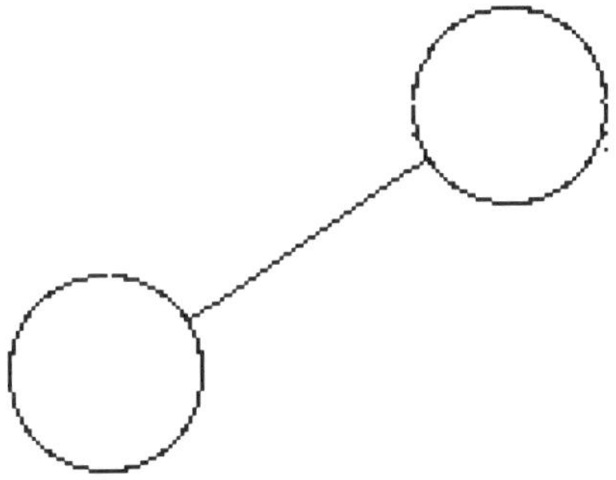

Figure 12-5. Eliminating Lines

In order to accomplish this we will use some of the more advanced graphics capabilities of the Macintosh. QuickDraw allows the definition of a region where anything drawn inside it will be displayed, but anything drawn outside it will not. It is called a clipRgn. Normally, the area defined by the clipRgn will be the entire drawing surface, and everything drawn will be displayed. By excluding from this the area taken up by the two nodes, anything drawn inside the node will not be displayed. We will simply create a new region that will temporarily replace the default clipRgn. There are several additional procedures we need to carry out this plan.

```
procedure GetClip(theRgn : RgnHandle)
```

The GetClip procedure changes the given region to one equivalent to the current clipping region. In a sense, it returns in theRgn a handle to the current clipRgn.

```
procedure SetClip(theRgn : RgnHandle)
```

The SetClip procedure changes the clipping region to the region pointed to by the handle theRgn.

Now let's look at the pseudocode for drawing the edge:

```
Save the current clipping region
Construct a new clipping region the same as the old
excluding the two nodes
Make the new clip region the current clip region
Draw a line connecting the two nodes
Restore the original clip region
```

The following procedure shows how it is implemented in the program:

```
{---------------------------}
{ Draw the edge specified by theEdge }
{---------------------------}
procedure DrawEdge(theEdge : EdgeHndl);
var
  p1, p2  :   Point;
  tempRgn,
  holdRgn :   RgnHandle;

  {-----------------------------}
```

```
  { Returns the point that is the center of the region }
  { specified by theRgn }
  {---------------------------}
  procedure centerRect(theRect : Rect; var p : Point);
  begin
    with theRect do
      begin
        p.v := (top + bottom) div 2;
        p.h := (left + right) div 2
      end
  end;

begin
  tempRgn := NewRgn;       { Allocate new clip region }
  holdRgn := NewRgn;       { Space to hold old clip region }
  GetClip(holdRgn);        { Get the current clip region }
  OpenRgn;                 { Create new clip region that }
    FrameRect(holdRgn^^.rgnBBox);{entire drawing window}
    DrawNode(theEdge^^.node1);   {excluding the nodes}
    DrawNode(theEdge^^.node2);   {that make up the}
  CloseRgn(tempRgn);           {end points of the edge}
  SetClip(tempRgn);      {Make the new clip region current}
  { Draw the edge from the center of one node to    }
  { the center of the other                          }
  centerRect(theEdge^^.node1^^.Shape, p1);
  centerRect(theEdge^^.node2^^.Shape, p2);
  Line(p1, p2);
  SetClip(holdRgn);    { Restore the original clip region  }
  DisposeRgn(tempRgn);{ Get rid of the temporary regions  }
  DisposeRgn(holdRgn)
end;
```

PRINTING PICTURES

While Turbo Pascal can easily print text to a printer, it has no facility to print graphics, and at first glance this seems like a mighty formidable task. However, printing graphics on the Macintosh is simpler than you might think. It requires working with the Toolbox's Print Manager, which contains all the routines necessary. Here are the steps involved:

Open and initialize the Print Manager

Set the print record to default values

Show dialog allowing user to change default values

If the user didn't cancel the job

open the printing document

open the page

draw whatever is going to be printed

close the page

close the printing document

print the document

Release memory for Print Manager

The Print Manager is designed for great flexibility so that it can be used with a wide variety of printers now and in the future. For instance, the LaserWriter did not exist when the Mac was created, but the Print Manager handles it just fine. To do this it uses several complex data structures, which will be discussed only in limited detail. For more information see "Printing from Macintosh Applications," in *Inside Macintosh.*

Printing from a Macintosh application is conceptually simple. When the user selects the Print option from a menu, the Print Manager is initialized. The program then displays a dialog box to get some information about the printing. From here on, printing is a two-stage process. First, the program creates a "port" to print with. The printing port is analogous to QuickDraw's GrafPort, and the program simply draws all the QuickDraw structures on the screen to the printing port. Of course, the program must be able to re-create what is on the screen, but with an object-oriented program such as TurboDraw this is simple. We just move through the data structures, redrawing all the objects to the port as we go. Next, what has been drawn to the port is saved by the Print Manager to a temporary file and then sent to the printer in a technique called **spooling**. Once everything is printed, close up the Print Manager.

The Print Manager maintains three data structures we are concerned with, the record types TPrint, TPrPort and TPrStatus. These three records have complex definitions that are not important at this point. Simply put, however, the TPrint record holds information such as the size and shape of the paper, number of copies, and type of printer. The TPrPort record defines the graphics environment in which we are drawing. TPrStatus is used to hold status information about how the print job is progressing. In the code that follows you will see a type THPrint. The "H" means that THPrint is a handle to TPrint. Similarly, TPPrPort is a pointer to TPrPort because of the extra "P."

To use the Print Manager routines, the Uses statement at the beginning of the program must list the MacPrint unit. Once that is done, all the Print Manager's routines and data structures are available for use. In order to use the Print Manager it must be opened, and after we are finished using it, it must be closed. The procedures that do this are

```
procedure PrOpen
procedure PrClose
```

Neither of these procedures takes any parameters, so both are quite easy to use. PrOpen loads the printer resources from the disk, which may take a second or two to complete. PrClose terminates all interaction with the Print Manager. These procedures can be called each time they are needed. However if you are going to print frequently during your application and wish to avoid the slight pause, call PrOpen just once at the start of the program. In our case, they can be called immediately before and after printing.

After the Print Manager has been initialized, we must allow the user to make some choices about how the print job should continue. If they are using an Image Writer, they can decide on the quality (draft, standard or high), the number of copies to be printed, and the type of paper. This information is kept in a record of type TPrint, which we must create and set with some default values. The record is created using the NewHandle routine. The Print Manager has a procedure (called PrintDefault) for setting the TPrint record to standard default values.

```
procedure PrintDefault (hPrint : THPrint);
```

The PrintDefault procedure fills the fields of a print record with default values; hPrint is a handle to the print record.

```
var
hPrint  :  THPrint;
  :
  :
hPrint := THPrint(NewHandle(sizeof(TPrint)));
PrintDefault(hPrint)
```

Now we can show the user a dialog box of printing options by using the PrJobDialog function.

```
function PrJobDialog (hPrint : THPrint) : Boolean;
```

The PrJobDialog displays the familiar dialog box used whenever you print from any Macintosh application. The dialog box for the ImageWriter is shown in Figure 12-6. The dialog box the user sees is dependent upon the print driver installed and selected by the user with the Chooser desk accessory. This makes the printer transparent to the program creating the output. PrJobDialog takes a parameter of type THPrint and returns True if the user responds OK and False otherwise (Cancel).

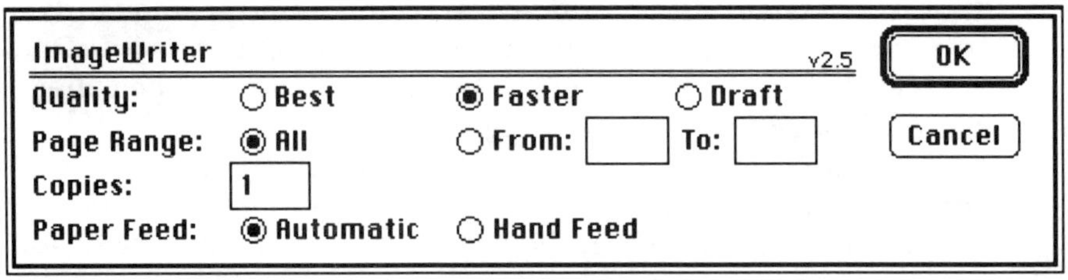

Figure 12-6. The ImageWriter Dialog Box

The next step is to create a port to draw in. To do this we use the PrOpenDoc function.

```
function PrOpenDoc (hPrint : THPrint; pPrPort : TPPrPort; pIOBuf
: Ptr) : TPPrPort;
```

The PrOpenDoc function creates a printing port and returns a pointer to it as the value of the function. The parameter hPrint is the current print record with the values entered by the user into the dialog box. We will pass NIL for the other parameters to indicate that we will accept the Print Manager's default values for these.

```
thePPort := PrOpenDoc(hPrint,  NIL,  NIL);
```

Next we open a page for drawing, draw to the port, close the page, and close the document.

```
procedure PrOpenPage (pPrPort : TpPrPort; pPageFrame
:TpRect);
```

The PrOpenPage procedure initializes one "page" of output for the printer. The parameters are the printer port we are using and Nil to represent that no scaling is to be performed.

```
procedure PrClosePage (pPrPort : TpPrPort) ;
```

The PrClosePage procedure finishes up the current page of printing and ejects the page if necessary.

```
procedure PrCloseDoc (pPrPort : TpPrPort) ;
```

The PrCloseDoc procedure finishes up the printing of the document associated with the printer port specified.

```
PrOpenPage(thePPort, NIL);
DrawAll;                          { Routine that draws everything}
PrClosePage(thePPort);
PrCloseDoc(thePPort);
```

DrawAll is a procedure in the program that draws all the objects to the part as discussed.

Finally, we call a Print Manager procedure to do the printing.

```
PrPicFile(hPrint, NIL, NIL, NIL, prStatus);
```

The PrPicFile procedure performs the spooling and printing process. The only two parameters to worry about are hPrint, which is the print record, and prStatus, which is a record passed as a variable parameter containing information on the printer status.

To end we simply clean up any dynamically allocated memory and close the Print Manager. The whole procedure follows.

```
procedure DoPrint;
 var
  hPrint  :   THPrint;
  thePPort:   TPPrPort;
  prStatus:   TPrStatus;
 begin
  PrOpen;
  hPrint := THPrint(NewHandle(sizeof(TPrint)));
  PrintDefault(hPrint);
  if PrJobDialog(hPrint) then
      begin
       thePPort := PrOpenDoc(hPrint, NIL, NIL);
       PrOpenPage(thePPort,NIL);
       DrawAll;
       PrClosePage(thePPort);
       PrCloseDoc(thePPort);
       PrPicFile(hPrint, NIL, NIL, NIL, prStatus)
      end;
  DisposHandle(Handle(hPrint));
  PrClose
 end;
```

LOADING AND SAVING THE DATA STRUCTURES

To be useful, a Tubro Draw program must be able to save a diagram to disk and be able to recall it later. As we have seen, for some types of programs this is quite easy; all that has to be done is write a file of all the information being stored in memory. However, in an object-oriented drawing program, it's not quite so simple. We must find some suitable way to organize and store the information we are working with. The first problem is that we have two different types of objects represented, nodes and edges. The second problem is that each of our objects has a relationship with one or more other objects. Saving handles in a disk file is useless because the memory location it holds will be meaningless when the program is reloaded into a different area of memory. We can get around this problem by numbering the nodes in the order in which they are stored in the linear linked list. We will assign the first node in the list number 0, the second node number 1, and so on. If we use figure 12-2 as an example, node A is numbered 0, node B is numbered 1, and node C is 2. It is easy to save the nodes and preserve their number; simply go through the linked list and write the nodes to disk. The first node in the disk file will be record 0, the next node is record 1, and so forth. The order in which they are written will be the same order they are read back later. The only information we need to record in the file for nodes is the rectangle that defines them and the shape of the node. It is not necessary to store the link handle to the next node because that information is preserved in the order in which the nodes are stored.

Saving the edges is only slightly more complicated. An edge can be defined by the nodes that it connects. Using our numbering scheme, in Figure 12-2 edge x connect nodes 0 and 1, and edge y connects nodes 0 and 2. We must traverse the list translating the handles to nodes into node numbers before the edges can be stored to disk. We will write a function Hdnl2Num, which translates the node handle into the node number. This function simply traces through the node list looking for a matching handle and keeping track of the number of the node examined. When it finds a match it returns the number of the node.

Two in One

It is much simpler to work with files having a single kind of record rather than two different types. We will therefore use a variant record to place the representation of both nodes and edges into the same type of record. The declaration for this record is

```
SaveRec = record
   case tag : Boolean of
      TRUE : (Shape    :   Rect;          { Node }
              kind     :   Integer);
      FALSE: (node1    :   Integer;       { Edge }
              node2    :   Integer);
   end;
```

There is a tag field of type Boolean that determines if a particular record holds a node or an edge. If the tag is True, the record uses the variables Shape and Kind to represent a node. If tag is False, the record uses the variables Node1 and Node2 to hold an edge. The file we use to save our diagram will be of type SaveRec. To save, we will traverse through the nodes, transferring from the node structure into the file. The same kind of operation will be done to save the edges.

FILENAMES

In order to comply with the standard Macintosh User Interface, we must when saving a file display a dialog box for entering the filename.This dialog box is displayed by the Toolbox's SFPutFile procedure.

```
procedure SFPutFile (where : Point; prompt : string; origName :
                     string; dlgHook: ProcPtr; var Reply :
                     SFReply);
```

The SFPutFile procedure displays the standard Save File dialog box as shown in figure 12-7. The parameters designate where on the screen to display the dialog box, a prompt for the user, the name of the last file used by the program (to do a check), a hook to an additional dialog box (for our use it's Nil), and the information entered by the user in a record in which the name entered is held in the name field. Other fields that indicate whether the user clicked on Save or Cancel are also contained in this record, but we will ignore them here and assume a click in the Save button for simplicity. We will use a procedure called NewFileName to handle the SFPutFile procedure. SFPutFile is part of the Toolbox's Package Manager and requires the unit PackIntf to be in the Uses statement at the beginning of the program.

```
procedure NewFileName(var fname : STring);
var
  reply : SFReply;
  where: Point;
begin
  where.h := 60; where.v := 50;
  SFPutFile(where, 'Save Document
    as:',fname, NIL, reply);
```

```
  fname := reply.fname
end;
```

In this example, Where is a point that determines the location of the top left-hand corner of the dialog box that appears on the screen. The string 'Save Document as:' is the message displayed in the dialog box. The string fname contains a default name to present to the user. For more detail on all the available features of SFPutFile, see the Package Manager chapter of *Inside Macintosh*.

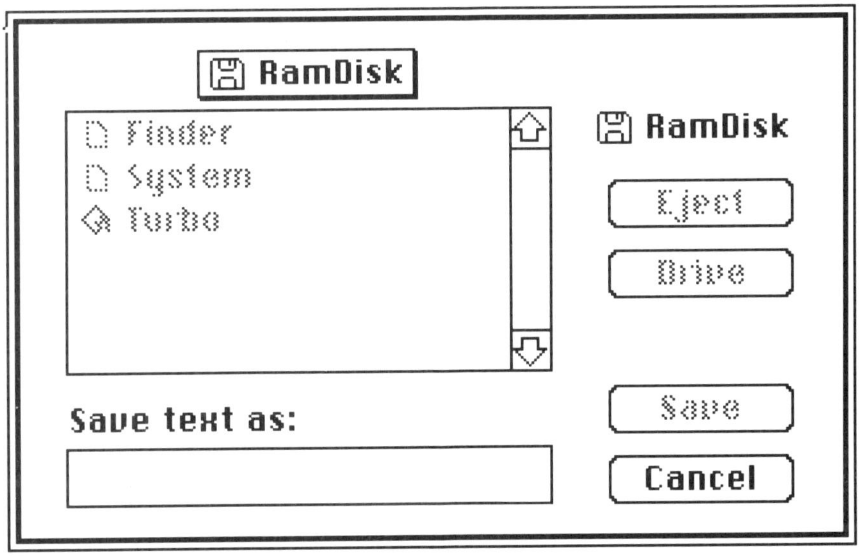

Figure 12-7. The Save Dialog Box

There is also a comparable procedure called SFGetFile that displays a dialog box for opening a file that already exists on disk, as shown in figure 12-8. We use this in our function OldFileName when loading our diagram back into memory.

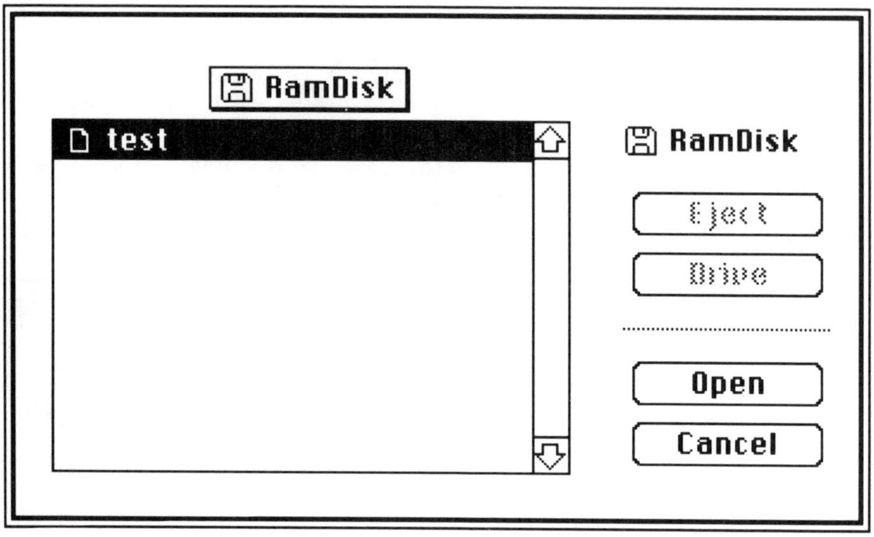

Figure 12-8. The Open Dialog Box

The code that creates this dialog box is analogous to that of NewFileName and can be found in the source code for TurboDraw at the end of the chapter.

Here is the code for the entire TurboDraw program:

Listing 12-1. The Complete TurboDraw Program.

```
program TurboDraw;
uses
  Memtypes,QuickDraw,OSIntf,ToolIntf,PackIntf,MacPrint;
const
  fileM     = 1;                    { Number of File menu}
  printItem = 1;                    { Print choice in File menu }
  loadItem  = 2;
  saveItem  = 3;
  quitItem  = 5;              { Quit choice in File menu   }
  MaxEdges  = 10;            { Maximum number of edges on a node }

type
  ToolType = ( NoTool, RectTool, OvalTool, RndRectTool, LineTool);
  NodePtr     =    ^Node;
  NodeHndl    =    ^NodePtr;
  Node = record
    Shape       :   Rect;       { Handle to structure holding shape }
    kind        :   ToolType;     { Type of shape for this node }
```

```
    link         :   NodeHndl    { Handle to next node in node list}
  end;
  EdgePtr      =   ^Edge;
  EdgeHndl     =   ^EdgePtr;
  Edge = record
    node1        :   NodeHndl; { Handle to node on one side of edge}
    node2        :   NodeHndl;   { Handle to node on other side}
    link         :   EdgeHndl    { Handle to next edge in edge list}
  end;

  SaveRec = record
    case tag : Boolean of
      TRUE : (Shape       :   Rect;          { Node }
              kind        :   ToolType);
      FALSE: (node1       :   Integer;       { Edge }
              node2       :   Integer);
    end;

var
  fileMenu    :   MenuHandle;
  doneFlag    :   Boolean;      { Becomes true when Quit is chosen }
  theEvent    :   EventRecord;
  currTool    :   ToolType;     { Type of tool that is current }
  NodeList    :   NodeHndl;     { Handle to list of nodes }
  EdgeList    :   EdgeHndl;     { Handle to list of edges }
  fname       :   String;       { Hold filename on disk of current
diagram }
  EdgeSet     :   array [1..MaxEdges] of EdgeHndl;
  Tools       :   array [RectTool..LineTool] of Rect;
{-----------------------}
{ Draws a line from point p1 to point p2}
{-----------------------}
procedure Line(p1, p2 : Point);
begin
  MoveTo(p1.h, p1.v);
  LineTo(p2.h, p2.v);
end;
}-----------------------}
{ Erases a line from point p1 to point p2}
{-----------------------}
procedure EraseLine(p1, p2 : Point);
begin
  PenMode(patXor);
  Line(p1, p2);
  Line(p1,p1);
end;

{-----------------------}
{ Wait for screen to do vertical refresh in  }
{ order to minimize flicker during animation }
{-----------------------}
procedure WaitRefresh;
var
```

```
  tickValue       :   LongInt;
begin
  tickValue := TickCount;
  repeat until (tickValue <> TickCount)
end;
{---------------------------}
{ Draw the shape specified by tempRect and kind}
{---------------------------}
procedure DrawShape(tempRect : Rect; kind : ToolType);
begin
  WaitRefresh;
  case kind of
    RectTool    : FrameRect(tempRect);
    OvalTool    : FrameOval(tempRect);
    RndRectTool : FrameRoundRect(tempRect,15,15);
    LineTool    : Line(tempRect.topLeft, tempRect.botRight)
  end
end;

{---------------------------}
{ Draw the node specified by theNode}
{---------------------------}
procedure DrawNode( theNode : NodeHndl);
begin
  DrawShape(theNode^^.Shape, theNode^^.kind);
end;

{---------------------------}
{ Returns a handle to region corresponding to theNode}
{---------------------------}
function Node2Rgn(theNode : NodeHndl) : RgnHandle;
var
  tempRgn     :   RgnHandle;
begin
  tempRgn := NewRgn;
  OpenRgn;
    DrawNode(theNode);
  CloseRgn(tempRgn);
  Node2Rgn := tempRgn
end;
{-------------------------}
{ If the point loc is inside a node then WhichNode}
{ returns the address of the node otherwise it}
{ returns NIL}
{-------------------------}
function WhichNode(var loc : Point) : NodeHndl;
var
  CurrNode    :   NodeHndl;
  tempRgn     :   RgnHandle;
begin
  CurrNode := NodeList;
  WhichNode := NIL;
  while CurrNode <> NIL do
```

```
    begin
      tempRgn := Node2Rgn(CurrNode);
      if PtInRect(loc, CurrNode^^.Shape) then
        begin
          WhichNode := CurrNode;
          CurrNode := NIL
        end
      else
        CurrNode := CurrNode^^.link;
        DisposeRgn(tempRgn)
    end
end;
{--------------------------}
{ Draw the edge specified by theEdge}
{--------------------------}
procedure DrawEdge(theEdge : EdgeHndl);
var
  p1, p2  :   Point;
  tempRgn,
  holdRgn :   RgnHandle;
  {----------------------------}
  { Returns the point that is the center of the region}
  { specified by theRgn}
  {----------------------------}
  procedure centerRect(theRect : Rect; var p : Point);
  begin
    with theRect do
      begin
        p.v := (top + bottom) div 2;
        p.h := (left + right) div 2
      end
  end;
begin
  tempRgn := NewRgn;              { Allocate new clip region}
  holdRgn := NewRgn;              { Space to hold old clip region }
  GetClip(holdRgn);               { Get the current clip region}
   OpenRgn;                         { Create new clip region that}
    FrameRect(holdRgn^^.rgnBBox); {entire drawing window excluding}
    DrawNode(theEdge^^.node1);     { the nodes that make up the end }
    DrawNode(theEdge^^.node2);     { points of the edge}
  CloseRgn(tempRgn);
  SetClip(tempRgn);            { Make the new clip region current}
{ Draw the edge from the center of one node to the center of the
other }
  centerRect(theEdge^^.node1^^.Shape, p1);
  centerRect(theEdge^^.node2^^.Shape, p2);
  Line(p1, p2);
  SetClip(holdRgn);           { Restore the original clip region   }
  DisposeRgn(tempRgn);        { Get rid of the temporary regions   }
  DisposeRgn(holdRgn)
end;
{--------------------------}
{ Erase the edge specified by theEdge}
```

```
{--------------------------}
procedure EraseEdge(theEdge : EdgeHndl);
var
  p1, p2  :   Point;
begin
  PenMode(patXor);
  DrawEdge(theEdge)
end;
{--------------------------}
{ Allows user to create a node or edge by}
{ dragging the mouse.  When the user releases the}
{ button the node or edge is added to the node}
{ or edge list}
{--------------------------}
procedure CreateNode;
var
  tempRect    :   Rect;
  startP,
  currP       :   Point;
  {--------------------------}
  { Add a new node to the node list}
  {--------------------------}
  procedure AddNewNode;
  var
    NewNode     :   NodeHndl;
  begin
    { Create a new node and make it first node in NodeList }
    NewNode := NodeHndl(NewHandle(sizeof(Node)));
    NewNode^^.link := NodeList;
    NodeList := NewNode;
    NewNode^^.kind := currTool;
    NewNode^^.Shape := tempRect
  end;
  {--------------------------}
  { Add a new edge to the edge list}
  {--------------------------}
  procedure AddNewEdge;
  var
    NewEdge     :   EdgeHndl;
  begin
    NewEdge := EdgeHndl(NewHandle(sizeof(Edge)));
    NewEdge^^.node1 := WhichNode(startP);
    NewEdge^^.node2 := WhichNode(currP);
    if (NewEdge^^.node1 <> NIL) and (NewEdge^^.node2 <> NIL) then
      begin
        EraseLine(startP, currP);
        NewEdge^^.link := EdgeList;
        EdgeList := NewEdge;
        DrawEdge(NewEdge)
      end
    else
      begin
        DisposHandle(Handle(NewEdge));
```

```
        EraseLine(startP, currP)
      end
  end;
begin   {--------- CreateNode ------------}
  PenMode(patXor);
  GetMouse(startP);
  currP := startP;
  Pt2Rect(startP, startP, tempRect);
  while Button do
    begin
      DrawShape(tempRect, currTool);
      GetMouse(currP);
      if currTool = LineTool then
        SetRect( tempRect, startP.h, startP.v, currP.h, currP.v)
      else
        Pt2Rect(startP, currP, tempRect);
      DrawShape(tempRect, currTool)
    end;
  if (currTool >= RectTool) and (currTool <=RndRectTool) then
    AddNewNode
  else if currTool = LineTool then
    AddNewEdge
end;{---------- CreateNode ------------}
{---------------------}
{ Draw all edges in the edge set}
{---------------------}
procedure DrawEdgeSet;
var
  count   :   Integer;
begin
  count := 0;
  while EdgeSet[count] <> NIL do
    begin
      DrawEdge(EdgeSet)[count];
      count := count + 1
    end
end;
{---------------------}
{ Erase all the edges in the edge set}
{---------------------}
procedure EraseEdgeSet;
var
  count   :   Integer;
begin
  count := 0;
  while EdgeSet[count] <> NIL do
    begin
      EraseEdge(EdgeSet[count]);
      count := count + 1
    end
end;
{-------------------------}
{ Returns True if theNode overlaps another node}
```

```
{-------------------------}
function Collision(theNode : NodeHndl) : Boolean;
var
  CurrNode    :   NodeHndl;
  tempRgn     :   RgnHandle;
  function Overlap(node1, node2 : NodeHndl) : Boolean;
  var
    r1, r2, tempRgn : RgnHandle;
  begin
    r1 := Node2Rgn(node1);
    r2 := Node2Rgn(node2);
    tempRgn := NewRgn;
    SectRgn(r1, r2, tempRgn);
    Overlap :=  not EmptyRgn(tempRgn);
    DisposeRgn(r1);
    DisposeRgn(r2);
    DisposeRgn(tempRgn)
  end;
begin
  CurrNode := NodeList;
  Collision := FALSE;
  while CurrNode <> NIL do
    begin
      if CurrNode = theNode then
        CurrNode := CurrNode^^.link
      else
        if Overlap(CurrNode, theNode) then
          begin
            Collision := TRUE;
            CurrNode := NIL
          end
        else
          CurrNode := CurrNode^^.link
    end
end;
{-------------------------}
{ Allows the user to move the node around the screen.  If the user
moves }
{ the node on top of another node then put it back into its old }
{location.  After the node has been moved erase the edges that }
{connected to the node at its old location and redraw at the new }
{ location}
{------------------------------}
procedure MoveNode(var  theNode : NodeHndl);
var
  oldLoc,
  newLoc          :   Point;
  tempRect        :   Rect;
  temp            :   Rect;
begin
  tempRect := theNode^^.Shape;
  PenMode(PatXor);
  GetMouse(oldLoc);
```

```
  while Button do
    begin
      GetMouse(newLoc);
      DrawNode(theNode);
      DrawNode(theNode);
      OffsetRect(theNode^^.Shape, newLoc.H - oldLoc.H, newLoc.V
 oldLoc.V);
      oldLoc := newLoc
    end;
    if Collision(theNode) then
      theNode^^.Shape := tempRect
    else
      begin
        CollectEdges(theNode);
        temp := theNode.^^.Shape;
        theNode^^.Shape := tempRect;
        EraseEdgeSet;
        DrawNode(theNode);
        theNode^^.Shape := temp;
        DrawEdgeSet;
        DrawNode(theNode)
      end
end;
{---------------------}
{ Create the menu bar}
{---------------------}
procedure SetUpMenus;
var
  i           :   Integer;
  appleTitle  :   String[1];
begin
  InitMenus;           { Initialize the Menu Manager }
  fileMenu := NewMenu(fileM,'File');
  AppendMenu(FileMenu,'Print;Load;Save;(-;Quit');
  InsertMenu(FileMenu,0);
  DrawMenuBar;
end;
{---------------------}
{ Make rect opposite color}
{---------------------}
procedure flipRect(theRect : Rect);
begin
  InsetRect(theRect,2,2);
  InvertRect(theRect)
end;
{---------------------}
{ Make no tool current}
{---------------------}
procedure UnSelectTool;
begin
  if currTool <> NoTool then
    flipRect(Tools[currTool]);
  currTool := NoTool
```

```
end;
{---------------------}
{ Make theTool the current tool}
{---------------------}
procedure SelectTool(theTool : ToolType);
begin
  UnSelectTool;
  currTool := theTool;
  flipRect(Tools[currTool])
end;
{---------------------}
{ Print the diagram on the printer}
{---------------------}
procedure DoPrint;
var
  hPrint  :   THPrint;
  thePPort:   TPPrPort;
  prStatus:   TPrStatus;
begin
  PrOpen;
  hPrint := THPrint(NewHandle(sizeof(TPrint)));
  PrintDefault(hPrint);
  if PrJobDialog(hPrint) then    { Allow the user to choose printer
options }
    begin
      thePPort := PrOpenDoc(hPrint, NIL, NIL);
      PrOpenPage(thePPort,NIL);
      DrawAll;
      PrClosePage(thePPort);
      PrCloseDoc(thePPort);
      PrPicFile(hPrint, NIL, NIL, NIL, prStatus)
    end;
  DisposHandle(Handle(hPrint));
  PrClose
end;
{-----------------}
{ Save the diagram to a disk file }
{-----------------}
procedure DoSave;
var
  Save        :   File of SaveRec;
  SaveBuf     :   SaveRec;
  CurrEdge    :   EdgeHndl;
  CurrNode    :   NodeHndl;
  {------------------}
  { Allows the user to choose a filename }
  { for the file.  Presents fname as a}
  { default choice}
  {------------------}
  procedure NewFileName(var fname : String);
  var
    reply       :   SFReply;
    where       :   Point;
```

```
    typeList    :   SFTypeList;
  begin
    where.h := 60; where.v := 50;
    SFPutFile(where,'Save Document as:',fname,NIL,reply);
      fname := reply.fname
  end;
  {---------------------}
  { Returns the node number of the node}
  { pointed to by theHandle}
  {---------------------}
  function Hndl2Num(theHandle : NodeHndl) : Integer;
  var
    NodeCount   :   Integer;
  begin
    NodeCount := 0;
    CurrNode := NodeList;
    while CurrNode <> NIL do
      begin
        if CurrNode = theHandle then
          CurrNode := NIL
        else
          begin
            CurrNode := CurrNode^^.link;
            NodeCount := NodeCount + 1
          end
      end;
    Hndl2Num := NodeCount
  end;
begin
  NewFileName(fname);
  rewrite(Save, fname);
  CurrNode := NodeList;
  while CurrNode <> NIL do
    begin
      SaveBuf.tag := TRUE;
      SaveBuf.Shape := CurrNode^^.Shape;
      SaveBuf.kind := CurrNode^^.kind;
      Write(Save, SaveBuf);
      CurrNode := CurrNode^^.link
    end;
  CurrEdge := EdgeList;
  while CurrEdge <> NIL do
    begin
      SaveBuf.tag := FALSE;
      SaveBuf.node1 := Hndl2Num(CurrEdge^^.node1);
      SaveBuf.node2 := Hndl2Num(CurrEdge^^.node2);
      Write(Save, SaveBuf);
      CurrEdge := CurrEdge^^.link
    end;
  close(Save)
end;
{-----------------}
{ Save the diagram to a disk file.}
```

```
{------------------}
procedure DoLoad;
var
  Save    :   File of SaveRec;
  SaveBuf :   SaveRec;
  CurrNode     :    NodeHndl;
  NewNode      :    NodeHndl;
  NewEdge      :    EdgeHndl;
  {----------------------}
  { Allows the user to choose a filename from }
  { the files that are on a disk}
  {----------------------}
  procedure OldFileName(var fname : String);
  var
    reply        :    SFReply;
    where        :    Point;
    typeList     :    SFTypeList;
  begin
    where.h := 60; where.v := 50;
    SFGetFile(where,'',NIL,-1,typeList,NIL,reply);
    fname := reply.fname
  end;
  {----------------------}
  { Returns a handle to the node that has the }
  { number specified by theNum}
  {----------------------}
  function Num2Handle(theNum : Integer) : NodeHndl;
  var
    NodeCount    :    Integer;
  begin
    Num2Handle := NIL;
    NodeCount := 0;
    CurrNode := NodeList;
    while CurrNode <> NIL do
      begin
        if NodeCount = theNum then
          begin
            Num2Handle := CurrNode;
            CurrNode := NIL
          end
        else
          begin
            CurrNode :CrrNoe\.link Nodecount := NodeCount + 1
          end
      end
  end;
begin
  OldFileName(fname);
  NodeList := NIL;
  CurrNode := NIL;
  EdgeList := NIL;
  {$I-}
  reset(Save, fname);
```

```
  while not eof(Save) do
    begin
      read(Save, SaveBuf);
      if SaveBuf.tag then
        begin
          NewNode := NodeHndl(NewHandle(sizeof(Node)));
          NewNode^^.link := NIL;
          NewNode^^.kind := SaveBuf.kind;
          NewNode^^.Shape := SaveBuf.Shape;
          if NodeList = NIL then
            NodeList := NewNode
          else
            CurrNode^^.link := NewNode;
            CurrNode := NewNode
        end
      else
        begin
          NewEdge := EdgeHndl(NewHandle(sizeof(Edge)));
          NewEdge^^.node1 := Num2Handle(SaveBuf.node1);
          NewEdge^^.node2 := Num2Handle(SaveBuf.node2);
          NewEdge^^.link := EdgeList;
          EdgeList := NewEdge;
        end
    end;
  close(Save)
  {$I+}
end;
{----------------------------}
{ Do the action specified by theItem from the file menu }
{----------------------------}
 procedure DoFileMenu(theItem : Integer);
 var
   myPort  :   GrafPtr;
 begin
   case theItem of
   quitItem:    doneFlag := TRUE;
   loadItem:    DoLoad;
   saveItem:    DoSave;
   printItem:
    begin
      UnSelectTool;
      GetPort(myPort);
      DoPrint;
      SetPort(myPort)
    end;
    end;
   DrawAll;
   DrawPallete
 end;
{--------------------------}
{ User click in the menu Bar take appropriate action }
{--------------------------}
procedure DoCommand(mResult: LONGINT);
```

```
var
  theItem:    Integer;
  theMenu:    Integer;
begin
  theItem := LoWord(mResult);      { Which item in the menu }
  theMenu := HiWord(mResult);      { Which menu }
  case theMenu of
    fileM:
      DoFileMenu(theItem);
  end;
  HiliteMenu(0)            { Turn off highlighting in the Menu Bar }
end;
{---------------------}
{ Check to see if user clicked in one of  }
{ of Toolboxes.  If so, set currTool.     }
{ Returns True if user click in Toolbox   }
{---------------------}
function WhichTool(location : Point) : Boolean;
var
  i           :   ToolType;
begin
  WhichTool := FALSE;
  for i := RectTool to LineTool do          { For every tool }
    if PtInRect(location, Tools[i]) then  {check if it is selected}
      begin
        WhichTool := TRUE;          { A tool was selected }
        if currTool <> i then { If click not in current tool  }
          SelectTool(i)     { select the tool }
        else                { Click in tool already selected}
          UnSelectTool;     { then unselect it }
      end
end;
{---------------------------}
{  Click in the drawing window and take appropriate action }
{---------------------------}
procedure HandleClick(whichWindow : WindowPtr; location : Point);
var
    tempNode :   NodeHndl;
begin
  GlobalToLocal(location);
  if not WhichTool(location) then  { If clicked in the palette set
                                     the tool }
    if currTool <> NoTool then
      CreateNode            { Tool selected create node or edge }
    else
      begin
        tempNode := WhichNode(location); { Check if click in node }
        if tempNode <> NIL then
          MoveNode(tempNode)             { Move the node }
      end
 end;
{---------------------}
{ Do the appropriate thing for each event }
```

```
{---------------------}
procedure HandleEvent(theEvent : EventRecord);
var
  whichWindow : WindowPtr;
begin
  if theEvent.what = mouseDown then
    case FindWindow(theEvent.where, whichWindow) of
      inSysWindow  :                { Click outside window }
        SystemClick(theEvent, whichWindow);
      inMenuBar    :                { Click in menu bar    }
        DoCommand(MenuSelect(theEvent.where));
      inContent    :                { Click in the window  }
        HandleClick(whichWindow, theEvent.where)
    end
end;
{----------------------}
{ Initialize location of tools in the palette }
{----------------------}
procedure InitTools;
var
  i       :   ToolType;
  tempRect:   Rect;
begin
  SetRect(tempRect, 2,5,38,40);
  for i := RectTool to LineTool do
    begin
      Tools[i] := tempRect;
      OffsetRect(tempRect,0,34);
    end;
  currTool := NoTool
end;
{-------------------------------}
{ Do all initialization for program including Toolbox stuff      }
{-------------------------------}
procedure Initialize;
begin
  SetUpMenus;              { Set up the menu structure }
  InitTools;               { Set up tool palette }
  EdgeList := NIL;         { No nodes or edges to start  }
  NodeList := NIL;
  DrawPallete;
  doneFlag := false;       { Not done with program yet}
  fname := '';
end;
begin              {--- Main program ---}
  Initialize;
  repeat
    if GetNextEvent(everyEvent, theEvent) then
      HandleEvent(theEvent);
  until doneFlag
end.               {--- Main program ---}
```

Do More

TurboDraw is a very complete and functional application, but like all programs more can always be added. Here are some suggestions for additions to TurboDraw:

1. Add the ability of writing text to the TurboDraw screen.
2. Add the ability to delete nodes and edges from a diagram.
3. Add the ability to do free-style drawing as well as structured drawing.
4. Add the ability to resize nodes after they are drawn.
5. Add the ability to connect nodes using arcs as well as lines.
6. Add the ability to add multisegment lines to connect nodes.

APPENDIX A

Table A-1. Turbo Pascal Reserved Words

and	goto	record
array	if	repeat
begin	in	set
case	label	string
const	mod	then
div	nil	to
do	nout	type
downto	of	until
else	or	uses
end	otherwise	var
file	procedure	while
for	program	with
function		

SINGLE CHARACTER SPECIAL SYMBOLS

$ ( ) + * , - . / : ; < = > @ [ ] ^ { }

CHARACTER PAIR SPECIAL SYMBOLS

<> <= >= := .. (* *) (. .)

APPENDIX B
Turbo Pascal Menu Summary

FILE MENU

The file menu contains options to save programs to the disk, restore programs from the disk, and print programs.

New

Opens a new window to allow you to start entering a new program.

Open

Displays a dialog box that allows you to recall a program already stored on the disk. A program residing on a different disk can be recalled by ejecting the current disk and inserting the new disk into the drive. A program is opened by double clicking on its name or by selecting the name and then clicking on the **Open** button. This is disabled if eight windows are already open.

Close

Closes the current editing window and erases its contents. If you haven't saved the program, you will be given a chance to do so. Disabled if no windows are open.

Save

Saves your program on the disk under the name it has been previously given (the name that appears on the top of the program window). If a program is new (named Untitled), a dialog box first asks for a name.

Save As . . .

Saves a new program with a name or saves an already named program with a new name. It also allows you to eject the disk in the disk drive or look at another drive so that you can save the program on a different disk.

Page Setup

Lets you select the size paper you are going to use in the printer with the standard page-setup dialog box. All settings are erased upon exiting Turbo.

Print . . .

Displays the standard print dialog box for the printer you are using.

Edit Transfer

Allows you to edit the list of programs found in the Transfer menu.

Quit

Closes all open editing windows and returns you to the Macintosh Desktop.

EDIT MENU

The Edit menu contains options that allow you to make changes to the text of your program.

Undo

Undoes the last editing changes you have made. You can also redo an undo. A handy little menu item!

Cut

Cuts any selected text out of your program and places it into the Clipboard. The Clipboard is a temporary storage area that allows you to pass information between programs.

Copy

Does the same thing as Cut, except it does not remove the selected text from the current program.

Paste

Inserts a copy of the Clipboard at the insertion point in your program or replaces the selected text with it.

Clear

Erases any selected text.

Shift Left

Shifts all the currently selected text one space to the left. Helpful in realigning text.

Shift Right

Shifts all the currently selected text one space to the right. Helpful in realigning text.

Options

Presents three options to customize your Turbo work environment. Tab Width sets the tabulator width between 1 and 8. The Auto Indent check box is used to set whether the auto indent is used while editing. The Startup Window check box is used to set whether an Untitled window comes up at the start of each session. None of the settings are saved upon exiting Turbo unless "Save Defaults" from the File menu is used.

SEARCH MENU

The Search menu contains options to easily locate and change text in the program window.

Find (Command-F)

Opens a dialog box that lets you enter a string to be searched for through the text of the active editing window. Searching starts at the current cursor position and proceeds downward.

Find Next (Command-D)

Starts to search for the next occurrence of the string entered via the Find or Change options.

Change (Command-A)

Similar to Find except that a string to replace the one found can also be entered. Each replacement of the string is verified with a dialog box.

Home Cursor (Command-H)

Moves the cursor to the top of the editing window currently active. This is the quickest way to jump back to the top of your program.

Window (Command-W)

Cycles through all the open editing windows.

Format Menu

The Format menu is used to customize the appearance of the text in the editing windows. It is broken into two main sections dealing with window layout and text size.

Stack Windows

Used to stack all open windows one behind the other with only the title bar of the inactive windows showing.

Tile Windows

Organizes all open windows into tiles so that all can show on the screen at once.

Zoom Window

Expands the active window so that it takes up most of the screen. If the window is already full size, it is shrunk back down. Also the name of a moderately successful band in the 1960s.

Text Size 9,10,12,14,18, and 24 Points

Used to set the text character size in the active window. All characters in a window must be the same size, but different windows can have different text sizes.

THE FONT MENU

Used to select the font of the text in the active window. Different windows can use different fonts, but all the text of a window must be the same font. The font names displayed will be dependent upon which are installed in the system folder you are using.

The Run Menu

The Run menu allows you to select different options for executing your program.

THE COMPILE MENU

The Compile Menu contains options to compile and run your programs

Run

Executes the program in the active window, compiling it to memory if necessary.

To Memory

Compiles the program in the active window to a file held in the Mac's memory. The file is erased if any editing is performed on the program.

To Disk

Compiles the program in the active window to a file on disk, producing a double-clickable application with the same name as the window.

Check Syntax

Parses a program checking its syntax. It is a good idea while writing a long program to use this option from time to time to remove syntax errors as you go.

Find Error

Positions the cursor at the statement in a program that caused the last run-time error.

Get Info

Displays some information about the size of the current program.

Options

Allows the programmer to set certain options for the compiler.

APPENDIX C
Compiler Error Messages

01 ';' expected
02 ':' expected
03 ',' expected
04 '(' expected
05 ')' expected
06 '=' expected
07 ':=' expected
08 '[' expected
09 ']' expected
10 '.' expected
11 '. .' expected
12 Begin expected
13 Do expected
14 End expected
15 Of expected
16 Interface expected
17 Then expected
18 To or downto expected
19 Implementation expected
20 Boolean expression expected
21 File variable expected
22 Integer constant expected
23 Integer expression expected
24 Integer variable expected
25 Integer or real constant expected
26 Integer or real expression expected
27 Integer or real variable expected

28 Pointer variable expected
29 Record variable expected
30 Ordinal type expected
31 Ordinal expression expected
32 String constant expected
33 String expression expected
34 String variable expected
35 Identifier expected
36 Type identifier expected
37 Field identifier expected
38 Constant expected
39 Variable expected
40 Undefined label
41 Unknown identifier
42 Undefined type in pointer definition
43 Duplicate identifier
44 Type mismatch
45 Constant out of range
46 Constant and case types do not match
47 Operand types do not match operator
48 Invalid result type
49 Invalid string length
51 Invalid subrange base type
52 Lower bound greater than upper bound
53 Invalid for control variable
54 Illegal assignment
55 String constant exceeds line
56 Error in integer constant
57 Error in real constant
58 Division by zero
59 Structure too large
60 Constants are not allowed here
62 Invalid type cast argument
63 Invalid '@' argument
64 Label defined already
65 Invalid file type
66 Cannot read or write variable of this type
67 Files must be var parameters
68 File components may not be files
70 Set base type out of range

71	Invalid goto
72	Label not within current block
73	Undefined forward procedure(s)
74	Program or unit expected
75	Error in type
76	Error in statement
77	Error in expression
78	Invalid external definition
79	Invalid external reference
80	Too many symbols
81	Too many nested scopes
82	Driver header not found
83	Too many variables
84	Expression too complicated
85	Segment too large
86	Unit not found
87	Duplicate or invalid unit number
88	Unit missing
89	Incomplete unit versions
90	Syntax error
91	Unexpected end of text
92	Line too long
93	Invalid compiler directive
94	Target address found in unit
95	Undefined external procedue(s)
96	Object file format error
97	Run-time support unit missing
98	Target address not found
99	Not enough memory

APPENDIX D
IOResult Codes

The following are the codes that will be returned by a call to the IOResult function when an error occurs:

−33	Directory file full
−34	All allocation blocks on the volume are full
−35	Specified volume doesn't exist
−36	Disk I/O error
−37	Bad filename or volume name (perhaps zero length)
−38	File not open
−39	Logical end of file reached during read operation
−40	Attempt to position before start of file
−41	System heap full
−42	Too many files open
−43	Volume not found
−44	Volume is locked by a hardware setting
−45	File is locked
−46	Volume is locked by a software flag
−47	One or more file open
−48	A file with the specified name already exists
−49	Only one access path to a file can allow writing
−50	No default volume
−51	Bad file reference number
−53	Volume not online
−54	Read/write permission doesn't allow writing
−55	Specified volume number is already mounted and online
−56	No such drive number
−57	Volume lacks Macintosh-format directory

−58	External file system error
−59	Problems during Rename
−60	Master directory block is bad; must reinitialize volume
−61	Read/write permission doesn't allow writing
−108	Not enough room in heap zone
−120	Directory not found
−121	Too many working directories open
−122	Attempted to move into offspring
−123	Attempt to do HFS operation on non-HFS file
−127	Internal file system error
−128	Text file not open for input
−129	Text file not open for output
−130	Error in numeric value during read from text file

APPENDIX E
Documenting a Program

The following program is presented for the purpose of providing a model for documenting a program. This particular program is only an example and should not be taken as the only way to document a program. The amount and detail of documentation that you should use in your program will depend on your application, its length, and its complexity.

Listing E-1. Program That Documents Programs.

```
program GradeBook;
{*****************************************************}
{*  Created 1/7/87        Programmer: M. Alan Zeldin  *}
{*                                                    *}
{*                                                    *}
{*  Functional Description:                           *}
{*  GradeBook maintains a file containing student     *}
{*  names and grades.  Weighted averages are computed *}
{*  when student information is displayed.   Students *}
{*  can be added or deleted from the file and student *}
{*  grade information can be modified.                *}
{*                                                    *}
{*  Implementation Description:                       *}
{*  Information is maintained in a file of records    *}
{*  that contain data about each student.  To find any *}
{*  specific record, a sequential search of the file  *}
{*  is performed.                                     *}
{*                                                    *}
{*  Implementation Restrictions (bugs):               *}
{*  Only the first student in the file with a given   *}
{*  name is accessible to the user.                   *}
{*                                                    *}
{*****************************************************}
 uses
```

```
 MemTypes, QuickDraw, ToolIntF, OSIntF
const
 FileName = 'STUDENTS';  { Name of file students are stored in }
 FileSize = 50;
 NumberExams = 6;
 Empty = '';          { Null string in LastName marks free record }
type
 Grades = array[1..NumberExams] of integer;
 NameType = string[15];
 StudentType = record
   LastName : NameType;
   FirstName : NameType;
   Exam : Grades;
  end;
var
 Choice : char;
{ Weight of each exam in average }
 Weight : array[1..NumberExams] of real;
 Student : file of StudentType;
 First, Last : NameType;     { Name of current student }
 Location : integer;         { Current location in student file }

procedure Menu;
{*********************************************************}
{* Displays all the program's functions and prompts the  *}
{* user to choose the desired function. If an invalid    *}
{* choice is made the computer beeps and waits for a     *}
{* a valid choice                                        *}
{*********************************************************}
begin { Menu }
 ClearScreen;
 Writeln('1. Modify a Student');
 Writeln('2. Add a Student');
 Writeln('3. Delete a Student');
 Writeln('0. Quit');
 Writeln;
 Write('Please Choose >');
 Read(Choice);
 while not (Choice in ['0'..'4']) do
  begin { Not a valid choice }
   SysBeep(5);
   Read(Choice)
  end
end; { Menu }

procedure InitFile;
{*******************************************************}
{* Open student file if it exists else create the file *}
{*******************************************************}
 var
  Count, Index : integer;
begin { InitFile }
 Open(Student, FileName);
```

```
  if EOF(Student) then           { File doesn't exist }
   begin
{ Write FileSize empty records into the file }
    for Count := 0 to FileSize do
     begin
      Seek(Student, count);
      Read(Student,StudentRec)
{ Initialize all records in file to be empty }
      with StudentRec do
       begin
        FirstName := Empty;
        LastName := Empty;
        for Index := 1 to NumberExams do
         Exam[Index] := 0
       end;
      Write(Student,StudentRec)
     end;
    Close(Student);
    Reset(Student, FileName)
   end
 end; { InitFile }

 procedure SetWeights;
 begin
  Weight[1] := 0.15;          { 15% of grade }
  Weight[2] := 0.15;          { 15% of grade }
  Weight[3] := 0.20;          { 20% of grade }
  Weight[4] := 0.15;          { 15% of grade }
  Weight[5] := 0.15;          { 15% of grade }
  Weight[6] := 0.20           { 20% of grade }
 end; { SetWeights }

 procedure GetName;
{******************************************** *}
{* Prompt user to enter name of a student    *}
{******************************************** *}
 begin { GetName }
  Write('Enter Last Name >');
  Readln(Last);
  Write('Enter First Name >');
  Readln(First)
 end; { GetName }

 function FindStudent (First, Last : NameType;
        var Count : integer) : Boolean;
{*******************************************************}
{* Returns True if the name is found in the file       *}
{* Returns False if the name is not found.  If the name *}
{* was found Count contains its position in the file   *}
{*******************************************************}
  var
   Found : Boolean;
 begin { FindStudent }
```

```
 Count := 0;
 Found := false;
 Seek(Student, Count);
 Read(Student, StudentRec);
{ Sequential search of file for matching name }
while (not eof(Student)) and (not Found) do
  begin
   with StudentRec do
    if (FirstName = First) and (LastName = Last) then
     Found := True
    else
     begin
      Count := Count + 1;
      Seek(Student, Count);
      Read(Student,StudentRec);
     end
  end;
 if not found then
  begin
   Writeln(First, ' ', Last, ' was not found. ');
   Writeln('Press <Return> to continue.');
   Readln
  end;
 FindStudent := Found
end; { FindStudent }

procedure DisplayStudentInfo;
{**********************************************************}
{* Display the contents of the current student record    *}
{* which is contained in Student^.  Calculate the average *}
{**********************************************************}
 var
  Index : integer;
  Average : real;
begin { DisplayStudentInfo }
 with StudentRec do
  begin
   ClearScreen;
   Writeln(' Last Name  : ', LastName);
   Writeln(' First Name : ', FirstName);
   Writeln;
   Writeln('1.  Exam1    : ', Exam[1]);
   Writeln('2.  Exam2    : ', Exam[2]);
   Writeln('3.  Final    : ', Exam[3]);
   Writeln('4.  Project1: ', Exam[4]);
   Writeln('5.  Project2: ', Exam[5]);
   Writeln('6.  Project3: ', Exam[6]);
   Average := 0;
   for Index := 1 to NumberExams do
    Average := Average + (Weight[Index] * Exam[Index]);
   Writeln('    Average : ', round(Average))
  end
end; { DisplayStudentInfo }
```

```
procedure Modify (Location : integer);
{****************************************************}
{*  Allows user to modify exam grades of the current *}
{*  student                                          *}
{****************************************************}
  var
   Choice : char;
   Value : integer;
begin { Modify }
 Seek(Student, Location);
 Read(Student, StudentRec);
 repeat
  DisplayStudentInfo;
  Writeln;
  Write('Enter Line to Change or 0 to Quit > ');
  Read(Choice);
  while not (Choice in ['0' . . '6']) do
   begin { Not a valid Choice }
    SysBeep(5);
    Read(Choice)
   end;
  Writeln;
  if Choice <> '0' then
   begin
    Write('Enter value > ');
    Readln(Value);
{ Convert choice into equiv integer for use as index }
    StudentRec.Exam[ord(Choice) - ord('0')] := Value;
   end;
 until Choice = '0';
 Write(Student,StudentRec)
end; { Modify }

procedure AddStudent (First, Last : NameType);
{*******************************************************}
{* Adds the student whose name is passed in to the file *}
{*******************************************************}
 var
  Added : Boolean;
  Count : integer;
begin { AddStudent }
{ Look for a record with no last name }
 Added := false;
 Count := 0;
 Seek(Student, Count);
 Read(Student, StudentRec);
{ Sequential search of file for free record }
while (not eof(Student)) and (not Added) do
  if StudentRec.LastName = Empty then
   begin { Found an empty spot }
    Seek(Student, Count);
    StudentRec.LastName := Last;
    StudentRec.FirstName := First;
```

```
      Write(Student, StudentRec);
      Added := True
     end
    else
     begin { Look at next spot }
      Count := Count + 1;
      Seek(Student, Count);
      Read(Student, StudentRec)
     end;
   if not Added then
    Writeln('File is full, Press <Return> to continue')
  end; { AddStudent }

  procedure Delete (Location : integer);
 {***********************************************************}
 {* Deletes the student at the place in the file specified *}
 {* by Location by putting an empty string into that       *}
 {* record.  The user is asked to verify the deletion      *}
 {***********************************************************}
   var
    Which : char;
  begin { Delete }
   Seek(Student, Location);
   Read(Student, StudentRec);
   with StudentRec do
    Writeln(FirstName, ' ', LastName);
   Write(' Delete (Y/N) > ');
   Read(Which);
   if (Which = 'Y') or (Which = 'y') then
    begin
     Seek(Student, Location);
     Read(Student, StudentRec);
     StudentRec.LastName := Empty;
     StudentRec.FirstName := Empty;
     Write(Student, StudentRec);
    end
  end; { Delete }

 begin { GradeBook }
  InitFile; { File doesn't already exist, create it }
  SetWeights;
  repeat
   Menu; { Show the choices }
   case Choice of
    '0' :
     ; { Do nothing }
    '1' :              { Modify a student }
     begin
      ClearScreen;
      GetName;
      if FindStudent(First, Last, Location) then
       Modify(Location)
     end;
```

```
   '2' :            { Add a student }
    begin
     ClearScreen;
     GetName;
     AddStudent(First, Last)
    end;
   '3' :            { Delete a student }
    begin
     ClearScreen;
     GetName;
     if FindStudent(First, Last, Location) then
      Delete(Location)
    end
  end { case }
 until Choice = '0';
 Close(Student)
end. { GradeBook }
```

APPENDIX F
Differences Between Turbo Pascal and Macintosh Pascal

Many programmers may switch from Macintosh Pascal to Turbo Pascal. This appendix notes their differences.

IMPLEMENTATION

The major difference between the two Pascals is in the way they are implemented. Macintosh Pascal is implemented via an interpreter reminiscent of interpreted BASIC. All program editing and execution is performed by the MacPascal interpreter. Once interpreted, a program written in Macintosh Pascal needs to be run in the Macintosh Pascal environment or with the aid of a run-time application. The major drawback of this is that Macintosh Pascal programs execute slowly, and it is not possible to develop a double-clickable application or a desk accessory, as is possible in Turbo. There is one advantage to working with Macintosh Pascal, and that is the superior debugging tools available in that language. Although Turbo is a compiler language, its environment provides many of the advantages of an interpreted system by presenting a unified environment where it is easy to jump from editor to compiler to application and back.

DATA TYPES

Both Pascals implement data types via the Mac's SANE package and thus are the same.

STRINGS

String handling is virtually the same in both systems. All the standard functions and procedures are the same. Macintosh Pascal has added two string procedures, Include and Omit. Macintosh Pascal does not support turning off range checking or any other Turbo compiler switch.

USER-DEFINED TYPES

Macintosh Pascal allows the reading and writing of the values of a user-defined type. Turbo Pascal permits only the Ords of user-defined values to be read or written.

FILES

There are significant differences in file handling between the two systems. Macintosh Pascal tries to implement file handling more consistent with the original Pascal definition, while Turbo varies from this standard in order to make file handling more consistent with other input/output operations. In Macintosh Pascal, there is a sharp distinction between sequential and random files. A sequential file can be open only to read or write, and no mixed operations are allowed. Turbo allows for mixed operations on either sequential or random files. Additionally, Turbo does away with the confusing and antiquated Get and Put procedures and the use of the file pointer. Instead, Turbo extends Read and Write to include all files. Here is a rundown on the differences in the file handling procedures.

Reset—Used in Macintosh Pascal to open a sequential file for read only. In Turbo it opens an existing file or rewinds an open file.

Rewrite—Used in MacPascal to open a sequential file for write only. In Turbo it creates and opens an existing file or erases an open file.

Open—Used in Macintosh Pascal to open a random file. Does not exist in Turbo.

Close—Same in both.

Seek—In Macintosh Pascal, Seek can only be used with a file opened for random access and automatically performs a Get. In Turbo, Seek only positions the file.

Get—Replaced by Read in Turbo.

Put—Replaced by Write in Turbo.

ADDITIONAL ROUTINES

Turbo implements additional functions and procedures not available in Macintosh Pascal (Table F-1).

Table F-1. Functions and Procedures Not Available in Macintosh Pascal

Exit	Int	ClearScreen	Lo	Halt
ClearEOL	MoveLeft	Swap	MemAvail	DeleteLine
MoveRight	HiWord	MaxAvail	InsertLine	FillChar
LoWord	Ord4	GoToXY	ScanEQ	SwapWord
Float	Pointer	KeyPressed	ScanNE	ReadChar
Hi				

APPENDIX G
Turbo Pascal Syntax Diagrams

ARGUMENT LIST

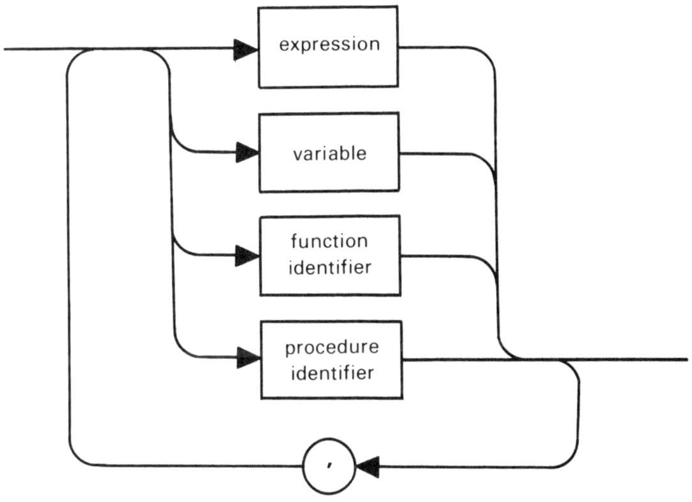

ARRAY TYPE

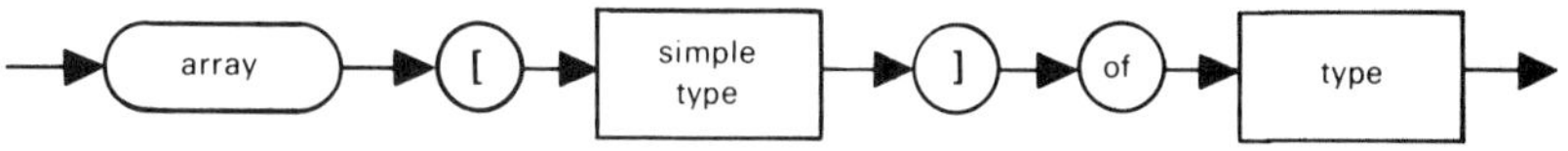

ASSIGNMENT STATEMENT

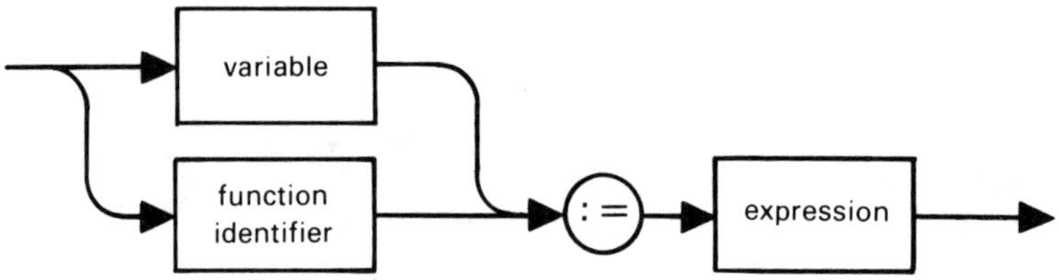

CASE STATEMENT

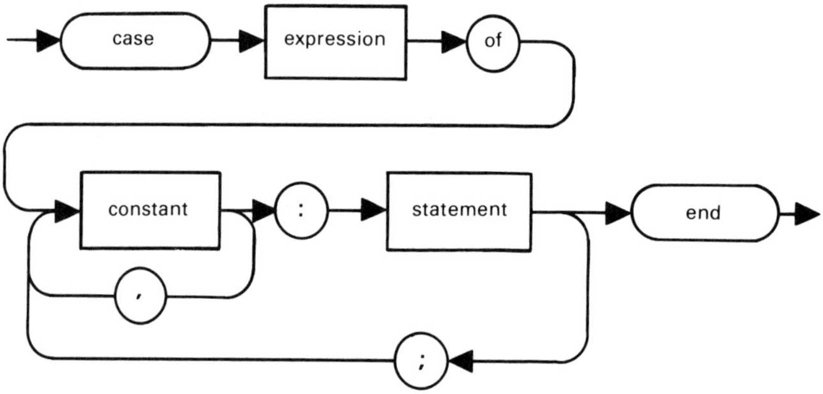

COMPOUND STATEMENT

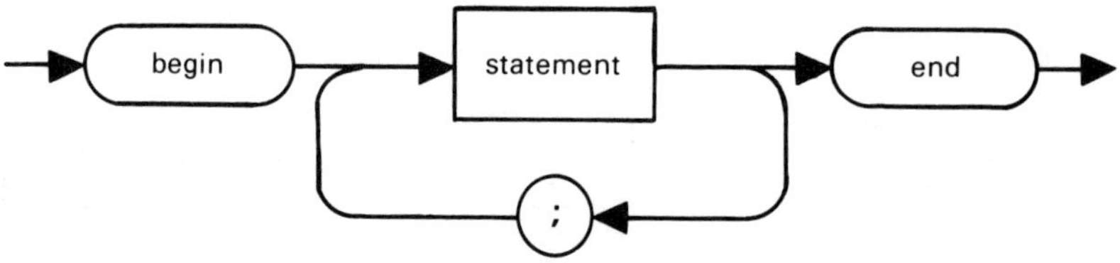

CONSTANT

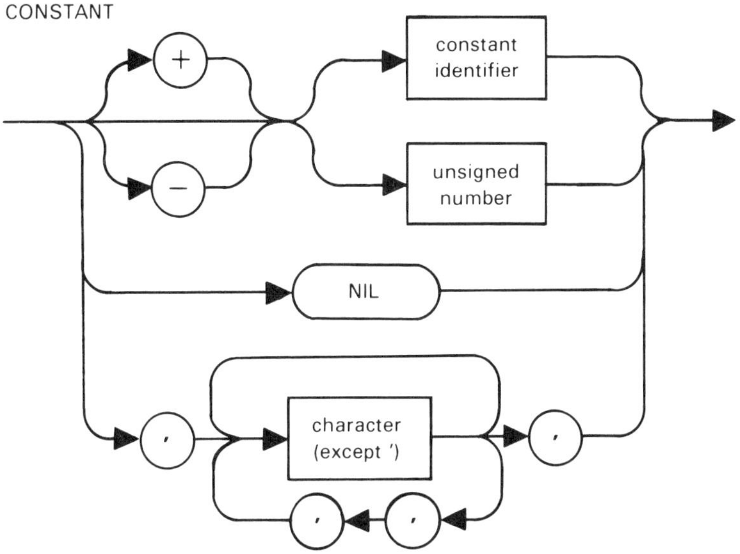

CONSTANT DECLARATION

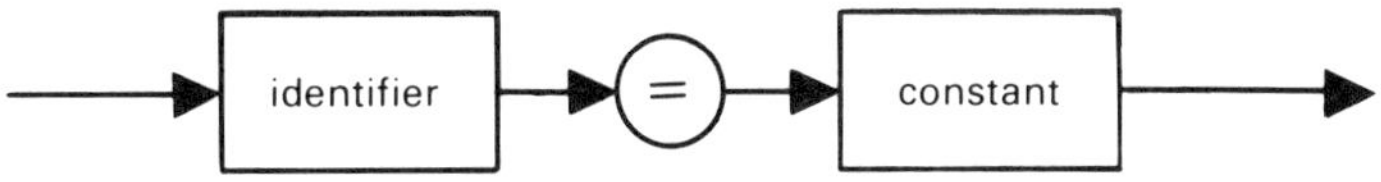

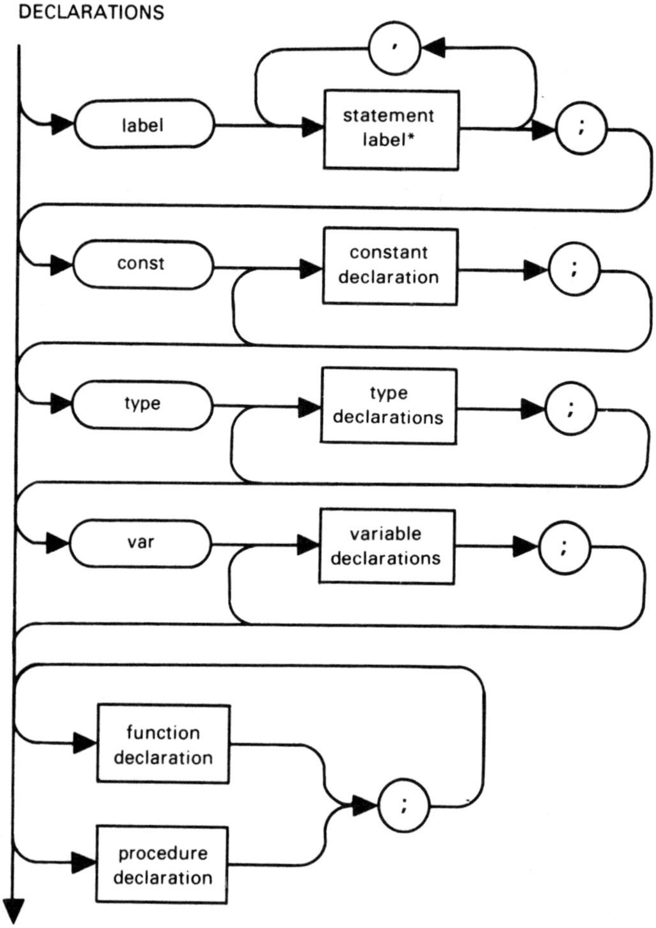

*statement label is one-to-four-digit unsigned integer

EXPRESSION

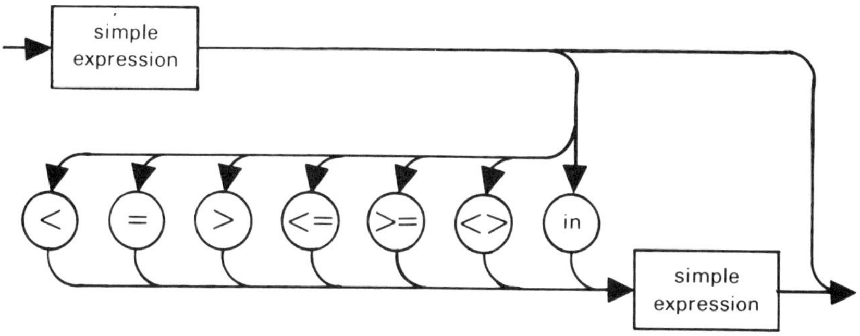

FACTOR

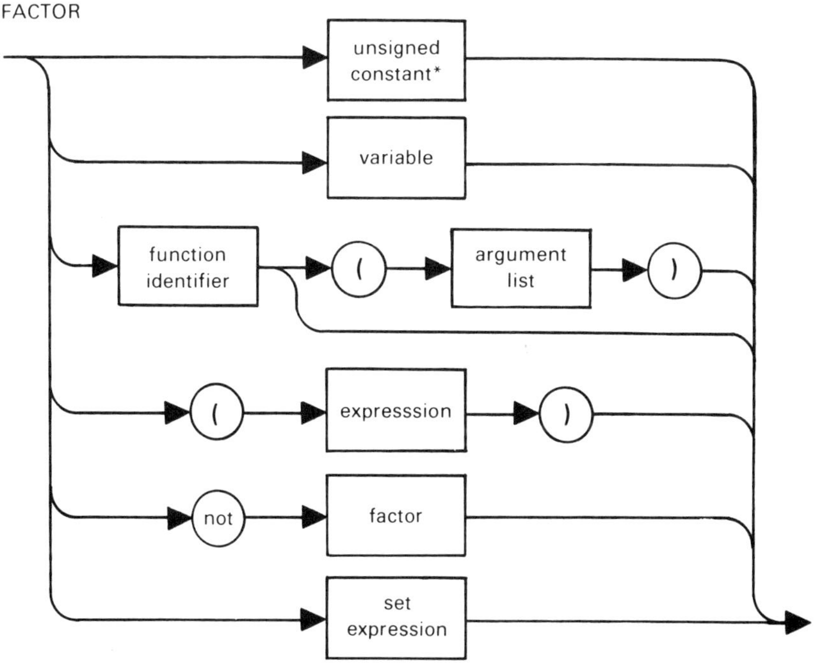

*An unsigned constant is a constant without a leading sign.

FIELD LIST

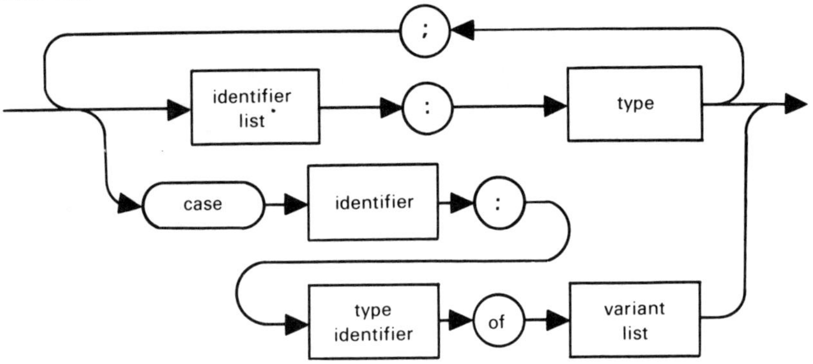

FILE TYPE

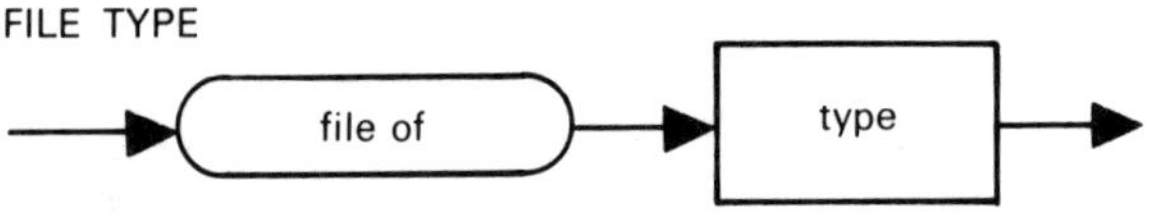

FOR STATEMENT

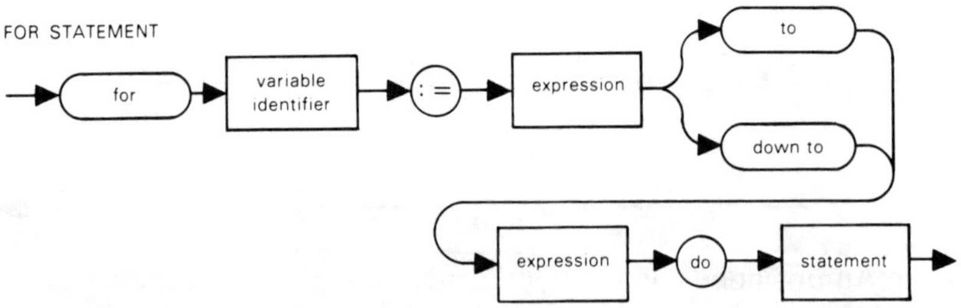

FUNCTION DECLARATION

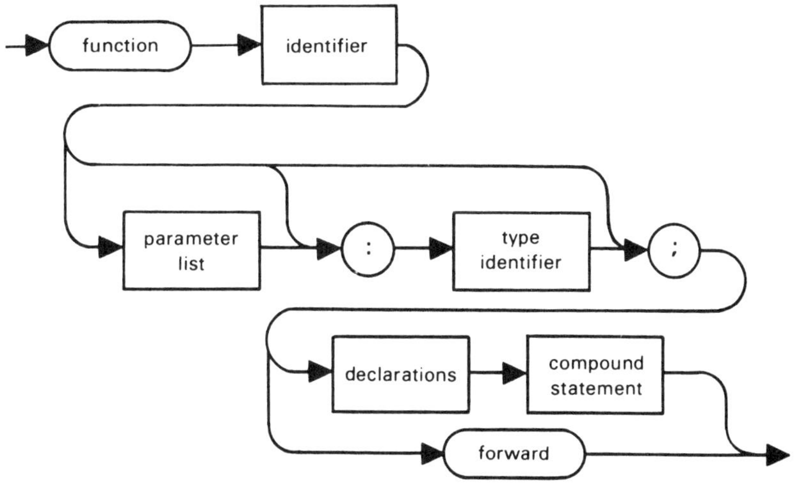

GOTO STATEMENT

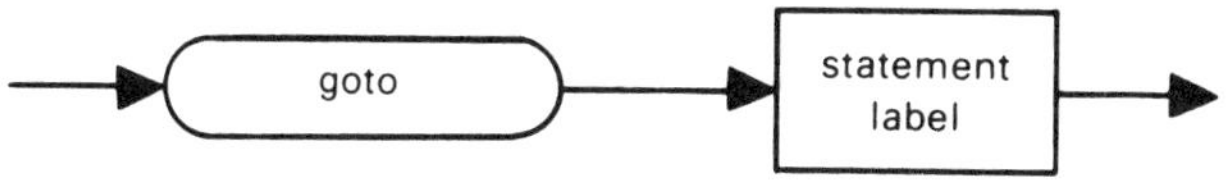

IDENTIFIER LIST

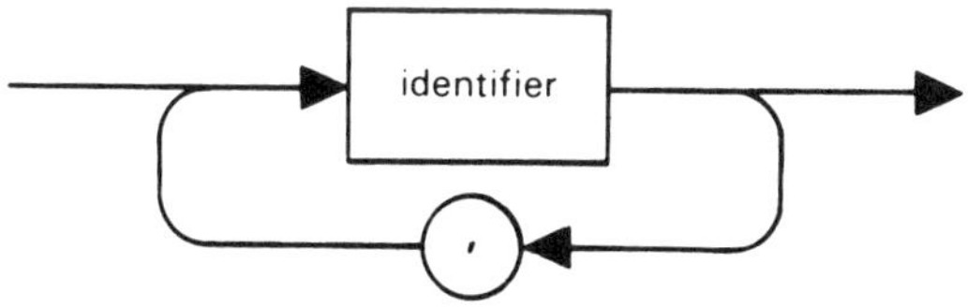

IF STATEMENT

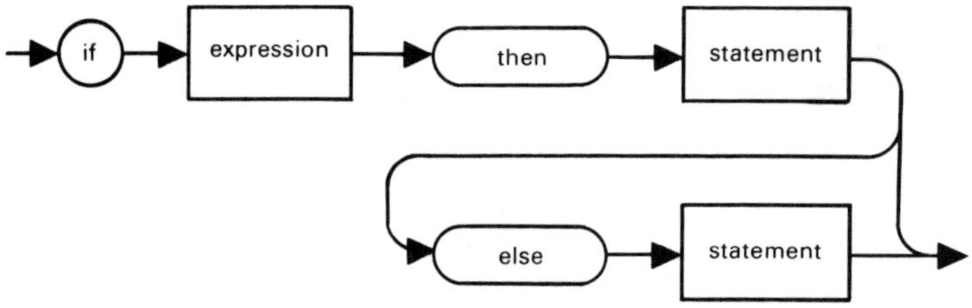

IF THEN STATEMENT

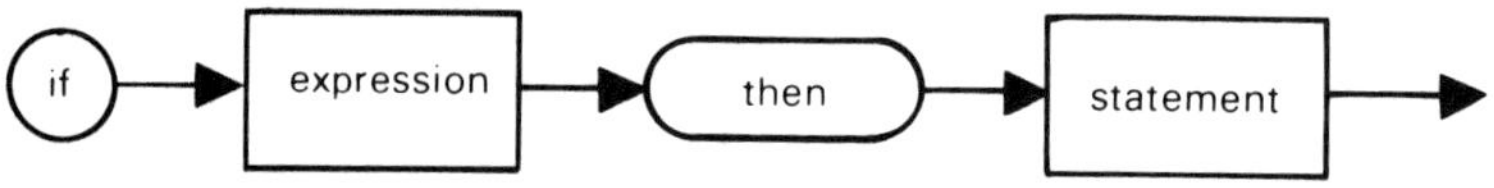

IF THEN ELSE STATEMENT

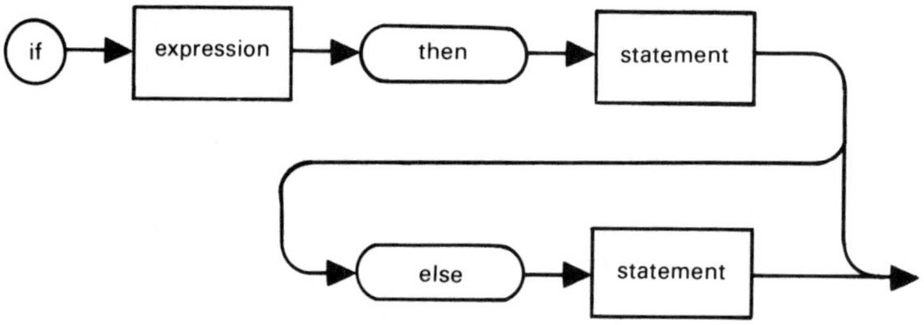

PARAMETER LIST

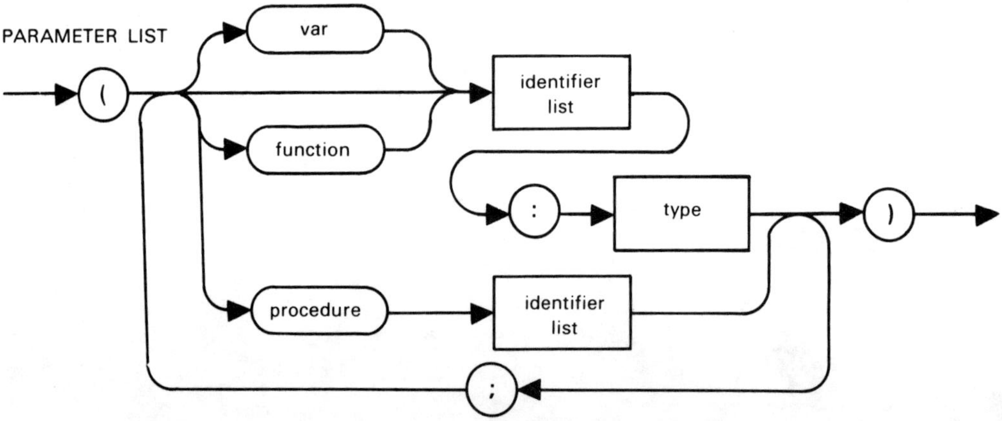

POINTER TYPE

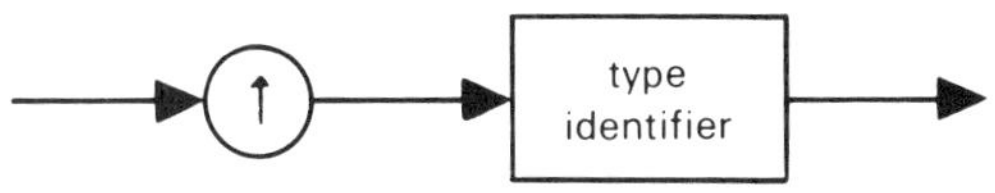

PROCEDURE DECLARATION

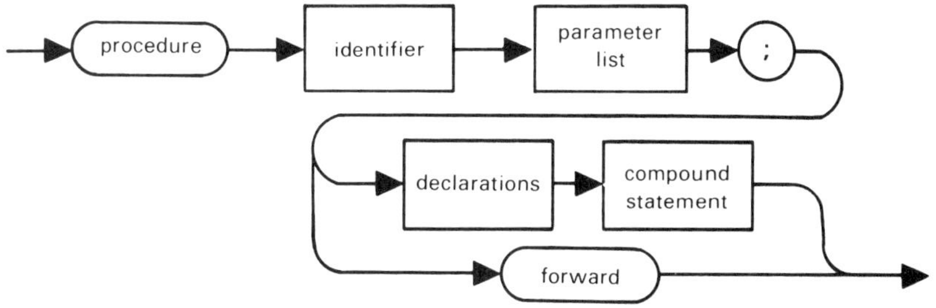

PROCEDURE STATEMENT

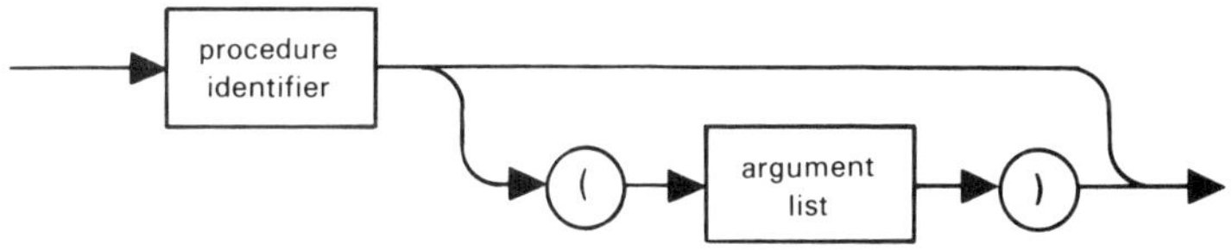

PROGRAM

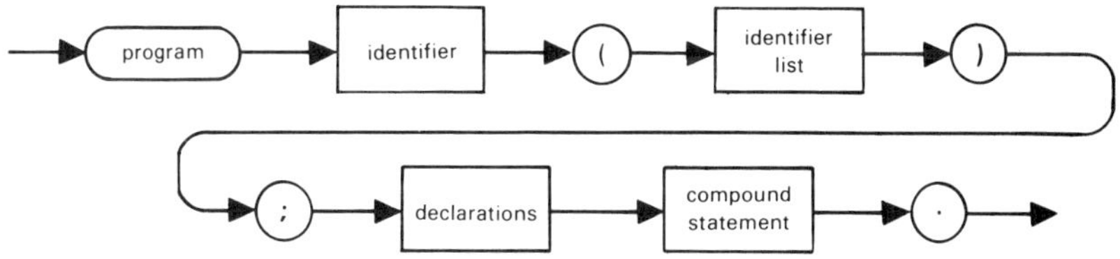

RECORD TYPE

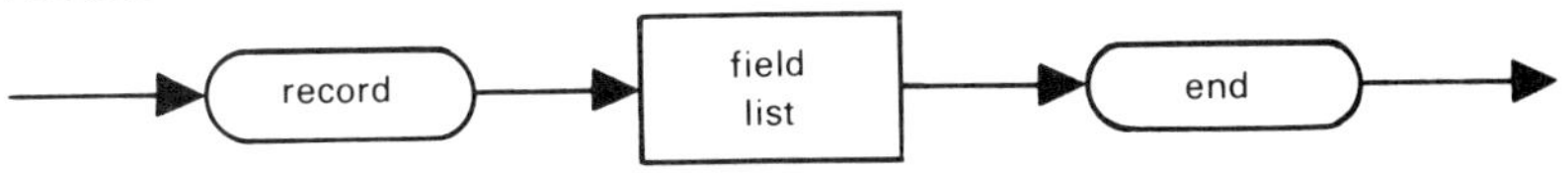

REPEAT STATEMENT

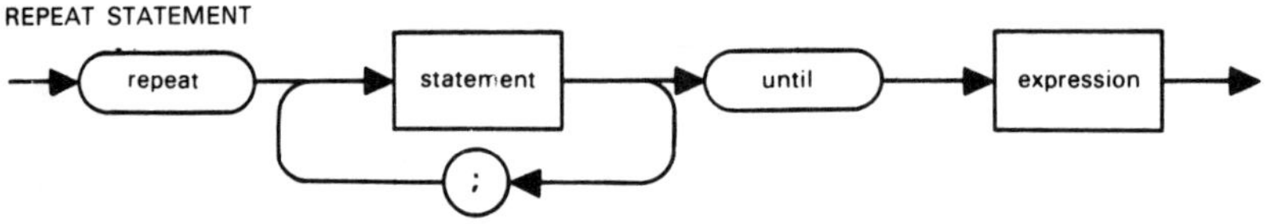

SCALAR TYPE

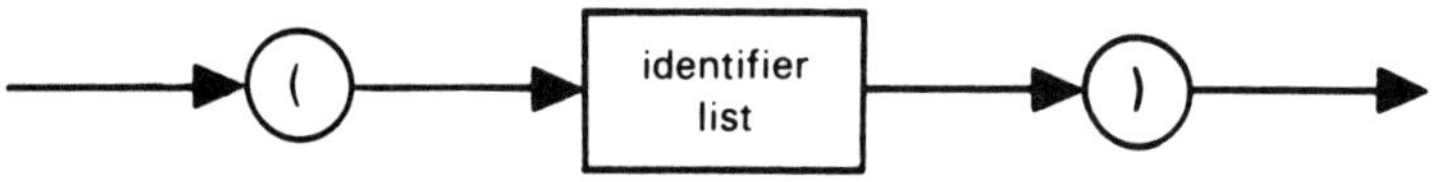

SET EXPRESSION

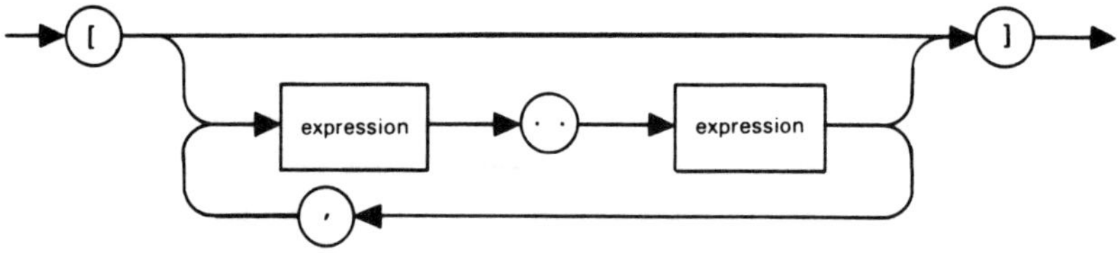

SET TYPE

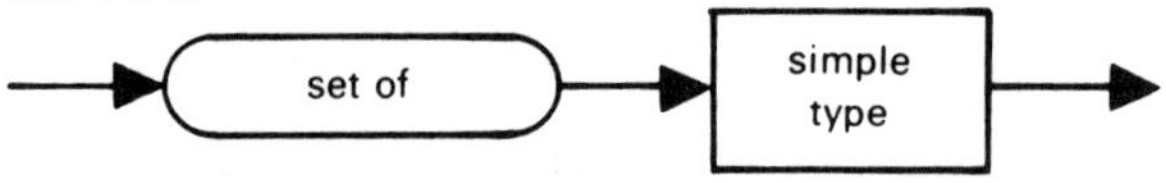

SIMPLE EXPRESSION

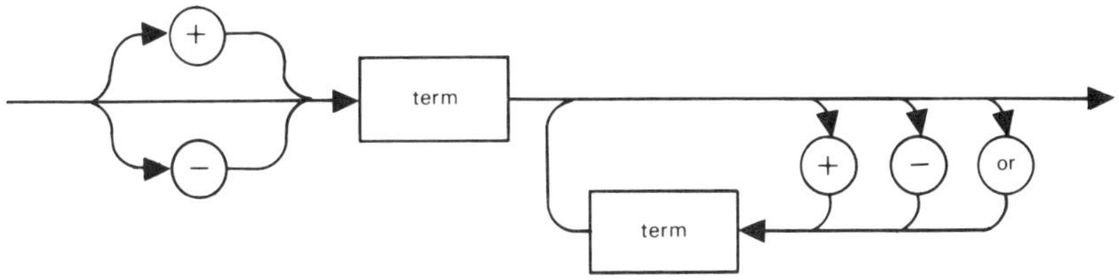

SIMPLE TYPE

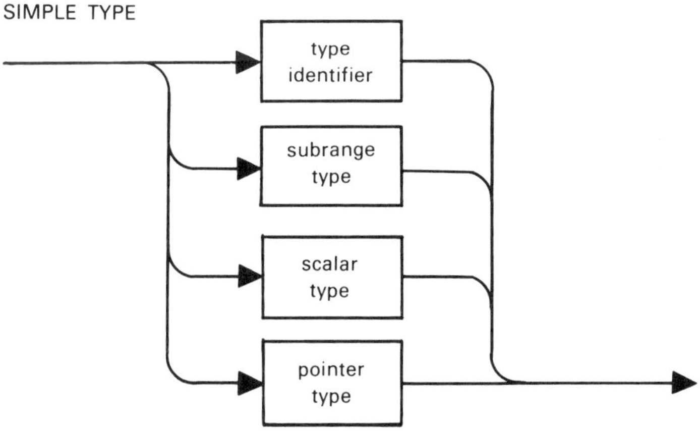

STATEMENT

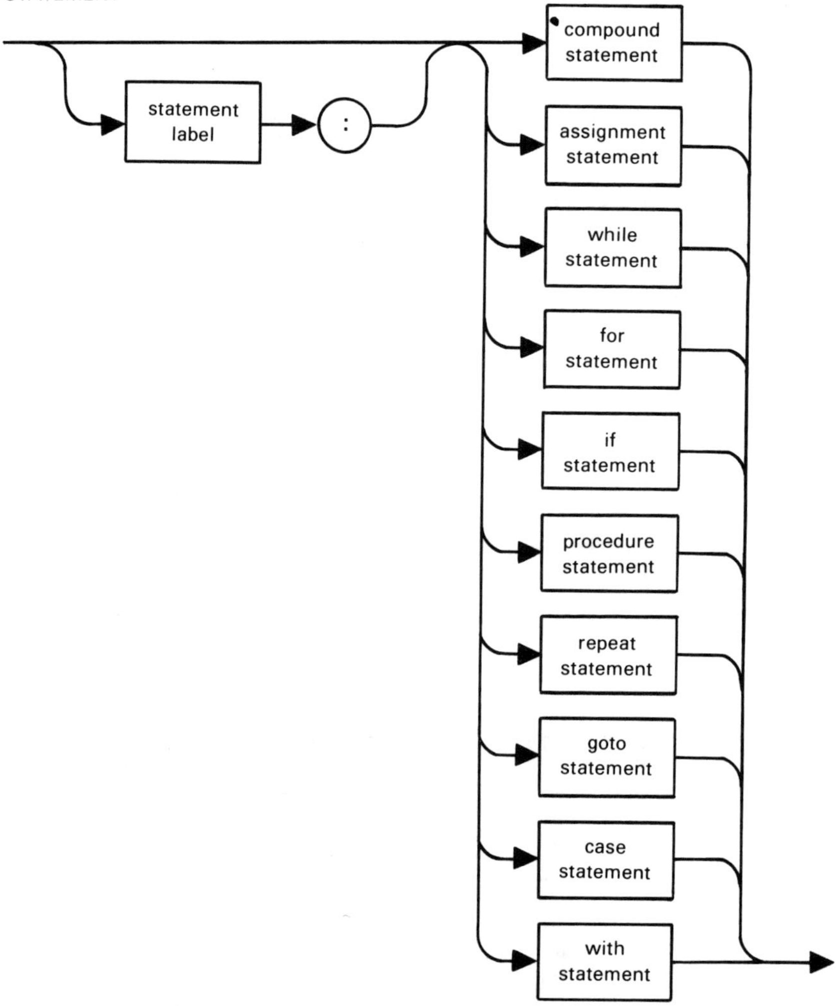

STATEMENT LABEL one-to-four-digit unsigned integer

SUBRANGE TYPE

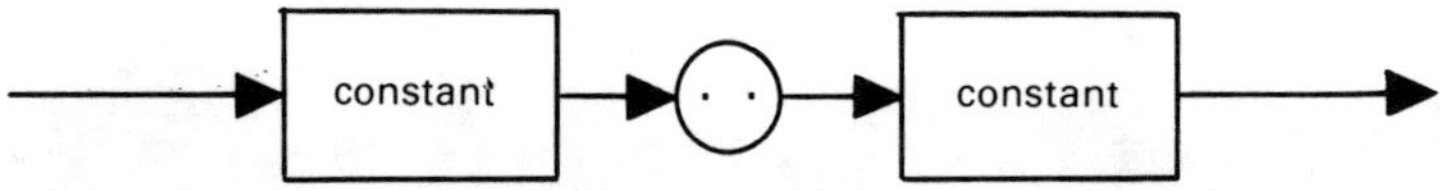

TERM

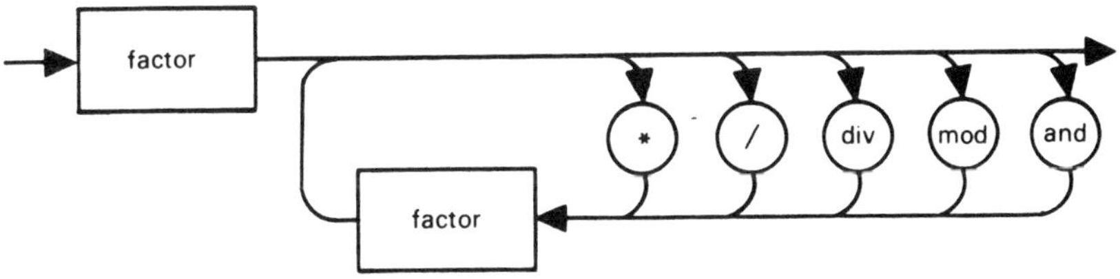

TYPE

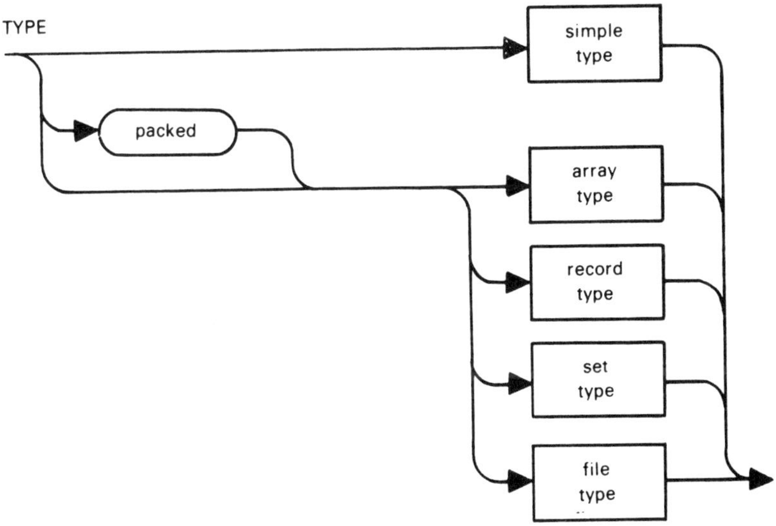

TYPE DECLARATION

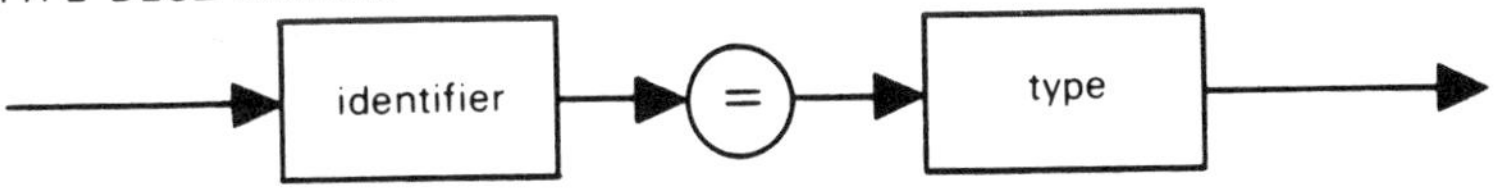

UNSIGNED NUMBER

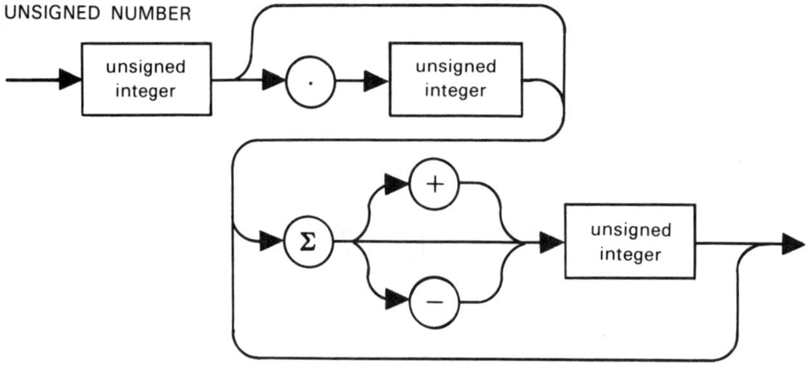

VARIABLE

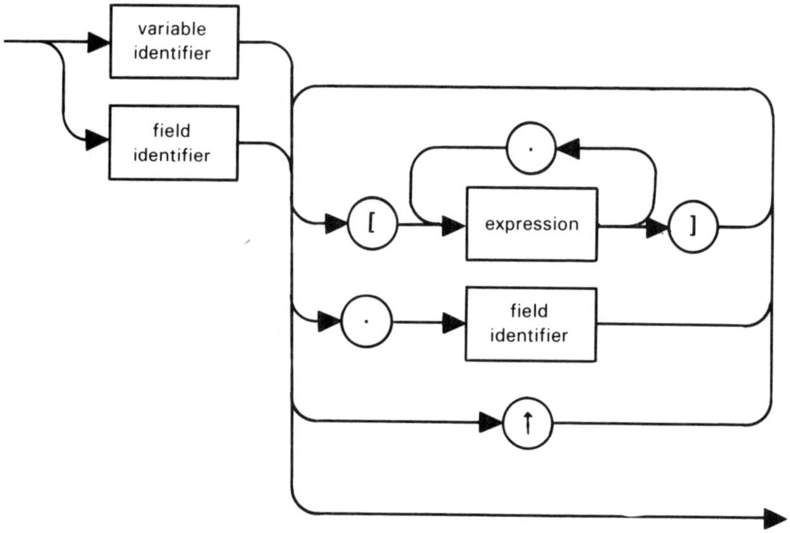

VARIABLE DECLARATION

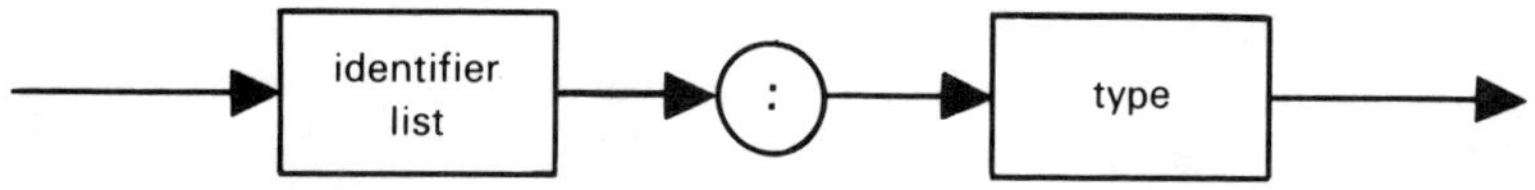

VARIANT LIST

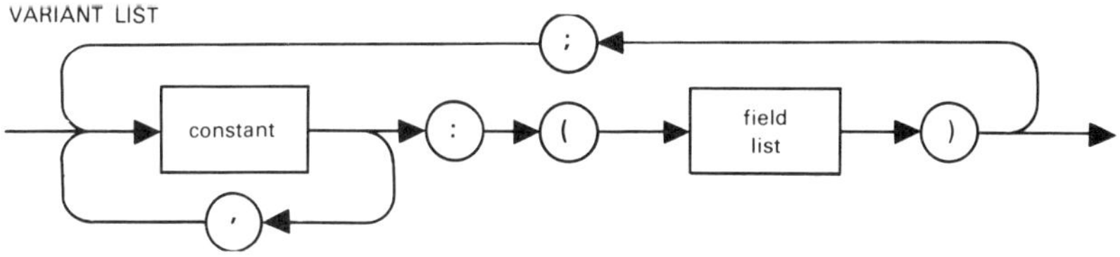

WHILE STATEMENT

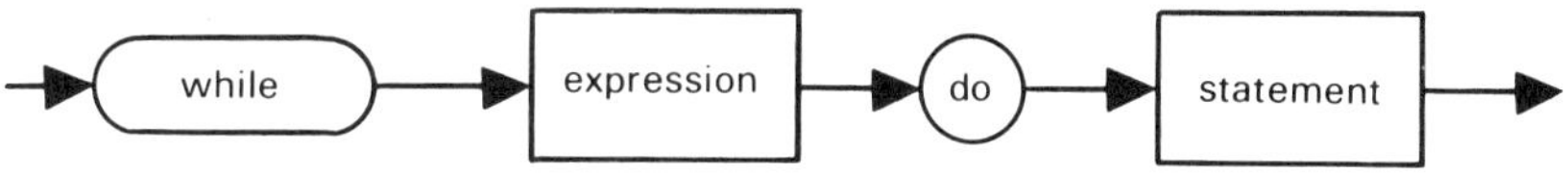

WITH STATEMENT

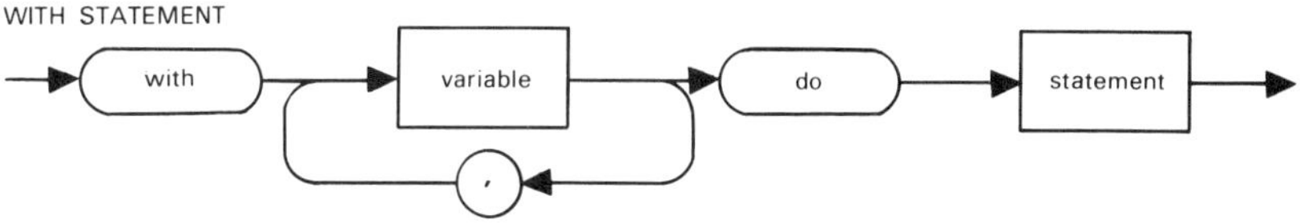

APPENDIX H
Units

One of the power features of Turbo Pascal is the use of units. A unit is a collection of constants, data types, functions, and procedures that is compiled separately from a program it is used in. There are two principal reasons why this is done. First, once a unit is written and compiled, the programmer need not worry about working with this code to include those functions into a program. Also, being compiled separately allows for speed-up of compile times (not a big problem in Turbo), since part of a program is already compiled and allows for the same code to be used in several programs. The second reason for using units is that they allow a very large program to be broken down into more manageable pieces, much like breaking down a program into procedures. Once it has been compiled, using a unit is similar to using any of the Toolbox routines or data types.

A unit is like a program, with some significant differences. A unit consists of two parts, the Interface and Implementation sections. Here is a generic unit:

```
unit identifier (unit)
interface
  uses (optional)
  {Public declarations}
implementation
 {Private declarations}
 {Procedures and functions}
begin
  {Initialization code}
end.
```

Three new reserved words are used with units, "unit," "interface," and "implementation." The unit starts with the reserved word "unit," followed by an identifier and a unit number, a positive number unique from other units. The reserved word "interface" marks the start of the unit. The interface section lists what will be seen by any program that is using the unit. Basically, this consists of procedure and function headings and declarations for variables and data types that can be used by the program calling the unit. The implementation section contains any declarations local to the unit (unavailable to a calling program) and the body of the functions and procedures.

For example, let's look at a unit that contains three routines for statistical work.

```
unit StatWorks (1);
Interface
  type
    ArrayType array[1 . . 100] of Integer;
   function Average(A : ArrayType; var ) : Integer;
   function Max (Num1, Num2 : Integer):Integer;
   function Min (Num1, Num2 : Integer):Integer;
Implementation
    procedure Average;
    var
      Ct, Sum : Integer;
     begin
       Ct := 0 ;
       Sum := 0;
       repeat
        Ct := Ct + 1;
        Sum := A[Ct] + Sum
       until A[Ct] <> -999;  {Sentinal value}
      Average := Sum/Ct
    end; {of Average}
   function Max (Num1, Num2 : Integer):Integer;
   begin
    if Num1 > Num2 then
       Max := Num1
     else
       Max := Num2
   end;
  function Min (Num1, Num2 : Integer):Integer;
   begin
```

```
      if Num1 = Max(Num1, Num2) then
         Min := Num2
       else
         Min := Num1
    end;
end. {Of Unit StatWorks}
```

By compiling this unit to disk, it will be saved with a suitcaselike icon. It can then be used in a program by including the unit name in a Uses statement and by using a compiler directive {U} to identify where the unit is, in this case {$U StatWorks}. Your program can now use these three functions, Average, Min, and Max, and the data type ArrayType freely as though they had been declared in the program.

Appendix I
The Macintosh Character Set

	0	1	2	3	4	5	6	7	8	9	A	B	C	D	E	F
0	NUL	DLE	SP	0	@	P	`	p	Ä	ê	†	∞	¿	–		
1	SOH	DC1	!	1	A	Q	a	q	Å	ë	°	±	¡	—		
2	STX	DC2	"	2	B	R	b	r	Ç	í	¢	≤	¬	“		
3	ETX Enter	DC3	#	3	C	S	c	s	É	ì	£	≥	√	”		
4	EOT	DC4	$	4	D	T	d	t	Ñ	î	§	¥	ƒ	‘		
5	ENQ	NAK	%	5	E	U	e	u	Ö	ï	•	µ	≈	’		
6	ACK	SYN	&	6	F	V	f	v	Ü	ñ	¶	∂	∆	÷		
7	BEL	ETB	'	7	G	W	g	w	á	ó	ß	∑	«	◊		
8	BS	CAN	(	8	H	X	h	x	à	ò	®	∏	»	ÿ		
9	HT	EM	)	9	I	Y	i	y	â	ô	©	π	…			
A	LF	SUB	*	:	J	Z	j	z	ä	ö	™	∫	⎵			
B	VT	ESC Clear	+	;	K	[	k	{	ã	õ	´	ª	Á			
C	FF	FS [◀]	,	<	L	\	l	|	å	ú	¨	º	Ã			
D	CR	GS [▶]	-	=	M	]	m	}	ç	ù	≠	Ω	Õ			
E	SO	RS [▲]	.	>	N	^	n	~	é	û	Æ	æ	Œ			
F	SI	US [▼]	/	?	O	_	o	DEL	è	ü	Ø	ø	œ			

Row and column headings are hexadecimal digits.
(Row16) + Column gives you the numeric code for the character.
The first 32 characters (DO-IF) and DEL (7F) are nonprinting control codes.
The shaded area is reserved for future use.

Bibliography

Aho, A., Hopcroft, J., and J. Ullman *Data Structures and Algorithms.* Reading, Mass.: Addison-Wesley Publishing Co., 1983.

American National Standard Pascal Computer Programming Language. ANSI/IEEE770X3.97-1983, IEEE/Wiley-Interscience, 1983.

Inside Macintosh. Apple Computer Inc., 1984.

Koffman, B. *Pascal, a Problem Solving Approach.* Reading Mass.: Addison-Wesley Publishing Co., 1982.

Chernicoff, *Macintosh Revealed.* Vols. I and II. Hayden Book Company, 1986.

Cooper, D. *Standard Pascal User Reference Manual.* New York: W. W. Norton & Co., 1983.

Gear, C. *Programming in Pascal.* Science Research Associates. Inc., 1983.

Goodman, P., and A. Zeldin *The MacPascal Book.* New York: Brady Books, 1984.

Goodman, P. *Advanced Macintosh Pascal.* Hayden Book Company, 1986.

Hamacher, C., Zvonko, V., and Z. Safwat *Computer Organization.* New York: McGraw-Hill Book Co., 1978.

Horowitz, E., and S, Sahni. *Fundamentals of Data Structures.* Computer Science Press Inc., 1976.

Jensen, K., and N. Wirth. *Pascal User Manual and Report.* New York: Springer-Verlag, 1975.

Kane, G., Hawkins, D., and L. Leventhal. *68000 Assembly Language Programming*. Berkley, Cal.: Osborne/ McGraw-Hill, 1981.

Kernighan, B., and P. Plauger. *Software Tools in Pascal*. Reading, Mass.: Addison-Wesley, Publishing Co., 1981.

Knaster, S. *How to Write Macintosh Programming*. Hayden Book Company, 1986.

Newman, W., and R. Sproull. *Principles of Interactive Computer Graphics*. 2nd ed. New York: McGraw-Hill Book Co., 1979.

Tiberghien, J. *The Pascal Handbook*. Sybex Inc. , 1981.

Wirth, N. *Algorithms + Data Structures = Programs*. Englewood Cliffs, N.J.: Prentice-Hall, 1976.

Index

ABOUT THE AUTHORS

Alan Zeldin is a software engineer in the New York/New Jersey metropolitan area. He holds a bachelor's degree in music, and a master's degree in computer science, and has taught computer science at Queens College of the City University of New York. His early claim to fame was *Spy's Demise*, a video arcade game for Apple, Commodore, and Atari computers. His current interests range from relation databases to computer-aided software engineering.

Paul Goodman holds a bachelor's and master's degree in computer science as well as a Juris Doctor. He is a partner in the New York City law firm of Elias and Goodman, P.C., where he concentrates on computer-related legal matters. He has frequently taught Pascal programming and is on the computer science faculty of Queens College. He is author of several other books and articles on both computer and legal topics. Every October he can be found near the back of the pack in the New York City Marathon.